Performing Medieval and Renaissance Music

The Emperor Maximilian I among his musicians. Woodcut by Hans Burgkmair the Elder (1473–1531) from *Der Weisskunig* series. Burgkmair designed 118 of the set of 251 woodcuts in this series. They date from 1512–1516.

Print from the collection of William and Dorothy Beckel.

Performing Medieval and Renaissance Music

an introductory guide

Elizabeth V. Phillips
and
John-Paul Christopher Jackson

Schirmer Books
A Division of Macmillan, Inc.
New York

Collier Macmillan Publishers
London

Schirmer Books
A Division of Macmillan, Inc.
866 Third Avenue, New York, N. Y. 10022

Collier Macmillan Canada, Inc.

Library of Congress Catalog Card Number: 85-18419

Printed in the United States of America

printing number
1   2   3   4   5   6   7   8   9   10

The following examples are reproduced from *Anthology
of Medieval Music*, edited by Richard H. Hoppin, by
permission of W. W. Norton & Company, Inc. Copyright ©
1978 by W. W. Norton & Company, Inc.: *Haec dies*; Leonin (?),
Alleluia: Nativitas; *Soli nitorem*; Guillaume de Machaut,
Dous amis.

Illustrations by Elizabeth Blair Matisz.

Library of Congress Cataloging in Publication Data

Phillips, Elizabeth V.
    Performing medieval and Renaissance music.

    Bibliography: p.
    Includes index.
    1. Music—500–1400—Performance.   2. Music—15th
century—Performance.   3. Music—16th century—Per-
formance.   I. Jackson, John-Paul Christopher.
II. Title.
ML430.5.P52   1986   780'.902   85-18419
ISBN 0-02-871790-2

To Our Students:
Past, Present, and Future

Contents

Appendices

List of Examples

List of Figures

Preface

Interest in the study and performance of early music has grown phenomenally in recent years. Scholars and performers alike are busily involved with performance-practice research of every description in an effort to keep pace with the thirst for knowledge in this area. Rarely has scholarly work had such a direct and immediate impact on musical performance as it has in the area of early music.

Around the world, interest in historical performance practices is demonstrated at both institutional and community levels, and by countless individuals. Across North America, colleges and universities have initiated programs in early music, usually centered around the collegium musicum. These programs, most of which are staffed by specialists, vary greatly from institution to institution. Similarly, at the community level one can cite both a few professional groups and numerous semiprofessional and amateur ensembles.

From time to time, groups at all levels have found themselves limited by inadequate library resources and incomplete expertise. Music of the Middle Ages and Renaissance presents enormous problems for the performer, yet information about historical performance practices has been restricted largely to scholarly articles of a specific nature. Valuable as these are, they have not always found their way into the hands of performers. As an alternative there has been no single book that addresses itself to the needs, both practical and scholarly, of this diverse and growing population of early-music enthusiasts.

As teachers and performers of early music for many years, the authors have perceived the need for a book such as this one. Over the years we prepared many sets of guidelines for our collegium students, in order to make them aware of style characteristics and of relevant scholarly literature. Our colleagues in the field urged us to make the results of our work more widely available.

The authors feel that this book can meet many of the needs of the performer of early music, whether involved in an academic program or in a community ensemble. In the following pages we offer recommendations suitable for nearly all types of music commonly included in the collegium repertory. Our suggestions are based on historical evidence, on research by other scholars, on evidence derived from the music itself, and on our practical experience. We have endeavored to separate fact from speculation in our remarks. We assume the responsibility for any errors. No guidebook can be all things to all readers, but the authors hope that this book will be a helpful companion for all those who love early music.

For the purposes of this book, the authors focus on the ensemble music of the Middle Ages and Renaissance. An examination of the Table of Contents will reveal that the subject of early music performance practice and its relationship to today's performers has been divided into three parts. Recommended projects are provided for topics within each of these parts. Appendices at the end of the book amplify selected areas of consideration. By dealing with the contents selectively, the instructor and student may use this book in connection with a one- or two-semester course in collegium performance or historical performance practice, and the general performer may adopt it as an ongoing reference tool.

This book is not intended to be an anthology of historical writings. It is not designed as a tutor for singing or playing early instruments. Neither is it a text for advanced-level study of historical performance practices. The bibliography, largely in English, is selective, and includes mainly secondary sources. The anthology of music comprises a representative selection of ensemble genres, but does not include solo repertories or dramatic music. Items in the anthology were selected for the purpose of allowing the reader to compare them with published facsimiles of original versions in manuscripts or prints.

The musical examples also give the reader an opportunity to become acquainted with many different editing practices. Although the examples have been re-autographed for this book, they show the original editors' choices of note values, *musica ficta*, text underlay, barring, etc. The authors hope that this diversity will prove stimulating to readers and useful to those who try preparing their own transcriptions from facsimiles. Readers who wish to know more about the editorial conventions affecting a particular example can, in most cases, find detailed explanations in the original edition from which the piece was borrowed.

This book was made possible in part by a grant from the National Endowment for the Humanities, by research grants from The University of Lethbridge, and by a West Georgia College Faculty Research Grant.

We also wish to acknowledge our sincere appreciation to the following persons and institutions for their assistance in the preparation of this book: Dorothy Beckel, Dr. William Beckel, Professor Dean Blair, Norbert Boehm, Phil Boon, Phil Boras, Dr. Paul Bowdre, Dr. Tilford Brooks, Carla Chiste, Dr. Robert M. Coe, Lucy Cross, Dr. Michael Fleming, Jessica Friedlander, Professor Kenneth Greene, Sheila Harrison, Dorothy Harrop, Dr. Douglas Hilt, Dr. Owen Holmes, Dr. René Immelé, Margaret Israel, Dr. Brian Jeffery, Dr. Roland Jordan, Dr. Edward Kottick, Elinor Lawson, Mark Lindley, Richard Mallory, Dr. Carol Marsh, Dr. Kevin Mason, Dr. Vondis Miller, Deborah Minkin, Kathryn Nelson, Dr. Paul Olson, Maribeth Anderson Payne, Dr. Paul Pisk, Dr. Steven Plank, Dr. Curtis Price, Dr. Carter Revard, Dr. Rhian Samuel, Michael Sander, Dr. Brent Shaw, Frances Stillwell, Stephen Toombs, The University of Lethbridge, Washington University in St. Louis, and West Georgia College.

Elizabeth V. Phillips
John–Paul Christopher Jackson

Performing Medieval and Renaissance Music

The Constitution of the Early Music Ensemble

INTRODUCTION

Part I examines the early music ensemble today and the resources for performance available to it. Historical instruments and singing are discussed, and recommendations are made for the establishment of collections of instruments, music, recordings, etc. The recommended projects at the end of this part are practical exercises for investigating resources. The material in Part I provides a background for the study of Parts II and III.

Chapter 1

The Collegium Musicum

The performance of early music today usually centers around the academic collegium musicum or a noninstitutional ensemble of similar makeup and function. Such an ensemble commonly sees as its goal the performance of Western art music written prior to 1750. For the purpose of this book, the authors focus on the performance of music of the Middle Ages and Renaissance. Our treatment of the ensemble repertory attempts to be comprehensive within these periods.

The origin of the collegium as an institution dates from the late sixteenth century, when informal gatherings of musicians provided opportunities for shared music-making and conviviality.

In the Baroque period greater musical emphasis was placed on similar gatherings. Such collegia, as represented by those of Telemann, Fasch, Bach, and others, included accomplished amateurs, students, and professionals. They afforded the participants excellent opportunities for performing and hearing the best contemporary music of the day. These groups were an important component of middle-class German and, later, German–North American life. Their demise resulted from the growth and popularity of the public concert.

The modern collegium began as the tool of musicologists. This type of study/performance group, as employed by Hugo Riemann (1849–1919) and Wilibald Gurlitt (1889–1963), focused its attention on "early music," and in doing so created an ensemble quite different from the original collegium concept. (This original concept survives today only in the form of campus "new music" groups.)

In North America the first modern collegia devoted to early music were those founded by Willi Apel (Harvard, 1938) and Paul Hindemith (Yale, 1943). Since that time the number of campus and community collegia has increased immensely. Paralleling and precipitating this increase has been the appearance of more music, better editions, more and better reproductions of historical instruments, and higher performance standards.

Modern collegia display considerable diversity. At one extreme are professional-quality ensembles of faculty and advanced students, with a generous supply of instruments, library resources, and funds. Such organizations feature frequent public performances and possibly accompany a degree program in early music performance. At the other extreme are groups with relatively modest resources and aspirations. These groups may function as extracurricular activities, noncredit courses, or perhaps performance laboratories for a music history or musicology curriculum.

Most groups find themselves somewhere between these extremes in terms of personnel, resources, scope of program, and role within the institution or community. Each director develops the type of ensemble that suits his or her special interests and abilities, and such an approach is entirely appropriate. At the same time, each ensemble reflects the setting in which it exists (just as musical organizations did in the Middle Ages and Renaissance!). The curriculum, budget, and philosophy of each organization help to determine the nature of its collegium.[1]

The collegium experience offers several benefits. Performance of music from all periods enhances understanding of the broad spectrum of musical literature and increases the performer's awareness of the nature of his art and its stylistic diversity. Performing early music can develop skills in the area of musicianship that prove valuable in the performance of music of every period. Because much early music uses only one performer on a part, all members of an ensemble become sensitive to the quality of their own contributions and aware of the relationship of their parts to the whole, as in any good chamber music experience. In addition, both singers and instrumentalists are challenged by this repertory's unique demands regarding tone color, rhythmic articulation, and embellishment, to name but a few special features. The presence of a collegium in the community or institution provides cultural enrichment, opportunities for participants and audiences, and a resource that may stimulate others to new endeavors. The growth of publications, research, and recording of early music attests to the validity of this repertory; that is, one deserving of performance.

Chapter 2

Resources for Performance

Successful performance of works from the early music repertory depends in part upon a firm understanding of the resources required for performance. Owing to the relative unfamiliarity of some of these resources, students of early music should acquaint themselves with this essential background at an early stage in their studies.

VOICES

In a very real sense, early music *is* vocal music. The vast majority of music written prior to 1600 was for voice(s) with or without instruments, and music that was originally intended for instruments alone owed much to vocal models.

The predominance of vocal music is a fact too often slighted by the modern collegium, which may find itself preoccupied by a fascination with the "authentic" sound of early instruments. Such a distraction is all the more understandable when one contemplates the difficulty of knowing anything at all about the "authentic" sound of the voice in the Middle Ages and Renaissance. Alas, there are no extant examples of these singers for us to study!

Historical accounts of the quality of tone produced by singers survive from a few witnesses. Although the ideal vocal quality was sometimes described as delicate, sonorous, etc., reports about actual singers were sometimes considerably less flattering, suggesting an extremely tight, nasal sound. From these contemporary descriptions, modern scholars and performers have drawn numerous conclusions about singing.[1] It must be remembered, however, that such accounts are at best very subjective, and that they range over several hundred years of singing practice. Today, for example, a singer may receive incredibly divergent criticism and review during a single performance season. Here, then, is the terrible problem: an age of vocal music, but what did it sound like?

One modern solution that seems to satisfy the requirements of the music quite well is the use of a clear, steady, rather forward-placed voice. This basically vibrato-free style permits purity of open harmonic consonances and clarity of contrapuntal lines.

If we cannot be more definitive about the sound of early voices, what can we say about their use? Here current knowledge is somewhat greater.

As a rule, sacred or secular polyphony written prior to 1400 was the repertory of soloists. Likewise the majority of secular categories after 1400 (chanson, lied, madrigal, etc.) may be thought of as music for one on a part, at least as an authentic option.

Choral singing occurred in the Middle Ages primarily in plainsong and perhaps also in some other monophonic repertory.[2] Choral polyphony did not appear as a standard practice until after 1400. The vast majority of Renaissance sacred music is intended for multiple singers on a part.

By today's standards, Renaissance choirs were generally quite small, ranging in size from perhaps 6 to 12 members in the early fifteenth century to about 20 to 30 members in the sixteenth century. Such ensembles were made up of differing combinations of male vocalists (basses, tenors, countertenors, soprano falsettists, boy altos, and boy sopranos).[3] In the sixteenth century, royal chapel choirs possibly permitted more participation by instruments than church choirs allowed,[4] but prior to that time, sacred choral music was sung *a cappella*, as a general rule.

The participation of women in the performance of both sacred and secular music is less well documented. Clearly, women in convents adopted some of the liturgical repertory for their use. The employment of tenor clefs as standard range indicators in medieval sources may simply represent convention (e.g., in the Codex Huelgas, a convent source). Some medieval monophony has poetry that presents a feminine point of view. Indeed, there are examples in this repertory that were composed by women. Iconographic evidence from Burgundian sources suggests that women were active performers in works from the chanson repertory. Pictures often show a female singer with a mixed group of instruments. In some paintings, the music is depicted as well, and in many cases it bears tenor clefs in spite of the treble performers. Such paintings probably represent amateur, upper-class music-making, in which women adapted works for their own use. This repertory contains many vocal parts, however, that are notated in the treble range, and some of these may well be intended for the female voice.[5] The sixteenth and early seventeenth centuries provide us with more certain repertory for the female voice (e.g., frottola, madrigal, chanson) as well as more accounts of actual performances.

Voices: Practical Ensembles

GROUP I—THE SMALL VOCAL ENSEMBLE. A large proportion of the non-choral literature of the Middle Ages and Renaissance can be performed by a group having these five singers available:

§ 1 soprano
§ 1 alto or countertenor
§ 2 tenors
§ 1 bass

Most of the remaining nonchoral literature can be accommodated by adding the following three voices:

§ 1 soprano

§ 1 alto or countertenor

§ 1 bass

GROUP II—THE MOTET CHOIR.   Required for Renaissance sacred music, this ensemble adds additional singers, resulting in the following totals:

§ 5 sopranos (male or female)

§ 5 altos (male or female)

§ 5 tenors

§ 5 basses

For Group II, mixed voices (men and women) may be the only practical solution today in lieu of trained falsettists and boy singers, but it is not the ideal solution. In a mixed choir it may be helpful to bridge the gap between male and female voices by creating some overlap; that is, by having some low female voices join on a tenor part and/or some high male voices join on an alto part. The exact distribution of these singers will depend on the number of voice parts and on considerations of tessitura, range, and balance.

INSTRUMENTS

A collegium that intends to perform music from all of the categories discussed in Part III needs extensive resources, particularly in its collection of instruments. A glance at any book on the history of instruments reveals the variety that existed in the Middle Ages and Renaissance.[6] Many types, great diversity in geographical and chronological distribution, and lack of standardization within a type (size, shape, materials, tuning, playing technique)—all contrast with the relative uniformity of twentieth-century instruments. Furthermore, names in the Middle Ages were not applied to instruments consistently. Different instruments with similar functions or playing techniques might share a common name; conversely, a single instrument might be referred to by several different names.

The reader is cautioned at this point to avoid a common misconception regarding the historical development of musical instruments, that evolution implies improvement. It must be remembered that some early forms of instruments remained virtually unchanged for hundreds of years, while others received various modifications, and still others underwent methodical developmental sophistication. The effectiveness of a musical instrument can be measured only by the degree of satisfaction that it provided to the people who used it and heard it.

Chordophones

Chordophones have always played an important role in Western art music. During the Middle Ages and Renaissance, a great diversity of both plucked and bowed types existed. The strings of these instruments were made from a variety of materials; for example, horsehair, silk, gut, or metal. Silk and gut strings have been used since ancient times, and metal strings may have existed as early as 1100. While gut was the most common material used in Europe, the individuality of an instrument perhaps extended to the performer's personal preferences for string material. Thus, the same kind of instrument might have been strung in different ways, according to local tastes.[7] Some instruments, of course, require specific string materials for optimum performance.

The use of the bow on string instruments in Europe began to entrench itself firmly from the eleventh century onward by way of Arabic Spain. Chordophones, which had been primarily plucked instruments in the early Middle Ages, appear in bowed forms with increasing frequency after this period, among them instruments of the rotta, lira, and fiddle types.

This application of bowing techniques to plucked instruments does not represent the introduction of new instruments for their own sake so much as it reflects the tastes of medieval society functioning under the purely musical requirements of a new musical system; that is, polyphony. That such techniques were perhaps widely in use in folk music is likely, at least in the folk art of Near Eastern cultures and perhaps that of Europe as well. Their adoption in the realm of serious art music must be viewed in part as an imitation of the vocal art and as coincidental with organal style and its drone-like characteristics.

Aerophones

Of secondary importance to strings for the performance of art music in the Middle Ages and Renaissance, aerophones, nevertheless, existed in considerable variety. Edge-tone, reed, and cupped-mouthpiece types are represented. Materials of construction include wood, horn, bone, cane, stone, clay, and metals.

Keyboards

During the Middle Ages, both chordophone and aerophone groups had mechanized representatives, although the latter were more important. In the Renaissance, a greater variety of keyboard chordophones began to appear.

Percussion Instruments

Percussion instruments are among man's oldest musical inventions. A great variety of percussion instruments was in use during the Middle Ages and Renaissance for military affairs, processionals and other ceremonials, and for dance. The specific use of these must, however, remain conjectural, owing to the completely unnotated nature of their music.

The survey in Appendix B will acquaint the reader with the principal medieval and Renaissance instruments known to us from writings and iconography. See also Appendix C, a list of instrument ranges and tunings.

Instruments: Practical Collections

The modern performer of early music, dependent upon available modern reproductions of historical instruments, can select specific instruments that suit only a small repertory. This is the solution of most collegia and other ensembles today, which usually emphasize sixteenth-century instruments in their choices. If the composer's original intentions are to be met, such an emphasis necessarily limits the scope of repertory to the sixteenth century. The authors would like to encourage the exploration of earlier literature, and we therefore offer the following as recommended collections that allow for a greater range of styles to be performed and that, at the same time, take into consideration matters of budget and practicality. While not always historically accurate, A-440 is the pitch standard of most modern reproductions, and this seems to be the most practical solution at present. Compromises in matters of range and tuning also occur in some modern reproductions.

GROUP I—THE BASIC COLLECTION.   This is a reasonably flexible and economical collection that can be expanded later.

*Strings**

1 lute, 8-course

1 vielle, 5 strings

4 viols: 1 treble in *d*, 2 tenors in G, 1 bass in *D*

1 psaltery

Winds

7 recorders (wide-bore): 2 sopranos, 2 altos, 2 tenors, 1 bass

4 crumhorns: SATB (Crumhorns are generally available in C and F, although historical instruments were made in other sizes and pitches; generally alto, tenor, and bass were a fifth apart.)

1 flute in *d'*

1 tenor sackbut in *B-flat*

FIGURE 2–1.   The authors examining a sordun in the collection of early instruments at The University of Lethbridge.

*In this book, pitches are identified as follows: the octave below middle C is labeled *c–b*; the octave below that, C–B, and below that, CC–BB; the octave above middle C, *c'–b'*; the octave above that, *c"–b"*. Specific pitch names are printed in italic type.

Percussion

1 tabor

1 tambourine

GROUP II—THE SECONDARY COLLECTION. This collection may be acquired after the basic collection. It allows an expansion of performance possibilities in both the medieval and Renaissance repertories.

Strings

1 oud (al'ūd); or 1 long-necked lute

1 harp

1 rebec

2 viols: treble and bass

Winds

1 smaller flute in *g'*

2 shawms: alto and tenor

1 or 2 cornetts in *a*

1 bass curtal (dulcian)

Keyboard

1 harpsichord (2 $\times$ 8', or 1 $\times$ 8' plus 1 $\times$ 4')

1 organetto (small portative)

Percussion

nakers

castanets, clappers, bells, etc.

Special categories of instruments are required for certain repertory; for example, the "consort lesson" ensemble, which comprises treble viol or violin, flute or recorder (there is controversy about which instrument and what size), lute, cittern, bandora, and bass viol. Unique coloristic ensembles such as this are fascinating, but they have a limited practical value, and should probably be reserved for groups that enjoy a lavish budget.

Selection of Instruments

When choosing instruments for an early music ensemble, one should pay particular attention to matters of pitch uniformity, maintenance implications, and "authenticity." Of course some compromises must occur, but the buyer is advised to purchase matched sets of instruments (recorders, flutes, crumhorns, etc.) from one maker at one time, in order to insure pitch and tonal agreement. One should avoid instruments that are based on conjecture (douçaine, soprano kortholt, etc.). Cheap instruments are no bargain, so buy to the limit of your budget.

The Bibliography includes reference works on historical instruments, instrument selection, and related topics of interest to the prospective buyer. One should also consult the various advertisements and registries published in journals devoted to early music and instruments, such as *Early Music, The Galpin Society Journal,* and the publications of societies specializing in lute, viol, recorder, harpsichord, etc. Addresses for several of these are listed in Appendix D.

Maintenance of Instruments

Most instruments require careful maintenance for optimum performance and long life. Early instruments are especially sensitive to climatic conditions. The person responsible for an instrument collection must become familiar with the needs of each instrument, whether stored or in use. Borrowers of instruments must be prepared to meet these needs.

As an illustration of the special care required by certain early instruments, the gemshorn may be cited. It can produce a tone only if properly humidified. While extremely moist or dry atmosphere could cause mold or cracking, changes of humidity within even a narrow band may create "voicing" problems. Other instruments have their own idiosyncracies related to temperature, humidity, handling, and general wear.[8]

MUSIC

We encourage performers of early music to consult both original sources and modern editions when studying and preparing early music for performance.

Original Sources

Original sources occur as manuscripts or as prints, many of which are available in facsimile editions. Facsimiles are important for a number of reasons. Firstly, they may be consulted as a check against ambiguity or errors found in modern transcriptions. Secondly, they provide the source for new transcriptions to be made by the performers themselves. The practice of making such transcriptions is valuable whether or not the work being transcribed exists in a modern edition. Lastly, facsimiles can be used directly for reading and performing music. In this way, the modern performer can share the same visual and intellectual experience as that which the original performers may have had.

Following are recommended facsimiles for a collection that will expose the performer to a large variety of repertory. While by no means complete, they represent many of the categories listed in Part III.

General

Apel, Willi. *The Notation of Polyphonic Music, 900–1600.* 5th ed., rev. Cambridge, MA: Medieval Academy of America, 1961.

Besseler, Heinrich, and Peter Gülke. *Schriftbild der mehrstimmigen Musik.* Musikgeschichte in Bildern, vol. 3, pt. 5. Leipzig: Deutscher Verlag für Musik, 1973.

Parrish, Carl. *The Notation of Medieval Music.* New York: Norton, 1957. Reprint. New York: Pendragon, 1978.

Publications of Mediaeval Musical Manuscripts. Brooklyn, NY, and Henryville, PA: Institute of Mediaeval Music, 1957–   .

Thirteenth Century

Anglès, Higini. *El Còdex musical de Las Huelgas: Música a veus del segles XIII–XIV.* 3 vols. Barcelona: Institut d'Estudis Catalans, 1931. Reprint. New York: AMS Press, 1977. Includes transcriptions.

Aubry, Pierre. *Cent motets du XIIIᵉ siècle: Publiés d'après le manuscrit Ed.IV.6 de Bamberg.* 3 vols. Paris: Rouart-Lerolle, 1908. Reprint. New York: Broude Bros., 1964. Includes transcriptions.

Beck, Jean. *Le Chansonnier Cangé: Manuscrit français n° 846 de la Bibliothèque Nationale de Paris.* Corpus Cantilenarum Medii Aevi, ser. 1, no. 1. 2 vols. Philadelphia: University of Pennsylvania Press, 1927. Reprint. New York: Broude Bros., 1964. Includes transcriptions.

Beck, Jean, and Louise Beck. *Le Manuscrit du Roi: Fonds français n° 844 de la Bibliothèque Nationale.* Corpus Cantilenarum Medii Aevi, ser. 1, no. 2. 2 vols. Philadelphia: University of Pennsylvania Press, 1938. Reprint. New York: Broude Bros., 1970.

Rokseth, Yvonne. *Polyphonies du XIIIᵉ siècle: Le Manuscrit H 196 de la Faculté de Médicine de Montpellier.* 4 vols. Paris: Editions de l'Oiseau-Lyre, 1935–1939.

Fourteenth Century

Carapetyan, Armen, ed. *An Early Fifteenth-Century Italian Source of Keyboard Music: The Codex Faenza, Biblioteca Communale, 117; A Facsimile Edition.* Musicological Studies and Documents, vol. 10. N.p.: American Institute of Musicology, 1961.

Reaney, Gilbert, ed. *The Manuscript London, British Museum, Additional 29987.* Musicological Studies and Documents, vol. 13. N.p.: American Institute of Musicology, 1965.

Fifteenth Century

Codex Tridentinus 87–93. 7 vols. Rome: Bibliopola, 1969–1970.

Petrucci, Ottaviano. *Harmonice musices Odhecaton A; Canti B numero cinquanta;* and *Canti C numero cento cinquanta.* Monuments of Music and Music Literature in Facsimile, 1st ser., vols. 10, 23, and 25. New York: Broude Bros., 1973, 1975, 1978.

Rehm, Wolfgang, ed. *Codex Escorial: Chansonnier, Biblioteca del Monasterio El Escorial, Signatur MS. V.III.24.* Documenta Musicologica, 2nd ser., vol. 2. Kassel: Bärenreiter, 1958.

Sixteenth Century

Corpus of Early Music. 30 vols. Brussels: Editions Culture et Civilisation, 1970.

Sternfeld, F. W., ed. *English Lute Songs 1597–1632: A Collection of Facsimile Reprints.* Menston, U.K.: Scolar Press, 1968– .

Tallis, Thomas, and William Byrd. *Cantiones Sacrae, 1575.* 6 partbooks. Leeds, U.K.: Boethius, 1976.

Modern Editions

Modern editions (transcriptions) are often categorized as either scholarly or popular. Scholarly editions range from an "urtext," in which nothing is altered except the most obvious errors in the original, to a text that includes more editorial suggestions, all of which should be clearly distinct from the original. In even the plainest of these editions, however, editors have had to make basic decisions that may alter the original in ways misleading to the performer. Reduction of note values, barring, *musica ficta*, specificity of pitch versus transposition, text underlay, and many other decisions are inescapable for the editor. Herein lies the value to the performer of consulting the original source and perhaps even of making one's own edition.

Modern Editions: Scholarly

Following are recommended scholarly editions for a representative collection. The reader should also consult additional sources cited in Part III.

General

Corpus Mensurabilis Musicae. N.p.: American Institute of Musicology, 1947– .

Early English Church Music. London: Stainer & Bell, Ltd. for the British Academy, 1963– .

Hoppin, Richard H., ed. *Anthology of Medieval Music*. New York: Norton, 1978.

Individual editions of the complete works of various composers, such as Byrd, Gesualdo, Lasso, Monteverdi, Obrecht, Palestrina, Senfl, and Victoria.

Lowinsky, Edward E., ed. Monuments of Renaissance Music. Chicago: University of Chicago Press, 1964– .

Marrocco, Thomas, and Nicholas Sandon, eds. *The Oxford Anthology of Music: Medieval Music*. London: Oxford University Press, 1977.

Musica Britannica. London: Stainer & Bell, Ltd. 1951– . 2nd ed., rev. 1966– .

Recent Researches in the Music of the Middle Ages and Early Renaissance. Madison: A-R Editions, 1975– .

Recent Researches in the Music of the Renaissance. New Haven and Madison: A-R Editions, 1964– .

Chant

The Liber Usualis, with Introduction and Rubrics in English. Edited by the Benedictines of Solesmes. Tournai: Desclée, 1952 and other editions.

Thirteenth Century

Anderson, Gordon A. *Notre-Dame and Related Conductus: Opera Omnia*. Collected Works of the Institute of Mediaeval Music, vol. 10. Henryville, PA: Institute of Mediaeval Music, 1979– .

Knapp, Janet, ed. *Thirty-Five Conductus for Two and Three Voices*. Collegium Musicum, 1st ser., no. 6. New Haven: Yale University Press, 1965.

Werf, Hendrik van der, ed. *Trouvères-Melodien I*. Monumenta Monodica Medii Aevi, vol. 11. Kassel: Bärenreiter, 1977.

Fourteenth Century

Apel, Willi, ed. *French Secular Music of the Late Fourteenth Century*. Cambridge, MA: Medieval Academy of America, 1950.

Schrade, Leo, et al., eds. Polyphonic Music of the Fourteenth Century. Monaco: Editions de l'Oiseau-Lyre, 1956– .

Fifteenth Century

Hanen, Martha K., ed. *The Chansonnier El Escorial IV.a.24.* Musicological Studies, vol. 36. 3 vols. Henryville, PA: Institute of Mediaeval Music, 1983.

Hewitt, Helen, ed. *Harmonice musices Odhecaton A.* Cambridge, MA: Medieval Academy of America, 1942. Reprint. New York: Da Capo, 1978.

Picker, Martin, ed. *The Chanson Albums of Marguerite of Austria: MSS. 228 and 11239 of the Bibliothèque Royale de Belgique, Brussels.* Berkeley and Los Angeles: University of California Press, 1965. Includes some sixteenth-century chansons also.

Pope, Isabel, and Masakata Kanazawa. *The Musical Manuscript Montecassino 871: A Neapolitan Repertory of Sacred and Secular Music of the Late Fifteenth Century.* Oxford: Clarendon Press, 1978.

Rehm, Wolfgang, ed. *Die Chansons von Gilles Binchois (1400–1460).* Musikalische Denkmäler, vol. 2. Mainz: B. Schott's Söhne, 1957.

Ringmann, Heribert, and Christian Väterlein, eds. *Das Glogauer Liederbuch.* Das Erbe deutscher Musik, ser. 1, vols. 4, 8, 85, 86. Kassel: Bärenreiter, 1954–1981.

Sixteenth Century

Einstein, Alfred. *The Italian Madrigal.* Translated by Alexander H. Krappe, Roger H. Sessions, and Oliver Strunk. 3 vols. Princeton: Princeton University Press, 1949. Reprint. 1971.

The English Madrigal School. Edited by Edmund Horace Fellowes. 36 vols. London: Stainer & Bell, 1913–1924. 2nd ed. The English Madrigalists. Revised by Thurston Dart. London: Stainer & Bell, 1956– .

Les Maîtres musiciens de la Renaissance française. Edited by Henry Expert. 23 vols. Paris: A. Leduc, 1894–1908. Reprint. New York: Broude Bros., 1963.

Monumentos de la música española. Edited by Higini Anglès. Barcelona: Consejo Superior de Investigaciones Científicas, 1941– . Selected volumes.

Modern Editions: Popular

Popular editions, often of individual pieces, generally include considerable editorial content. This content is not always set in relief from the original. The best popular editions render a genuine service to early music enthusiasts. The worst editions include remote transpositions; a dot, dash, or dynamic mark on nearly every note; fanciful translations and text underlay; and misleading indications of instrumentation—all with little or no reference to what was original. Needless to say, such editions are to be avoided.

When choosing a practical edition, look for one that is "clean." Make sure that the editor has differentiated the additions from the original. Are the original clef and incipit given? Are original time and proportion signatures shown? Are most suggestions confined to a preface? Is a clear translation provided? If the answer to these questions is yes, then the edition is probably a well-considered and reliable one. Fortunately, many popular editions are quite usable, and their numbers are such that it would be impossible to list them all here. Following are some series that offer high standards of scholarship at prices more affordable than those of editions designed mainly for libraries:

§ Anthology of Music (Cologne: Arno Volk Verlag)

§ Antico Edition (Newton Abbot)

§ Early Music Series (London: Oxford University Press)

§ Hortus Musicus (Kassel: Bärenreiter)

§ London Pro Musica Edition (London and Brighton)

§ Musica Britannica: Performing Parts for Mixed Consorts (London: Stainer & Bell)

§ Ogni Sorte Editions (Miami: Arnold Grayson)

RECORDINGS

The number of recorded performances of early music has increased significantly during recent years. Many of these newer releases offer an exciting blend of scholarship and musicianship, just what this book aims to encourage. Listening to such recordings is an invaluable aid to understanding general matters of style and specifics of performance practice.

In no other field of music have "traditions" of performance practice undergone such continual change. Since about 1960, recordings of early music have reflected a wide variety of approaches to the repertory. As new research and more secure musicianship (both technical and aesthetic) allow performers to present new solutions to performance problems, new recordings will replace old ones.

Because of this rapid rate of change, we have chosen not to recommend a basic collection of recordings.[9] Prospective buyers of early music records need to acquaint themselves with recordings and performers that reflect the state of the art. Reviews in music journals can be helpful in making these determinations.

PERFORMANCE OPPORTUNITIES

The type of programming done by an ensemble naturally reflects the kind of ensemble it is, as discussed in Chapter 1. While the "variety" program is still popular, the authors feel that both performers and listeners have much to gain from programs of concentration (see Chapter 3). A list of sample subject areas follows.

§ French Music of the Middle Ages

§ Songs of Pilgrims and Crusaders

§ Music and Poetry of Machaut

§ The Roman de Fauvel

§ Josquin and His Contemporaries

§ A Renaissance Dance Concert

§ Masterpieces of the Polish Renaissance

§ The Music of Orlando di Lasso
§ Music from the Intermedii
§ Music from the Court of Elizabeth I

Some of the foregoing programs, as well as many others, may combine musicians, dancers, and actors, and are ideal multidisciplinary projects for schools whose departments are interested in cooperative endeavors. Although these are large undertakings, they can be tremendously rewarding and worthwhile for the participants and public alike.

Material for programs of concentration exists for all types of early music ensemble. One need only explore the vast wealth of medieval and Renaissance music to locate a suitable theme.

PROJECTS FOR INVESTIGATING RESOURCES

1. Assess the resources available for performance, as outlined in this chapter, for your school or community ensemble.

2. Design several "specialty" program themes and investigate the repertory available and the performance forces needed for each.

3. Compile a bibliography dealing with practical performance and maintenance aspects of the early instrument that you play.

4. Compile a discography of currently available recordings of a particular repertory.

PART II

General Guidelines for Early Music Performance

INTRODUCTION

Part II of this book offers further information on the use and interpretation of resources described in Part I. The reader will find statements of philosophy, discussions of performance-practice problems, and practical guidance. Consideration is given to four topics of special interest to performers of medieval and Renaissance music: rhythm, musica ficta, text underlay, and ornamentation. The recommended projects that follow each topic are designed to increase both the reader's understanding of the principles involved and also the capacity to apply them in performance. The material in Part II is essential to the study of examples in Part III.

Chapter 3

Approaches to Performing Medieval and Renaissance Music

AUTHENTICITY

Performances of medieval and Renaissance music in recent years have shown that the repertory can be interpreted in differing ways and still maintain artistic validity and audience appeal. Like a Shakespeare play, a piece of early music can be clothed in various costumes, from period robes to modern dress, and it can be produced in a style dramatically stark or sumptuous. Because musicians can never recreate precisely an original performance situation, owing to insufficient information and lost resources, and because a piece of music might have had several legitimate interpretations in its composer's own lifetime, performers must make choices among the options that they perceive.

Performers can exercise options in three general areas: the "text" of the music as it is to be performed; the forces that are to be employed; and the method of interpretation. "Text" preparation involves determining the pitches, rhythms, form, words, text underlay, etc.—the script that the cast will follow. "Forces" include voices, instruments, even dancers or speakers—the cast of characters. "Method" is basically musical execution: tempo, balance, dynamics, phrasing, embellishment, etc.—a matter comparable to interpreting a role or directing a scene. Decisions in all of these areas may take historical evidence into account, if desired.

For the performer who chooses a historical approach to interpretation, documentary evidence and scholarly research provide many discrete items of information about period practices. Enough information exists to support fairly detailed reconstruction of original performances of some bodies of music. Other repertories rely at present largely on educated guesses and speculative approaches to interpretation. Like music of any period, including our own, music of the Middle Ages and

Renaissance may accommodate more than one "authentic" manner of performance, but the solutions for a given piece must all fit within parameters of interpretation intrinsic to the work.

So much tradition has vanished that many aspects of performance will always remain conjectural. Tone is an obvious and crucial example. Not only does the vocal tone of any style period remain a mystery, but so does instrumental tone to some extent. Even the most faithful reproduction of the best-preserved instruments cannot compensate for changes caused by aging. To duplicate the present sound of a museum instrument may be to render serious injustice to the original sound of that instrument when new or in its best playing condition. And as the reproduction ages, its tone, too, will change. Besides tone, traditions of pitch inflection, rhythmic freedom, and improvisation remain frustratingly beyond recovery.

Nevertheless, the authors feel that an "authentic" performance is the most satisfactory way to present a piece of music. A manner of interpretation that takes into account the composer's intentions and reproduces a style of performance from his lifetime, insofar as possible, can reveal and communicate the spirit of the music to greatest effect. The "authentic" approach is, however, only the point of departure; the principal responsibility of any performer is to select music of high quality and to perform it intelligently and musically. In the authors' experience, early music that is performed in an authentic manner and with competence arouses a strong, favorable response from audiences and performers.

For the purposes of this book, the authors advocate historically defensible choices in the preparation of text, selection of performance forces, and method of interpretation as the point of departure for performance. From that point on, some compromises are inevitable.

The modern concert performance is, of course, the first compromise made by performers who wish to present their music to the public. Large halls, large audiences, and considerations of programming preclude any authenticity of setting or recreation of original atmosphere. Besides imposing an artificial context, one that limits the intimacy of communication between performer and audience, the large concert hall simply does not accommodate the soft sounds and subtle nuances of most early music, a problem not solved by electronic amplification. Recordings may capture "authentic" sounds better than a live audience hears them, and the excellence of much recent recording compensates for the absence of communication and spontaneity.

Performers who give concerts in relatively small rooms, churches, etc., may be able to recreate historically "correct" sounds that are audible to all listeners. Those who concertize in larger halls sometimes resort to the use of instruments modified to produce more sound, and they select repertory that works effectively in the larger environment.

The problem of "authenticity" must be resolved by serious students of early music. Only by attaining knowledge of the subject and competence as performers can they bring life to this music and discover its full potential. At the same time, they will encounter the limits of present knowledge and performance techniques. Awareness of these possibilities and limitations provides the framework within which historically valid performances can be created today.[1]

QUALITY OF PERFORMANCE

Whatever choices the performer makes in preparing a piece of music, the audience will be stimulated by a performance that meets discriminating standards. The difficulty of the early music repertory must not be underestimated. Those wishing to encourage greater public interest in this music will serve their cause by presenting concerts of the highest attainable quality.

Mastery of technique is the first requisite for each individual performer, whether singer or instrumentalist, soloist or ensemble member. Such technique implies control of tone, pitch, attack, release, etc., all governed by a discerning ear and specific, well-trained reflexes. It also implies an intimate understanding of the particular instrument or voice, in order to work with its idiosyncracies in a flexible manner.

Ensemble skills are challenged as much in some early music as in twentieth-century literature. Especially because most groups perform without a conductor, singers and players must bring to the early repertory great sensitivity to rhythm, texture, and balance, as well as to intonation and to many other aspects of ensemble procedure. Performers who come to medieval or Renaissance music with ensemble techniques appropriate to later periods usually need to acquire further skills and to allow generous amounts of rehearsal time for preparing early works.

Employing the appropriate ensemble for a given work helps to insure a high standard of performance. Compromise, as stated previously, sometimes appears inevitable; still, the least compromise is generally the best. Knowledge of a particular repertory and its performance traditions allows the most informed judgment when change is necessary; for instance, substitution of women's voices for boys', or lute for vihuela. Substituting Baroque instruments for those of the Renaissance, however, or choral forces for solo singers, may distort the music nearly as much as synthesized renditions misrepresent the works of Bach. Modern instruments playing early music belong in the classroom, not on the concert stage.

The best possible acoustic environment for a given genre enhances its appeal considerably. Liturgical music usually profits from the resonance of a church's vaulted roof. Antiphonal works need separated spaces. *Haut* (loud) instruments sound good outdoors and possibly indoors, but *bas* (soft) instruments require indoor settings, sometimes quite intimate, for best effect.

A historically faithful rendition adheres to the complete original form, both musical and textual. If a piece is performed out of context—for instance, a liturgical motet, or one of a set of dances—it needs to be complete in its own right. Singing in the original language, with an authentic pronunciation, best conveys the interrelationship of music and text. A written or oral translation, even a synopsis, increases the audience's appreciation of vocal performances in foreign languages.

PRACTICAL CONSIDERATIONS

Performers inexperienced in the medieval and Renaissance repertory are advised to perform works for which they are best equipped; that is, those that permit maximum transfer of technique. Singers, of course, continue to sing, possibly modifying their tone production. Persons trained on a modern instrument adopt a close early counterpart.

Compositions that resemble works performed previously may be the easiest types to learn at first. For example, a cellist with string quartet experience might find that playing a viol in consorts yields better results than playing a rebec for monophonic dances, while a violinist who has played "country" music could find the opposite to be true. A lieder singer might prefer Dowland ayres to Machaut ballades, at least in initial encounters. Success with the relatively familiar can lead to exploration of the more unusual styles, instruments, and techniques.

The performer is encouraged to specialize on one instrument, or at most on one family, such as recorders. The advantages are obvious: the opportunity to develop competence, the minimizing of risks in performance, and the relatively small expense. (Incidentally, transporting more than one fragile, perhaps bulky instrument often proves difficult!) The attractions of learning several instruments may seem tempting; a small ensemble can offer a variety of styles and timbres while impressing the audience with its versatility. Many professional early music groups do just this. The novice, however, needs to perform well on one instrument before attempting to learn others.

Concentrating on the music of a single style period helps both instrumentalists and vocalists to achieve successful performances in a relatively short time. Such concentration permits small ensembles or soloists to master basic characteristics of the style and eventually to deal with its subtleties. In an educational setting, this approach aids students in developing aural familiarity with a style, a prerequisite for making independent judgments about stylistic performance within a chosen repertory.

The members of a newly formed early music group or class could find their combined experiences and instruments unsuited to any particular repertory. Bringing together an operatic tenor and an alto folk singer with an Elizabethan lute, a vielle, and a wide-bore soprano recorder might present practical problems, but not insurmountable ones. In this hypothetical situation, the performers would probably decide that certain duets and trios were stylistically acceptable, and that quintets were best avoided. Some compromises might be considered; for example, playing the lute with a plectrum in fourteenth-century repertory, or involving everyone in a heterophonic rendition of a medieval song. However, quantities of music exist that members of this group could perform "authentically," without branching into an inordinate number of style periods. Thus, radical compromises could be relegated to experiments in private, and more authentic solutions could be developed and presented to the public.

While encouraging early music performers to make the most of their available resources, the authors urge these performers—as individuals, groups, or institutions—to expand their resources, in order to improve and develop musically. Growth of this kind usually suggests capital expenditure for music, instruments, instruction, concert production, and ongoing expenses. Some of the most enterprising ensembles have the support of institutions, boards of directors, private patrons, or grants from governmental, corporate, or foundation agencies.

Even without external financial assistance, an early music group can develop interest and support within its own community. The group can recruit and train new members, experienced or novice, professional or amateur. It can recommend private instruction where available, or bring guest artists for workshops. (A concert presented by a guest artist may increase community awareness and appreciation of local early music activities.) Members of the group can seek out further resources (instruments, music, recordings) to borrow, rent, trade, or purchase. Schools, churches, and civic organizations may offer rehearsal space, opportunities for performance, and perhaps a degree of sponsorship.

In an educational context, early music performance flourishes where resources are adequate, scheduling is propitious, and students are encouraged to participate. If students can receive academic credit and obtain supplementary private instruction, they are more likely to continue in a group and to improve their skills. Students who desire course credit can use the suggested Projects in this book for class assignments. Their curriculum can also include supplementary reading and listening.

Some institutions coordinate their collegium repertory with courses in music history, theory, or literature; with programs in drama, history, art, dance, etc.; and with diverse events on the campus. Such cooperation is generally beneficial to all involved.

Success in early music performance is difficult to measure and often difficult to attain. The authors can offer some assurance that performers who demonstrate musical ability, resourcefulness, organizational skills, willingness to work, and enthusiasm are likely to prosper.

Chapter 4
Primary Recommendations for Performance

SCORE STUDY

Careful examination of the music is the first step in preparing a performance. We recommend obtaining the best available scores. Facsimiles should come from reliable sources and should be clearly readable. Modern transcriptions should be reliable editions—not merely accurate, but also faithful to the original conception of form, rhythm, etc. (see Chapter 2, "Music," p. 11). A good musical text provides a great deal of definite information. Beyond that, it may offer criteria for making decisions regarding performance.

Facsimiles

Facsimiles present the viewer with several basic formats.

MONOPHONIC MELODY. (See Figure 4-1.) If the melody is a song, the first lines of text are usually underlaid, and the remainder of the text follows.

SCORE. (See Figure 4-2.) Here the two or more parts are aligned vertically, to some extent. Normally the parts coincide at each margin.

CHOIRBOOK. (See Figure 4-3.) This format, an efficient use of writing space, places the parts in separate areas of one page or of facing pages. Choirbook arrangement suits pieces whose parts differ in the number of notes, although it may occur where all parts have similar length.

PARTBOOK. (See Figure 4-4.) The printing of music brought an increased appearance of small partbooks, collections of pieces containing the music for a single part (e.g., bassus) or for two parts (e.g., superius and tenor) of a larger ensemble.

TABLATURE. This category of notation, used for keyboard and string instruments, employs letters or numerals to indicate pitches or finger positions. Primarily a soloist notation, it also appears in chordal plucked-string parts of instrumental ensemble music and accompanied song.

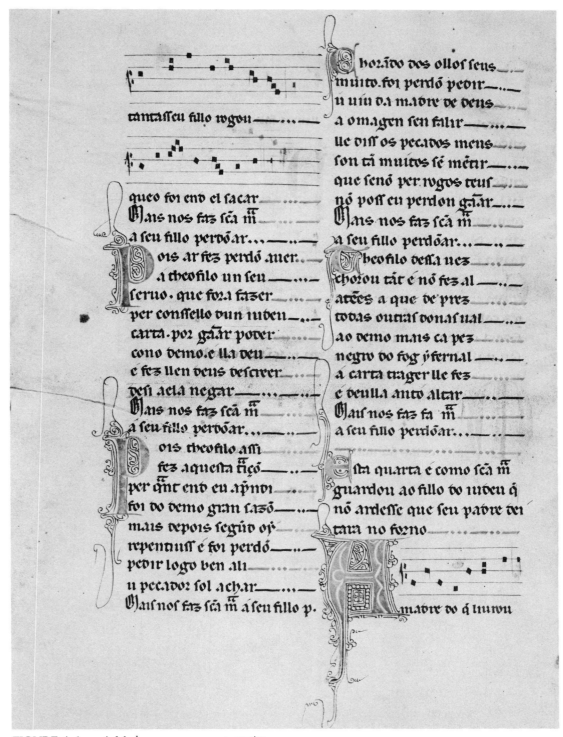

FIGURE 4–1a. A *Madre*: an anonymous cantiga.
Reproduced from "*Cantigas de Santa Maria*," MS. 10069, courtesy of the Biblioteca Nacional, Madrid.

FIGURE 4–1b.   *A Madre. (cont.)*

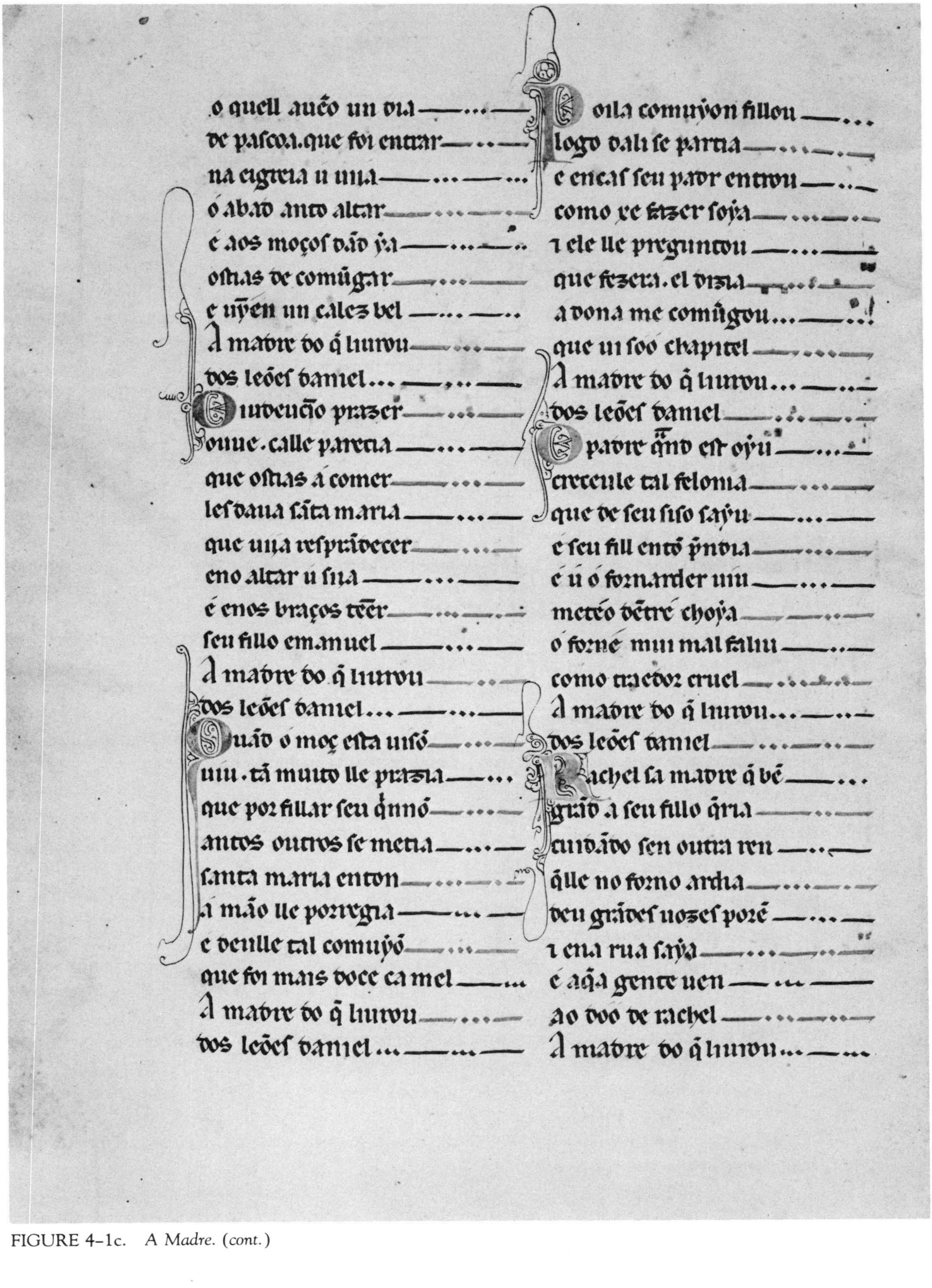

o quell aueo un dia
de pascoa. que foi entrar
na eigreia u uiia
o abad ante altar
e aos moços dão ia
ostias de comũgar
e uiien un cales bel
A madre do q liurou
dos leões daniel...
Iuueuçõ prazer
onue. calle parecia
que ostias a comer
les daua sãta maria
que uiia resprãdecer
eno altar u siia
e enos braços tēer
seu fillo emanuel
A madre do q liurou
dos leões daniel...
uão o moç esta uiso
uiu. tã muito lle prazia
que por fillar seu ãnõ
antos outros se metia
santa maria enton
a mão lle porregia
e deulle tal comuiõ
que foi mais doce ca mel
A madre do q liurou
dos leões daniel...

oila comuion fillou
logo dali se partia
e encas seu padr entrou
como xe fazer soia
7 ele lle preguntou
que fezera. el dizia
a dona me comũgou...
que ui soo chapitel
A madre do q liurou
dos leões daniel
padre ãno est oyu
crrceule tal felonia
que de seu siso sayu
e seu fill entõ pndia
e u o fornadeir uiu
meteo dētre choia
o forne mui mal faliu
como traedor cruel
A madre do q liurou
dos leões daniel
Rachel sa madre q bē
queria a seu fillo ãria
cuidãdo sen outra ren
qlle no forno ardia
deu grãdes uozes pore
7 ena rua saia
e aqa gente uen
ao doo de rachel
A madre do q liurou...

FIGURE 4–1c. *A Madre.* (cont.)

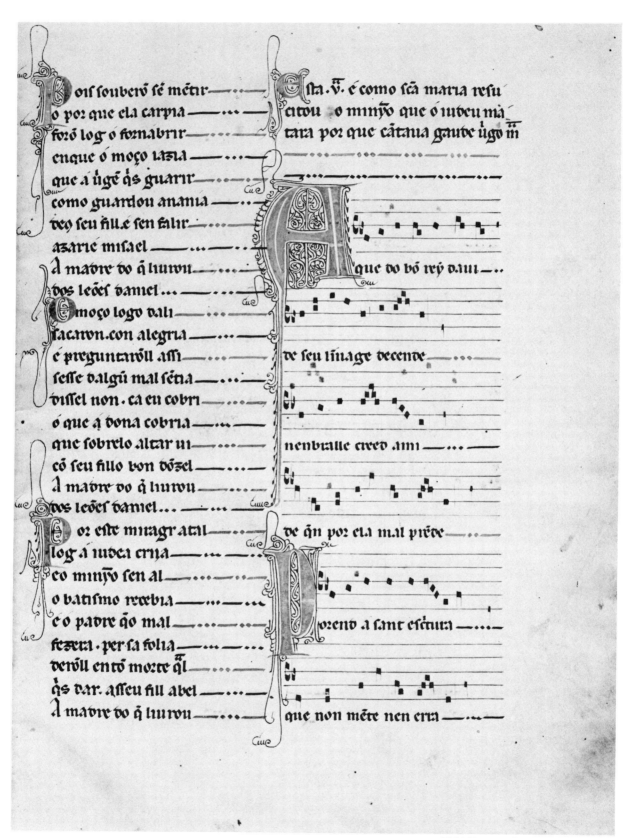

FIGURE 4–1d.   *A Madre.* (cont.)

FIGURE 4–2. *Laus Domino/Eius:* an anonymous motet.
Reproduced from Cod. Guelf. 1099 Helmst., courtesy of the Herzog August Bibliothek, Wolfenbüttel.

For purposes of study, the performer is advised to transcribe choirbook, partbook, and tablature facsimiles into score format. The facsimiles can be returned to later for rehearsing and performing.

Facsimiles allow the modern performer to come to terms with the music as the original performer did. Performing from a choirbook or partbook facsimile encourages independence of line and awareness of the ensemble. Without reference to a score, performers must devise new techniques for efficient sight-reading and rehearsal. Comparison of facsimiles from various sources of a work can provide considerable information and insight, as one source may correct the errors of another or show valid variants.

Facsimiles pose some problems, manuscripts more so than prints. For example, black-and-white photographs fail to show red ink, which affects notational values (see cover illustration). Most sources lack some ingredients needed for performance, such as complete text underlay or *musica ficta*. Surviving manuscripts rarely constitute a performer's version. Many are presentation copies, perhaps copied long after the time when a work and its style were in vogue. Even in manuscripts of the composer's own time and place, scribal errors occur in nearly

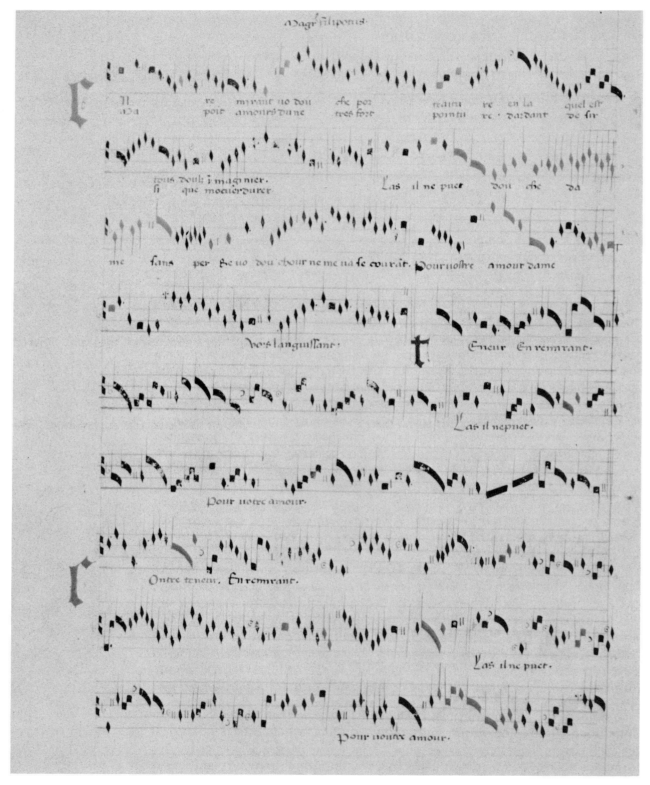

FIGURE 4–3. *En remirant*: a chanson by Philipoctus de Caserta.
Reproduced from MS. α M.5. 24, courtesy of the Biblioteca Estense, Modena.

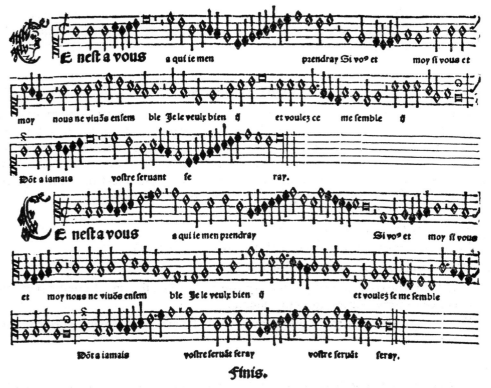

FIGURE 4-4a. Superius and tenor parts of *Ce n'est a vous*: a chanson by Pierre Certon. Reproduced courtesy of the Herzog August Bibliothek, Wolfenbüttel.

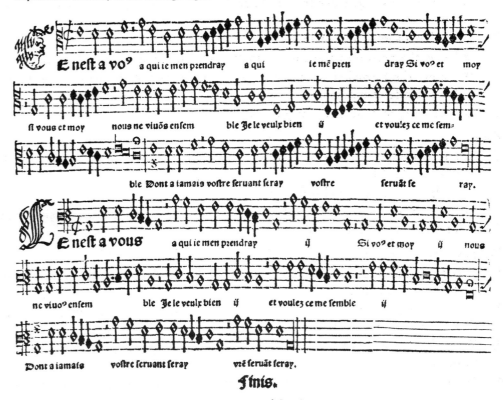

FIGURE 4-4b. Contratenor and bassus parts of *Ce n'est a vous*.

every source. The quality of calligraphy does not necessarily correlate with accuracy or reliability. These caveats are intended not to discourage the use of facsimiles but to draw attention to the challenges that they pose.

Score Analysis

A practical approach to score analysis can proceed from a general assessment of the design of the music to specific considerations of form, texture, pitches, text, etc. The following list outlines features that performers need to consider in preparing a piece of medieval or Renaissance music. The questions included under each heading represent the authors' recommended approach. Some questions suit only certain works; some pieces may require other questions.

General Character and Function of the Music
1. To what repertory does the work belong (see Part III)?
2. Who composed it, when, and where?
3. What was the occasion or purpose of the work (e.g., liturgy, dramatic performance, ceremony, entertainment, dancing)?
4. What qualities does the work convey in its length, complexity, sonority, and affect?

Text
1. Are the parts texted or textless? If textless, should text be provided? If texted, is the text complete? If incomplete, is it merely an incipit title, or should the part be texted and sung? Does the presence of text necessarily mean that the part is sung?
2. What language(s) and dialect(s) are employed?
3. What is the nature of the subject matter, and in what style is it presented?
4. What are the formal characteristics (e.g., length, meter, rhyme scheme, repetitions, stanzaic structure)?
5. Is borrowed textual material incorporated within the text?

Form
1. What determines the form of the work, considering music and text as a whole? Is it a standard form?
2. Does borrowed material influence the form?
3. What units make up the work (e.g., through-composed sections, musical repetitions with new text, refrains)?

Compositional Materials
1. What are the melodic characteristics (e.g., range, length, pitch sets, shapes, patterns, pitch centers)?
2. What harmonic procedures are employed? What constitutes consonance and dissonance? Is the work modal, tonal?
3. What is the nature of the meter (i.e., unmeasured, modal, mensural, proportional)?
4. What are the rhythmic characteristics? How do they relate to the overall quality of movement?

5. How does the composer create cadences?
6. Is borrowed material included? If so, how?

Phrase Structure and Texture

1. Does the piece exhibit monophony, homophony, polyphony?
2. Is imitation used, or canon? In what way?
3. What determines the phrase structure of a single part? Do its melodic and textual phrases coincide?
4. Do the parts exhibit simultaneous or overlapping phrases?

Extramusical Aspects

1. Was a nonmusical activity involved in the occasion for first performing this work (e.g., liturgical or dramatic action, dance, procession, carnival, wedding)?
2. Does the composition contain symbolism in its structure or its text? Are numerological considerations significant?

The Performer's Perspective

1. How would original performers have dealt with the score or parts from which they performed? What decisions would they have needed to make in rehearsal? What instructions might they have marked in their music?
2. What conventions and information did the original performers apply to this music (e.g., solmization, *musica ficta*, text underlay and repetition, ornamentation, interpretation of symbols, knowledge of common mensurations)?
3. How can modern performers best convey the spirit of this music within the limits of their resources and understanding?

DETERMINATION OF AN ENSEMBLE

Most sources of medieval and Renaissance music contain no reference to the appropriate vocal and/or instrumental performing forces. Therefore, performers today must learn which performing forces are historically documented for each style period and genre of music chosen for study. Such information has been gleaned by scholars from a variety of evidence. Furthermore, new evidence continues to be discovered, old evidence reinterpreted, and earlier conclusions modified.

When performers know the options, they must then make choices and perhaps exercise their own judgments. A case in point is secular polyphony of the thirteenth, fourteenth, and fifteenth centuries. For much of this music, evidence may be cited to support performance by singers only, or by a mixed vocal-instrumental ensemble, or (less often) by a group of instruments. It is conceivable that a particular piece might have been performed in all three ways, each appropriate to a particular place and time. When the performers have decided which mode of performance they intend to recreate, they will need to determine the particular voices and/or instruments to be used.

Structural Considerations

At this point a structural interpretation may be helpful. Although this approach has lost favor as the primary means of determining an ensemble, the authors find it useful for revealing practical, workable solutions when many possibilities exist.

This type of interpretation derives from the internal evidence of the music itself. That is, the nature of each part of the polyphony and the relationship of the parts are viewed as containing clues to the appropriate performing forces. Obviously, this approach relies on the performer's interpretation of the music; it also hinges on the individual's opinions of what sort of music suits each voice and instrument best. Taken to the extreme, structural interpretation implies that the composer had very specific performing forces in mind, that he wrote in a unique manner for each type of performer (voice or instrument, wind or string, plucked or bowed, etc.), and that we can discover his intentions by studying the score.

Is a melodic line ever inherently vocal or instrumental? One study shows that before 1600 the only criterion for an exclusively instrumental line is extreme width of range or the need for extremely rapid execution.[1] Nevertheless, singers seem to negotiate diatonic lines more successfully than frequent or wide leaps. The existence of a complete, underlaid text seems a strong indication that the composer, scribe, or printer thought that a line should be performed vocally.

The absence of text or the appearance of only an incipit may cause the performer to consider that a given line might be instrumental. As stated earlier, wide range, fast motion, or frequent leaps might also suggest the use of an instrument.

A melodic part with narrow range can accommodate a wind instrument; the higher the part, the greater the number of wind instruments available for choice. A melodic part with wide range may be more suited to a string instrument or to an aerophone with keyboard mechanism. Bowed strings are the obvious choices for most medieval parts of low range. By the sixteenth century many winds had low and fairly wide ranges.

Parts that contain many long notes and few rests suggest instruments that can sustain a tone. Sustained tone may be desirable for a part that helps to determine a cadence, especially for one that provides the lowest pitch. A sustained part that accompanies a solo voice can be performed most expressively on an instrument of variable volume and adjustable pitch. At the opposite extreme, a part that contains short notes, rests, and wide leaps, and does not contribute to cadence formation, might be assigned to a plucked instrument, because of its relatively rapid decay of sound. One can argue, however, that a composer who writes frequent rests wants precisely measured silences, which are more clearly articulated on a sustaining instrument.

An instrument used in an ensemble of any type must provide appropriate volume and timbre. Some instrumental music, including certain dances and works performed outdoors, is suited to loud instruments. (Loud instruments also carry well in a large concert hall.) Soft instruments work best with voices and with one another. In the authors' opinion, much polyphony attractively reveals its stratified textures when performed using a mixture of diverse timbres. Sixteenth-century music, on the other hand, often benefits from employing instruments of one family to reinforce a homophonic texture.

The relationships and functions of the parts can influence the choice of performing forces. Similar parts, especially ones written in canon or with considerable imitation or in uniform rhythm, may suggest similar instruments or voices. Unlike parts may appear more appropriate for contrasting instruments. A part that alternates texted passages with long, untexted melismas may work well when performed by a voice doubling or alternating with an instrument. This last solution, for example, has some support when applied to cantus parts of Burgundian chansons.[2]

Transposition

In addition to structural considerations, the determination of an ensemble may be influenced by questions of transposition. In the authors' opinion, ensembles of voice(s) with one or more instruments must usually maintain notated ranges because of instrument characteristics and in order to preserve normal sonorities and the correct interval relationships among parts. An exception to this principle might be those fifteenth-century chansons that have especially low tenors, whether the performer conceives those parts as instrumental or vocal; perhaps these works should be transposed upward.

Transposition permits a voice of any range to sing the monophonic song literature; however, some texts seem more appropriate for men, some for women. Vocal ensemble music for one singer per part without accompaniment also offers some options with regard to transposition and voice types. Some of these works have both soprano-range and bass-range parts, so that extremes of register govern the degree of transposition possible. A portion of the repertory can be performed by an ensemble of adult male voices. Indeed, sonority and blend tend to favor such an ensemble when skilled countertenors are available. Even when female sopranos take part, a countertenor voice may sound better than a woman's alto voice on an inner part.

Renaissance choral works are almost exclusively sacred, hence intended for male voices. A *cappella* performance was the norm, and the number of singers was small (see Chapter 2, "Voices," p. 5). Parts in soprano range were sung by adult falsettists or boys or, later in the period, castrati.[3] Some authorities suggest that transposition upward by a minor third or so is appropriate to sixteenth-century English church music.[4] Such transposition could necessitate assigning a different type of voice to a given part.

Blend and balance are important in determining the best voice for a part, and they are even more critical in choosing the best instrument. Instruments offer a broader spectrum of volume, timbre, range, and sustaining power. One instrument may seem more appropriate for a particular subject or situation than another. In describing and classifying instruments, medieval and Renaissance writers were aware of these factors.[5]

When one takes into account all the voices and instruments historically appropriate to a given genre, and then considers the possibilities of transposition and the characteristics of the music—range, function, and nature of each part and of the piece as a whole—the choices usually narrow to a very few. Among these options, the final determination of an ensemble depends on the available singers and instruments, on the circumstances of performance, and ultimately on the performer's personal taste.

PITCH

Early music ensembles performing in this day and age must make decisions about pitch standards and about temperament, decisions that were not so problematic for the medieval or Renaissance musician. In performing compositions of their own generation with instruments of the day, period musicians used some agreed-upon level of pitch, or what was then available on fixed-pitch instruments. And they applied a conventionally acceptable temperament, possibly without even being aware of doing so.

Evidence suggests that the actual frequency of a notated pitch easily varied by as much as a perfect fourth from one place to another. Museums today possess dozens of period wind instruments, many of which have been scientifically measured. These instruments exhibit a variety of pitch levels; a large group of sixteenth-century instruments lies within the range of approximately A-410 to A-465 (a difference of about a whole step).[6] Early organs show considerably wider variance, from a perfect fourth below to a major third above A-440.[7] A fixed-pitch instrument, therefore, was played in combination only with other instruments constructed at the same pitch level or at a level that accommodated a conventional transposition.

Most modern reproductions are manufactured to perform at A-440 (see Chapter 2, "Instruments: Practical Collections," p. 8). In actual fact, they may produce an optimum tone quality at a level somewhat higher or lower than that standard. And certain makers choose to construct replicas of period instruments that use some pitch standard other than A-440. An ensemble today must thus exercise care in combining instruments and forethought in acquiring them. A standard of A-440 might not even be one of the "authentic" options, but merely a practical compromise.

Vocal ensembles and choirs performing *a cappella* can transpose a work to make its compass suit their voices. As mentioned earlier in this chapter, some music appears to require a pitch standard higher than A-440. Several explanations have been offered for the various combinations of clefs used in the fifteenth and sixteenth centuries; for example, as prescriptions for transposition, or for non-transposition (sometimes resulting in unusually high or low tessitura), or for the use of certain types of voice.[8]

Knowledge of the temperaments used in the Middle Ages and Renaissance comes from arithmetical systems promulgated in theoretical treatises and from practical writings concerned with the tunings of instruments and with the proper sounds of intervals. Both theoretical and practical evidence indicates that a shift from Pythagorean toward mean-tone tuning occurred in the mid-to-late fifteenth century.[9]

The Pythagorean tuning system contains pure fifths (except for one "wolf" fifth) and no pure thirds. Such a system naturally favors harmonic intervals of fifths, rather than thirds, on strong beats and at cadences. Most medieval music displays these characteristics, treating thirds as imperfect consonances and fifths as perfect consonances.

Mean-tone temperaments, on the other hand, incorporate pure or nearly pure thirds and narrow fifths. The syntonic comma characteristic of this system is distributed in various ways; for instance, 2/7-, 1/4-, 1/5-, and 1/6-comma tunings. Music that employs thirds as harmonic consonances benefits from mean-tone temperament: Certain thirds and triads sound particularly stable.

Changing compositional procedures in the fifteenth century coincided with the adoption of mean-tone temperament. The melodic and harmonic thirds that increasingly appeared in early-fifteenth-century composition are those that sound most pure in Pythagorean tuning. With the change from three-part to four-part texture, from fauxbourdon to triads used in the context of contrary motion and imitation, and with an expanding harmonic vocabulary came the diminishing significance of the pure fifth and the greater attraction of the pure third.[10]

Music of the late fifteenth and sixteenth centuries requires a greater concern for harmonic intonation than earlier music does. The extreme independence of line in most earlier music demands careful melodic intonation at all times, along with attention to harmonic consonances, particularly at cadences. Harmonic intonation is somewhat less crucial for ensembles that combine disparate sonorities within stratified textures; indeed, precise intonation may be physically impossible for some combinations. By way of contrast, later Renaissance music not only embodies many triads, but also utilizes them frequently in homophonic textures and in settings that call for blending in ensembles of solo voices or of like instruments. These factors, together with the greater number of parts sounding simultaneously and the wider overall compass, focus attention on the accuracy of harmonic intonation.

Temperaments other than strict Pythagorean and mean-tone were formulated by a few theorists or necessitated by some instruments. Marchettus de Padua, for example, suggested in the fourteenth century a system of intervals that included an unusually high leading tone.[11] If his system were applied to the performance of trecento works, cadences would resolve from a very wide major sixth to the octave, emphasizing the change from dissonance to consonance. Chromaticism in certain unusual works of the late fourteenth and late sixteenth centuries defies the use of a rigid temperament or of fixed-pitch instruments.[12] The puzzling "secret chromatic art" of the Renaissance motet also operates outside of a fixed temperament.[13]

Equal temperament, although never advocated in medieval and Renaissance arithmetical speculations, can occur as an attribute of fretted instruments. If the strings of lutes and viols are tuned to distribute the comma among the third and fourths of open strings, and if the frets are spaced for equal semitones, equal temperament results (or very nearly equal, given the variables of strings and of instruments). Some Renaissance composers and writers discussed tuning strings and adjusting frets in a way that more nearly achieves mean-tone temperament.[14]

A modern performer accustomed to equal temperament must respond to the challenge of learning to hear and perform in other temperaments. Early music performed in equal temperament loses some of its harmonic zest. Performing this music with truly pure thirds or pure fifths where appropriate enhances its affective potential.

FORMS

In the preceding chapter, performers were encouraged to render the complete musical and textual form of a work. Just as a play, a painting, a sonnet, or a concerto needs to be experienced in its entirety, so too a composition from the early music repertory deserves a complete performance in order to be appreciated fully.

The early music revival in its beginning stages justified some curtailing of forms by the need to present variety in a concert or on a recording, as well as by the fear of boring an audience with long pieces unfamiliar in style and sonority.

Truncated or misarranged forms resulted occasionally from misunderstandings by editors and performers. Audiences now are more informed and receptive, new editions correct the errors of the old, and the art of historical performance practice has reached a high level of professional competence. For these reasons, deliberate compromises of form are seldom necessary. Some compositions, however, remain unclear and require decisions by the performer. (See, for instance, Example III-15. Note that Arabic numerals refer to chapters and Roman numerals to parts; Example III-15 is in Part III.)

Instrumental versions of vocal works can sound pointlessly repetitive when all internal repeats of the vocal model are observed. If the source provides no written-out variations, the performer may wish to rethink the form. Categories include solo lute, vihuela, and keyboard arrangements of sacred and secular polyphony, as well as textless ensemble settings.

LANGUAGES

Vocal music of the Middle Ages and Renaissance displays a wonderful array of languages and dialects. If these works are sung in original languages with "authentic" pronunciations, as the authors have recommended, the modern singer needs proficiency in pronunciation and, to some extent, in translation.

Language has always been an evolving means of communication, fertilized by cross-cultural interchange, refined by social and regional preferences, enriched by invention and even by misunderstanding. A moment's reflection on today's international language, English, its history and variety, suggests the variations that must have existed within Latin, for instance, the international tongue of earlier times. As with English and Latin, so to some extent with early French, Italian, German, etc.: "High" poetic versions coexisted with common dialects, each of which changed over time and varied according to place and culture.

These changing patterns of language make it difficult for today's performer to know what systems of pronunciation to apply. Scholars sometimes disagree over details or discourage rigid rules. At the same time they have deduced considerable information on such matters as consonants, vowels, and stress patterns, through analysis of rhyme, comparison of orthography, and similar techniques.

Performers, then, must try to determine the particular version of the language used in a text, after which they have to decide on an appropriate pronunciation scheme. Few musicians have the expertise for this, but they may be able to consult a specialist in a college or university language department. The authors have received valuable assistance from such linguists, who have usually been intrigued as well as cooperative.

An expert can also help in translating texts. Although many editions contain excellent translations and useful glossaries, these may fail to disclose symbolism, allusions, and double meanings.

The effort to determine "authentic" pronunciation might not seem important if the audience is ignorant of the language; however, listeners seem to react favorably to the sonority of historic pronunciations (see Appendix E). Audiences respond even more fully when they know the meaning of a text. Hence the authors urge singers to provide printed or oral translations, either complete or condensed.

Chapter 5
Rhythm

Rhythm is the vital force of music, the flow that gives meaning to pitches, timbres, and words. Its durations can be captured, at least approximately, in notation. Its more subtle dimensions—tempo, stress accent, note grouping, phrasing—elude quantification and depend on the performer's sensitivity to a given style.

A good performing edition of medieval or Renaissance music normally translates the rhythm symbols of the original source into a standard twentieth-century frame of reference, so that performers can read the music easily. The edition usually reduces note values; it may add time signatures, bar lines, ties, fermatas, and even accents; it groups notes with beams and sometimes with phrase markings; and it may suggest metronome settings and tempo changes. Rarely does any vestige of the original notation survive. For example, the semibrevis, in essence the same symbol as today's whole note, was once the unit of pulse. Now the quarter note or half note commonly assumes that function.

More important to performers than the transcription of symbols is the fact that an edition sometimes forces the music into only one of several possible rhythmic interpretations. The editor's decisions about note values, meter, tempo, etc., reflect what that individual considers to be valid performance practice. Depending on the category of music, editorial constraints on rhythm vary from scarcely significant to total organization.

Rhythmic interpretation is one of the knottiest problems faced by serious performers of early music. The evidence in treatises and in notation contains enough ambiguities and inconsistencies to preclude any definitive approach to rhythm for some repertories. Some other types of music show clear metric organization, but require that performers determine the nuances.

In order to make informed decisions, performers of early music must acquire a basic understanding of early rhythmic notation systems. The development of notation during the Middle Ages largely concerned rhythm: making durations of pitches and rests more specific; and providing for increasingly complex relationships of durational values, both simultaneous and successive. Renaissance notation underwent some cosmetic changes, while retaining many features of late medieval rhythm. The *tactus* governed the relationship of the note value to real time and organized the "proportions" that characterize much Renaissance music. Readers are urged to consult the textbooks on notation cited in the Bibliography.

NOTATION

In order to indicate the correspondence of repertories to systems of rhythm and notation, a brief summary follows. References to rhythmic interpretation also appear in Part III.

Monophonic Music: Plainsong, Secular Song and Dance, Conductus, Lauda

This body of music is subject to numerous rhythmic interpretations because much of its notation (*neumes*) indicates neither duration nor meter. Scholarly suggestions for performance range from free rhythm (no regular note values), through measured rhythm (irregular groupings of precise note values), to metrical rhythm (regular groupings in binary or ternary meter). Poetic meters are sometimes invoked to support metrical interpretations.

Thirteenth-Century Polyphony: Organum, Clausula, Motet, Conductus, Hocket

Most of this music is governed by modal rhythm, a system that organized durations into six somewhat variable patterns of long and short notes. Notation symbols represent these patterns (*rhythmic modes*), rather than indicating precise durations. Like neumes, modal notation might have served a largely mnemonic function. Hence its ambiguities need not have disturbed performers in the Ars Antiqua.

Experts continue to debate the applicability of modal interpretation to some monophonic song literature and to the organal voice of organum duplum in the style of Leonin.[1]

Modal rhythm imposes a regular pulse within a triple meter. Stress accentuation at the beginning of an *ordo* is often implied by consonant intervals and stressed syllables. This type of rhythm characterizes much thirteenth-century music even after the changes in notation described by Franco of Cologne (ca. 1260). Stratification of rhythmic activity among the various parts became increasingly apparent during the course of the century.

Fourteenth-Century French and Italian Polyphony; Early Fifteenth-Century Music

Following the significant developments of late-thirteenth-century notation, fourteenth-century mensural notation introduced numerous symbols to indicate durations and developed a hierarchy of meter (*mensuration*) to prescribe their relationships. France and Italy used different but comparable notation systems, which later merged to some extent.

The rhythm of this music is basically metrical: stress accentuation occurs fairly regularly, compounded of text placement (where it can be ascertained), harmonic consonance, contrapuntal activity, and factors that contribute to a sense of rhythmic arrival (long notes, especially in all parts; long notes following several short notes or following syncopation or following disparate contrapuntal rhythms). Although French music employs more dissonance than Italian does, both have clear phrase units marked by definite points of arrival.

French music of the fourteenth century contains much rhythmic complexity. Isorhythm, for example, organizes a part into patterns that are more structural than audible. The extreme manifestation of notational intricacy appears in certain compositions from the late fourteenth century, when "mannered" notation permitted composers to specify subtleties of duration and relativity unmatched until our own time. This rhythm avoids the metrical straitjacket. In order to sound flexible it actually demands great precision and ensemble skill from performers.

Much early-fifteenth-century music reflects a return to simpler rhythmic organization. Particularly in the secular repertory, compositions feature articulated pulse, audible meter, clear phrasing, and distinct rhythmic cadences. Syncopation and hemiola add occasional impetus to the rhythmic flow.

Late Fifteenth- and Sixteenth-Century Music

The major notational innovation in this period is a system of proportional time signatures, which expand the possibilities of mensural relationships. Used primarily in sacred music, proportional notation accommodates elaborate rhythmic canons. In most music a notated rhythm indicates more or less the durations that a composer conceived in imagining the sound of the music. Proportional canons, by way of contrast, seem to generate the composition, making other elements secondary to the rhythm. However, the proportions are scarcely audible in performance. Simultaneous employment of different proportions usually produces independent contrapuntal rhythms.

Proportional relationships were exercised to a degree in all mensurally notated repertories. From the fourteenth century through the Renaissance and beyond, note colors were altered in order to indicate a change from normal values. This practice could indicate three notes in the time of two (*hemiola*) without a change of time signature; later the proportion *sesquialtera* accomplished the same result and the two notations were used interchangeably. Editors differ on rhythmic interpretation of these notations, as to whether or not the three notes always indicate equal triplets.[2] Coloration in red ink is difficult to detect in black-and-white photo reproductions; transcribers must be alert to its possibility (see Figure 4-3).

Rhythm in the late fifteenth and sixteenth centuries encompasses many styles of organization. An audible pulse characterizes much of the music, but regular stress accent occurs chiefly in dances and lighter secular vocal music. Most music of this period gains interest in performance by revealing the alternation of regular and irregular stress patterns. Often these patterns do not coincide in the various parts. The rhythmic interplay of contrasting simultaneous patterns characterizes most Renaissance polyphony.

TEMPO

Renaissance musicians measured tempo according to the most stable indicators available, the human heartbeat or a normal walking pace. Given human variability, these measurements allow the performer considerable latitude. Performers also know that a "correct" tempo depends somewhat on the acoustical environment (indoors or out, large hall or small, resonant or "dead"), and on the size and sonority of an ensemble. Thus a guide to performance practice can suggest some considerations for determining tempo, but cannot provide metronome markings for early music.

The unit of notation that approximates the human pulse shifted from the *longa* of the early thirteenth century to the *brevis* in the later thirteenth, the *semibrevis* in the fourteenth, and the *minima* in the sixteenth century. The reason for this trend was the continuing subdivision of notes into smaller and smaller values: brevis, semibrevis, minima, semiminima, etc. Thus the brevis is commonly transcribed from modal notation as an eighth note, from Franconian notation as a quarter note, from mid-fourteenth-century mensural notation as a half note or larger value, and from sixteenth-century notation (without proportional alteration) as a whole note or dotted whole note.

The concept of *tactus*, first mentioned in 1482,[3] relates time signatures to a fixed unit of real time, such as a person's pulse. Performers were instructed to beat time so that one down-up cycle (the tactus) would equal one pulse beat, normally corresponding to the semibrevis.[4] The usual tactus gives equal duration to the down and the up motions. Certain proportions require an unequal tactus, the first motion lasting twice as long as the second. Scholars have disagreed on the speed of the tactus, interpreting it from M.M. 30 to 80.[5] Obviously the duration of the tactus depends on the judgment of a knowledgeable performer; tactus is thus not a totally fixed quantity. Furthermore, it indicates only speed, not accent.

The idea of tactus, despite its elasticity, provides several important determinants of tempo for music from Ockeghem's time until the end of the Renaissance:

1. Tempo should relate the unit of beat to the semibrevis of a standard mensuration, commonly **C**.

2. Proportional time signatures appearing simultaneously or successively within a piece relate to the standard semibrevis tactus; however, their interpretation is not always obvious.

3. The tactus of a piece, once determined, remains unvaried throughout the work.

4. Separate sections of a work, each having its own time signature (e.g., dance pairs, some Mass movements), may call for proportional relationships.

One last word of caution: Sixteenth-century composers frequently gave the proportional time signature **¢** to pieces that have duple meter in all parts, where **C** would be theoretically more appropriate. This convention requires modern performers to decide on the tempo: tactus equal to the brevis (strict proportion); normal tactus equal to the semibrevis; or a somewhat faster tactus equal to the semibrevis. Glareanus (1547) discusses accelerating the tactus by changing **C** to **¢**,[6] and modern scholars generally agree with this interpretation.[7]

The tempo of dance music used for dancing depends not only on its time signature but also on the step patterns of the particular dance. Dance manuals of the sixteenth century provide valuable descriptions of step patterns and other movements. Knowledge and practice of these patterns helps immensely in interpreting dance rhythms. Stylized dance music, not intended for actual dancing, may require a slower tempo to accommodate the composer's ornamentation.

RHYTHM GROUPINGS IN RENAISSANCE MUSIC

Most of this repertory contains note groupings of irregular lengths. A performance that reveals the rhythmic groupings of each part of a polyphonic composition gives vitality to the music. Points of articulation or stress accentuation often do not coincide with modern editorial bar lines. The authors have developed the following guidelines for interpreting the rhythm of sixteenth-century music. Observation of these guidelines, of course, does not obviate the performer's responsibility to present musically sensitive phrasing.

1. Beats are grouped in twos or threes. The duple group is the ordinary unit; triple groups are exceptions.

2. A long note marks the beginning of a group.

3. Long notes are strong; short notes are weak.

4. Within a group, longer notes do not follow shorter ones. An isolated note between the end of one group and the beginning of the next should be treated as unaccented and phrased with the preceding group.

5. Sometimes duple or triple groups occur at a level of note value longer or shorter than the basic unit of pulse.

6. In ambiguous situations the harmonic context determines which notes are strong and which are weak.

7. Rhythm groups frequently coordinate with word accents, especially in sixteenth-century music with a Latin or Italian text. When long and short syllables are not set to long and short notes, respectively, the singer must decide whether the word accent should prevail or whether the underlay should possibly be altered (see Chapter 7).

8. Articulation of groupings is made on instruments by shortening the last note of a group, creating a brief silence before the beginning of the next group. (Consecutive notes on one pitch can be similarly separated.) The effect of accentuation results naturally from such separation; no increased intensity of dynamics or timbre is required. Voices can make separations where a new syllable occurs at the beginning of a group. If the syllable does not change, a slight dynamic inflection will bring out the rhythm grouping.

Example 5-1 illustrates the application of these guidelines to a Kyrie by Ockeghem (Example III-19). Groupings are indicated at quarter-note and half-note levels. Solid curved lines indicate duple groupings. Dotted curved lines indicate triple groupings. An X shows an isolated note. A two-beat or three-beat group may be occupied by a single note. Brackets indicate ligatures.

EXAMPLE 5–1

PROJECTS FOR RHYTHM

1. Study the four facsimiles in this book (Figures 4-1 to 4-4). What type of notation does each facsimile represent? What information does each piece provide about duration?

2. Compare the facsimiles of Figures 4-2, 4-3, and 4-4 with the transcriptions in Part III. Prepare your own transcription for a portion of each work.

3. Choose a modern edition of a Franco-Flemish instrumental work. Mark the rhythm groupings. Organize an ensemble to read the piece with your articulations, and evaluate the result.

4. Devise several practical ways to notate rhythm groups in editing early music (various kinds of bar lines, phrase marks, accents, note shapes, etc.). Write a few measures of your piece from Project 3 in each of these notations. Which one is easiest to read? Ask other musicians what they think.

Chapter 6
Musica Ficta

Musica ficta is the term commonly used today for the practice of adding accidentals in order to alter certain notated pitches in early music.[1] The term usually refers to accidentals placed above notes in modern editions. (Its original meaning was somewhat different, also related to pitch alteration.) Modern *musica ficta* brings intervals into conformity with established principles of style. It raises or lowers certain notated pitches as composers would have expected in performances in their own time. Rules for *musica ficta*, then, are essentially guides for performers, who are obliged to make particular pitch changes whether indicated or not. In the Middle Ages and Renaissance a performer was expected to know the appropriate rules and to apply them to a melodic line.

In order to understand the material that follows in this chapter, the reader unfamiliar with modal theory is advised to consult the following entries in the *Harvard Dictionary of Music:* "Church modes," "Hexachord," "Solmization," "Musica ficta, musica falsa."[2]

Medieval music acknowledged a scale that comprised the diatonic pitches from G (*gamma ut*, or *gamut*) to *e″* plus *b♭* and *b♭′*, thus 22 notated pitches. (Absolute or relative pitch is not at issue here.) All these pitches belong to the pitch class that was called *musica recta*. All other pitches belong to the pitch class called *musica falsa* or *musica ficta*.

The accidental signs that differentiated B-flats from B-naturals, when applied to other pitches, created *musica falsa*. These signs functioned not only to raise and lower pitches, but also to indicate where half-steps should occur; that is, where a singer should substitute *mi–fa* for the normal solmization syllables. The flat was sung *fa*, the sharp or natural, *mi*.

At first, *musica falsa* comprised only a few chromatic inflections: F-sharps, C-sharps, E-flats. Gradually *musica falsa* encompassed greater numbers of pitches from which to select. Through a type of modulation called *mutatio* (mutation), the hexachord shifts in the direction of either flats or sharps. By 1430, treatises speculated on more remote extensions of the system than musical practice required.[3] It has been suggested that "key" signatures have the effect of transposing *musica recta*. For example, if E-flats become part of a *musica recta* pitch class, then B-naturals become *musica falsa*. *Musica recta* thus maintains its limited number of pitches. Mixed or partial signatures, furthermore, indicate the simultaneous occurrence of two or more sets of *musica recta*.[4]

In the foregoing, hypothetical case, where *musica recta* includes E-flats, the source does not need flat signs before every B and E. Signs generally appear where the performer needs them: where a pitch inflection must be other than the anticipated one, or where uncertainty might arise. Scribal practices were inconsistent, however, as comparison of concordant manuscript sources generally reveals.

Printed music presents similar discrepancies. Not only did copyists and printers observe local customs, but they also made errors, reorganized the placement of notes on the page, and added or deleted accidentals in sometimes mistaken attempts to convey the intent of the original source. In working with a source, scholars must decide whether explicit accidentals illustrate common practices or whether common practices were so well understood that accidentals show exceptions to those rules.

When confronting an original source the performer must answer several questions about each accidental that appears:

1. Is it correct, or is it a possible scribal or printing error?
2. Does it function as a "key" signature, indicating a transposed mode for an entire piece or section?
3. Does it apply to one note, or to an entire phrase or staff line?
4. Does it imply the alteration of other pitches? (For instance, E-flat implies the use of B-flat; C-sharp implies B-natural and F-sharp.)
5. Does it affect the following pitch, does it give advance warning of an upcoming inflection or mutation, or does it (in rare cases) follow the affected pitch?[5]
6. Does it alter the pitch that is signed, or does it indicate *mi–fa* in an irregular way? (For example, the pitch G-flat rarely occurs as a performed pitch; an F followed by a G-flat indicates *mi–fa* and may mean F-sharp followed by G-natural.[6] Also, a flat sign before *f″* warns that this note lies outside the gamut and that it must be sung *fa* on the pitch *f″*.[7])
7. Is it a "cautionary" sharp; could it mean other than what it appears to mean?[8]

In a polyphonic piece these questions may best be answered in the context of all the parts.

After coming to terms with the significance of *recta* and *ficta* accidentals in the source, performers are ready to consider adding other accidentals to their performing editions. Most performers prefer a working score in standard modern format, with bar lines and key signatures controlling the duration of pitch inflections. Some persons prefer to perform only from a facsimile, recreating original performance conditions. For study purposes, however, some type of score is invaluable. It should show all the pitch alterations implicit in the original source but not individually signed. Some of these alterations may be debatable. This is not to say that they are optional, but rather that we cannot be certain of the intent of the source.

Most practices that evolved in the Middle Ages persisted in the Renaissance. Additional rules apply to fifteenth- and sixteenth-century music. Treatises generally reflect practices of an earlier generation, so a rule might apply to music composed shortly before the theory was expressed. The following paragraphs supply more detailed guidelines for *musica ficta* rules and their exceptions. These guidelines have been derived by the authors from primary and secondary sources and from practical application.

RULES THAT ORIGINATED IN THE MIDDLE AGES

Use perfect melodic intervals of the fourth, fifth, and octave. Avoid the melodic tritone, usually by altering the second pitch of an interval. Lowering the note above *la* to a

Chapter 7
Text Underlay

Vocal music, in both manuscripts and prints, usually requires some editorial alignment of text with music. Rarely did scribes or printers provide complete correspondence between syllables and notes. Economical use of vellum or paper dictated the placement of text in a small amount of space, and custom perpetuated the practice of grouping words together at the beginning of a phrase of music, rather than meting them out to their notes. Singers may have prepared the underlay in rehearsals; also, every established ensemble probably maintained a set of conventions regarding underlay.

In music sung one on a part, each soloist might have been allowed some latitude in text placement. However, uniformity was probably maintained in homophonic and imitative settings. The only texts that permitted certainty of underlay were complete texts having syllabic settings (i.e., the same number of notes and syllables). Today, performers and editors must make decisions about underlay where a text is incomplete or where syllables and notes do not correspond in number.

Only a few treatises, mainly from the sixteenth century, provide rules for text underlay in music, and these primarily for texts in Latin. Experts have speculated about the application of these rules to music of earlier centuries and to texts in other languages.[1] In the absence of other sets of rules, editors must deduce their own, based on their understanding of the particular language and musical style under consideration.[2] A general rule for underlaying text is to coordinate word accents and musical accents. However, even so basic a rule does not apply to a relatively unstressed language, such as French; and the usual equivalence between long note and musical accent is absent in some styles; for instance, Ars Antiqua motets in rhythmic mode two and Ars Nova melodies with "appoggiaturas."

According to theorists, a ligature indicates that only one syllable may be sung on the pitches that comprise that symbol.[3] In some instances, adherence to this principle results in a text underlay that may seem awkward to modern performers. Furthermore, this principle appears to be contradicted by a particular body of fifteenth-century sacred music for which no instruments were used; in this music, singing the complete text demands setting ligatures with multiple syllables.[4] Many editions use a closed bracket to connect pitches that are transcribed from a ligature.

INCOMPLETE TEXT UNDERLAY

Let us examine the matter of incomplete text underlay, by considering compositions that have the following characteristics:

1. No text underlaid at all. Such a piece may be identified by a title somewhere in the source, or by concordance with another source. Its text may exist in a nonmusical source, such as a collection of poetry.

2. One or more incipits (the first few words of a line of text), and no complete text. An incipit may function as a title for an instrumental part or as an abbreviated text for a vocal part.

3. Text underlaid completely in one or more voices, with incipits or no text in other parts.

4. The first lines of text underlaid, and the remaining lines following, without music. Sometimes the subsequent lines or stanzas differ from the first in number of syllables or in stress patterns.

5. Far more music than text, perhaps with repetition of musical phrases. Sometimes a line of text is followed by some kind of indication to repeat preceding text.

6. Text containing abbreviations. Latin texts, particularly in manuscript sources, contain a great number of conventional abbreviations. Often an abbreviation is indicated by a line drawn over or through a letter.

Before attempting to underlay text to music in categories 1 and 2 in the preceding list, one must decide whether the piece as it exists in a particular source is intended for vocal performance. Texting practice is frequently consistent within a source and possibly reflects performance traditions associated with the place and time of the source (see, e.g., Example III–20).

Compositions that belong to category 3 originated in the fourteenth, fifteenth, and early sixteenth centuries, for the most part. Some of these works seem suited to more than one possible ensemble of voices and/or instruments (see Examples III–11, 12, 14, 15, and 26). If a part having partial text or none is determined to be vocal, it can sometimes use the text and underlay found in another part (e.g., an untexted part canonic with a texted one).

In order to accommodate extra lines of text (see number 4 in the preceding list), the singer must be prepared to rearrange the correspondence of notes and syllables. In some languages, elision takes care of excess syllables. Otherwise, subdivision of single notes is necessary to accommodate extra text. Such subdivisions must follow the natural flow of verse and music (see Example 7-1).

EXAMPLE 7-1   Robert Cooper, *I have been a foster* (Example III-23)

Where the amount of music obviously exceeds the amount of text (category 5) and the text appears to be complete, repetition of some words usually balances the situation. The letters *ij* (prototype of the modern ditto mark) indicate to the performer that an appropriate portion of the text that was just sung should be repeated. Instead of *ij*, the first word of a previous phrase may appear in the source. Often the associated melodic line resembles an earlier section of music, so that corresponding words fit easily. Sometimes the melodic line is completely different, requiring the singer to examine other voice parts, other sections of the music, or other works in the style for clues. If no such clues exist, performers must apply their own judgments in setting repeated text. Zarlino (1558) directed singers to repeat phrases of text that are complete in their meaning, rather than individual words or syllables.

Other possible solutions for surplus music include melismatic or instrumental performance. In the polyphonic conductus, for example, long untexted caudae have been considered to be instrumental sections or vocal melismas. Likewise, many chansons of the Burgundian repertory begin or conclude with textless phrases that may be performed vocally, although rendition by an instrument is also a possible solution (see p. 34).

Abbreviations (item 6) range from obvious to obscure, and may require considerable knowledge of the language. Dictionaries offer some help. Nonmusical sources of text are less likely to contain the kinds of abbreviation that serve as shorthand reminders to singers already familiar with the words.

Instructions for text underlay appear in an anonymous manuscript (ca. 1440) and in writings by Gafori (1496), Lanfranco (1553), Vicentino (1555), Zarlino (1558), Stocker (ca. 1570), and Luchini (after 1588), among others. Topics treated by these writers include the following: repetition of words and phrases; elision of words; preferred vowel sounds for melismas; correspondence of long notes with long syllables, and of short notes with short syllables; the division of a long note or of a dotted note to accommodate two syllables; and the placement of syllables on first, penultimate, or final notes, on ligatures, on dotted notes, on notes following dotted notes, on short notes, on notes following short notes, and on consecutive notes of one pitch.[5] While there are many points of agreement among these authors, some earlier rules appear to admit more exceptions. The later rules impose more consistency and also show concern for expressive declamation, a concern that later crystallized in Italian monody.

PROJECTS FOR TEXT UNDERLAY

1. Obtain a facsimile of a texted Burgundian or Flemish chanson and one or more transcriptions made from that source. Compare the text underlay in the original with that in the edition(s). If the editor has not set all the lines of text, try underlaying the remaining text.

2. Obtain a facsimile of a trecento ballata that is fully texted in the cantus only. Underlay the text in the cantus. Try fitting the text to the tenor also, and possibly to the contratenor, if there is one. Compare your results to editions in *Polyphonic Music of the Fourteenth Century* or in *Corpus Mensurabilis Musicae*, vol. 8.

3. Read Zarlino's ten rules for text underlay. (See the English translation in Oliver Strunk, *Source Readings in Music History* [New York: Norton, 1950], 260–61; or in the five-volume edition [New York:

Norton, 1965], 2: 70–71.) Choose a late-sixteenth-century motet—
for example, one by Lassus or Palestrina—and arrange its text to
conform to those rules as closely as possible. Also try setting a
sixteenth-century Kyrie or Agnus Dei, in order to become familiar
with melismatic underlay.

Chapter 8

Improvisation and Ornamentation

The well-trained medieval or Renaissance musician was expected to be proficient at creating counterpoint or at embellishing a written part stylistically.[1] Most treatises and tutors give at least passing reference to the art of improvisation. Numbers of instruction books from the late sixteenth century deal exclusively with ornamentation.

Music created by the performer, as distinguished from music specified by another composer, may be classified as follows:

1. Original and extemporaneous music; a piece not based on any preexistent musical material.
2. Counterpoint; a melodic line performed simultaneously with one or more composed parts.
3. Ground bass variation; a melodic line improvised on a repeated pattern of chords derived from a ground bass melody.
4. Diminutions; figuration patterns that break up the long notes of a composed part into shorter notes.
5. Graces; embellishments applied to a single note or to a cadence formula.

Because all of these categories of improvisation aim to produce music that sounds fresh and spontaneous, their results may look somewhat similar when notated. Nevertheless each classification represents an isolable approach to ornamentation, as described in the following paragraphs.

ORIGINAL IMPROVISATION

An original improvisation occurs only once. After that it is a composition that can be performed by anyone, especially if it is recorded on paper or electronically. Thus there exist few if any notated historical examples of spontaneously improvised music. Our sources of information are compositions in the style of improvised performance; examples of cadences, figuration patterns, counterpoint, etc. in trea-

tises and manuals; and written instructions and descriptions of improvisatory practices. Capturing improvisation on paper is a difficult task, as anyone who has tried to
notate jazz or ethnic music will confirm. Thus the sources of information on medieval and Renaissance improvisation probably fall short of the mark as guides to
actual practices.

Works that resemble original free compositions comprise mainly solo instrumental pieces: preludes, toccatas, ricercari (e.g., Example III–21a), and the like, for
lute, organ, harpsichord, viol, or other solo instruments. Such works are generally
brief, and perhaps call for rhapsodic interpretation. Ensemble improvisation is
mentioned by Ortiz (1553), who suggests the possibility of duet improvisation on
viol and harpsichord, using imitation.

COUNTERPOINT

Improvised counterpoint took many forms during the Middle Ages and Renaissance. Medieval treatises describe ways to add new counter-melodies to chant,
thereby creating organum. Strict rules prescribe suitable intervals and voice-leading
for this type of music, whether composed or extemporized.[2] In a similar vein,
English discant accompanies plainchant with improvised counterpoint in one added
voice as the norm.[3] Medieval hocket was sometimes improvised vocally on
plainchant.[4]

English faburden, an early Renaissance successor of discant technique, adds
two new parts to a *cantus firmus:* a part in parallel fourths above the plainchant, and
a part in thirds and fifths below the chant. Continental fauxbourdon, in contrast,
calls for one improvised part to function as the middle voice between two composed parts. The new part moves in parallel fourths below the *cantus firmus,* which
is set in the top voice. It has been suggested that fifteenth-century polyphonic
hymns that incorporate fauxbourdon harmony represent a refined version of a
practice of improvising on plainchant hymns.[5]

"Countering," yet another method of improvising polyphony on a chant melody, also includes ornamentation of the chant. Fourteen rules for this unusual
practice exist in a Scottish treatise copied ca. 1580.[6]

Tinctoris, in a treatise dated 1477, describes how singers can add a contrapuntal part to preexisting music. Although this process (*cantare super librum*) appears to
have been thought out in advance, rather than extemporized, the counterpoint was
not necessarily written down.[7] One or more contrapuntal parts could be added to a
chant, to a tenor borrowed from polyphony, or to composed polyphony. This
process differs somewhat from composition, both because the counterpoint is
created by singers and because each added part is expected to fit only with the
tenor. Nevertheless, Tinctoris commends counterpoint that takes into account the
relationship of all the parts when there are three or more.[8] Other theorists continued throughout the sixteenth century to discuss the singing of counterpoint.

In the realm of instrumental music, the fifteenth-century *basse danse* depended
upon improvisation for its very existence. Several theories have been proposed
regarding performance of this genre (see Appendix A 2a).

GROUND BASS VARIATION

Variations on grounds constitute a category of Renaissance counterpoint different from the improvised polyphony discussed previously. A stock ground bass pattern (e.g., passamezzo antico, romanesca) comprises a series of bass notes, each with an implied harmony. The chord pattern is repeated several times, providing a framework for melodic invention by an instrumentalist. Performers on some chordal instruments could supply the ground for their own solo variations or for variations played by another instrument. Commonly each variation explores only one or two melodic motives, through such devices as repetition, sequence, and inversion. Numerous composed examples appear in the treatises and instrumental repertory of the sixteenth century.

DIMINUTIONS

Like variations on a ground, diminutions allow a soloist to create melodic figuration against composed harmonies. This category gives to one performer at a time the opportunity to embellish one or more parts of an existing polyphonic composition. The technique involves dividing long notes into shorter ones and filling in disjunct intervals.

Sixteenth-century treatises provide many formulas and guidelines.[9] For example, diminution figures should begin and end on the pitches that they connect; they should be consonant with intervening strong beats; they should avoid frequent leaps, and a leap should return by step; and a figure should stay within an octave. Exceptions occur to all these conventions, of course. Most categories of sixteenth-century ensemble music are suitable for the application of diminution: sacred and secular vocal polyphony, accompanied solo song, and dance.

In vocal polyphony, one singer can ornament a part throughout a piece, particularly the bass or superius line. Or all the parts can be ornamented in turn, a passage or phrase at a time. Treatises indicate that only one part should be ornamented at a time, by only one performer at a time.[10] An instrumental version of a sixteenth-century polyphonic vocal work is likely to apply far more embellishments than a vocal ensemble would improvise. Written examples for viol and harpsichord (e.g., Example III–30) or for solo bowed, plucked, and keyboard instruments frequently contain elaborate diminutions. Solo keyboard manuscripts from the fifteenth century (e.g., Codex Faenza 117 and the Buxheimer Orgelbuch) reveal similar approaches to ornamented transcription.

Accompanied solo singers similarly have more license to add ornamentation than ensemble singers have. Virtuosity is not to be pursued, the authors feel, at the expense of proper pronunciation, tempo, or text underlay. On this last point, the underlay must accommodate diminutions, so that they occur on appropriate syllables and vowels. The "florid song" repertory of the late sixteenth century offers ample evidence of solo vocal ornamentation.[11]

Dance music is a prime candidate for improvised ornamentation, particularly dances containing repeated strains. Although the sources of simple polyphonic dances rarely include written-out diminutions, many sixteenth-century stylized dances composed for keyboard, lute, or "broken consort" exhibit extravagant embellishment. On the basis of those examples, the authors think that the superius part of a simple polyphonic dance may receive somewhat similar treatment, provided the correct tempo for dancing can be maintained.

GRACES

The final category, graces, comprises embellishments of single notes and of cadences.

Practices of ornamenting chant and organum cannot be deduced with certainty from surviving examples and descriptions. There is evidence to indicate that the added voice of organum duplum was embellished beyond its already florid written state. Jerome of Moravia (late thirteenth century) mentions graces used in singing organum and chant.[12] Fifteenth-century chant also received some type of gracing or diminution, as Tinctoris writes concerning *cantus regalis*.[13]

The sixteenth-century theorists distinguished isolated graces from the more uniformly pervasive diminutions and variations discussed previously. Certain graces that might be considered trills decorate notes within a phrase and at cadences. The former type begins on a principal note, alternating with the upper or lower neighbor, occasionally using the interval of a third rather than a second. The cadential trill alternates the leading tone with its resolution, usually starting on the dissonant tonic note. Several other graces are codified late in the century, foreshadowing baroque ornamentation practices.[14]

Treatises on ornamentation offer instructions and examples designed primarily for the novice. They undoubtedly do not give away all the secrets of practicing virtuosi. Although the manuals claim that singers and instrumentalists employ the same devices, it seems likely that skilled performers evolved a stock of figurations that displayed their art to best advantage. "Spontaneous" improvisation develops from the application of familiar, well-tried formulas to familiar musical material.

In preparing to ornament a piece of early music, today's musicians can proceed in similar fashion. First, they should become thoroughly familiar with the chosen composition or ground, performing it at the correct tempo without embellishment. Next, they should learn some of the appropriate figurations and rehearse them until they feel comfortable. Finally, they can begin adding embellishments. Cadences are the places to ornament first, then notes or intervals within a phrase. Modern performers who practice improvisation in early music may wish to heed the opinions of such authorities as Josquin and Zarlino, both of whom deplored the excesses of ornamentation added by some performers.

PROJECTS FOR IMPROVISATION AND ORNAMENTATION

Improvising on a tenor, ground bass, or polyphonic work requires knowing the piece well and having the opportunity to practice with the accompanying music. The authors recommend making a tape recording of the accompanying music and using it as a background for practicing appropriate counterpoint, variations, diminutions, or graces. Improvising in a public concert needs such preparation in order to sound secure and convincing.

1. Chordal-instrument players (keyboard, lute, etc.) who wish to improvise short preludes and ricercari should play a number of such works in a single style, until its characteristics become familiar. If the original fingerings can be ascertained, use them, so that your fingers automatically move in stylistic patterns. Borrow and combine some of the characteristic musical gestures to form short phrases. Build these into longer sections, until a complete piece results.

2. Singers who wish to improvise counterpoint should try adding a part to chant using the guidelines of Tinctoris. His eight rules appear with musical examples in Johannes Tinctoris, *The Art of Counterpoint (Liber de arte contrapuncti)* (trans. and ed. Albert Seay, Musicological Studies and Documents, vol. 5 [n.p.: American Institute of Musicology, 1961], 132–141); a condensed version of the rules appears in Gustave Reese, *Music in the Renaissance* (rev. ed. [New York: Norton, 1959], 144); Latin text and musical examples are in Edmond de Coussemaker, ed., *Scriptorum de Musica Medii Aevi, Nova Series* ([Paris: Durand, 1864–1876; reprint, Hildesheim: Georg Olms, 1963], 4: 147–153). Memorize the chant before preparing your new part.

3. Melodic instrument players who wish to improvise counterpoint should study the two "quinta boz" examples provided by Diego Ortiz in his *Trattado de glosas* (Rome, 1553), ed. Max Schneider ([Kassel: Bärenreiter, 1967], 83–85, 103–106). These pieces illustrate both the addition of a fifth part to four-part polyphony and the ornamentation of an added part. Examine Ortiz's procedures and apply them to a simple chanson or madrigal, first as composition, then as improvisation.

4. Select a ground bass pattern and study several composed variations on it, perhaps works for a variety of instruments (keyboard, lute, vihuela, viol). Instrumentalists should play several sets of variations written for their instrument, if such works exist. Ortiz's *recercadas* on grounds (see Project 3) provide models useful not only to viol players but also to players of other single-line instruments. Prepare a recording of your ground played several times in succession. Practice improvising variations on your instrument. As an exercise, singers might enjoy improvising vocalises in the style of instrumental variations.

5. If you play a chordal instrument, provide the ground bass accompaniment for someone else performing variations. Listen carefully to the ensemble and adapt your accompaniment (texture, tessitura, rhythm, etc.) to suit the sound of the other performer and the character of each variation.

6. Choose a sixteenth-century chanson or madrigal relatively straight-forward in style. Obtain either the diminution treatise by Ortiz (see Project 3 [English translation of the text by Peter Farrell, *Journal of the Viola da Gamba Society of America*, 4 (1967): 5–9]) or that of Girolamo dalla Casa, *Il vero modo di diminuir* ([Venice, 1584], facs. ed. [Bologna: Forni, 1970]). Study the tables of diminutions and the examples of decorated compositions. Memorize one part of your selected work. Prepare a composed ornamented version. Try improvising on the part with a live or recorded accompaniment.

7. Use the same piece as in Project 6 or select another. Look at the examples of sixteenth-century graces given in Howard Mayer Brown, *Embellishing Sixteenth-Century Music* (Early Music Series, no. 1 [London: Oxford University Press, 1976], 1–16), and in the manuals of Ortiz and dalla Casa (see Project 6). Ornament the cadences in one part and then add graces at other appropriate places. Practice improvising graces with your live or recorded accompaniment.

PART III

The Early Music Repertory:

Specific Recommendations for Performance

INTRODUCTION

*After studying the material in Parts I and II of
this book, the reader may apply information
about resources and performance to the preparation
of specific pieces of music.*

*Part III is a compendium of examples of the principal
genres of ensemble music from the Middle Ages and
Renaissance, together with recommendations for their
performance. These examples were selected because
original versions of most of them appear in facsimiles
generally available to the reader for study and
comparison. Each example consists of a complete
transcription of a representative work or significant
section of that work.*

Most of the transcriptions in this section are based on sources represented by published facsimiles; in some cases, only a variant version is available in facsimile. Each transcription is prefaced by general commentary and suggestions for performance of both the example and the body of works that it typifies. Bibliographic references cite original sources, facsimiles, modern editions, and recordings. Some recordings are out of print; multiple identification numbers are sometimes provided to assist in locating recordings.

Recommended projects follow the examples. These exercises are designed to assist the performer in developing a method for dealing with performance-practice issues. They offer further opportunities to apply principles discussed earlier in the book. The performer will also want to refer to the Checklist of Performance Considerations (Appendix F).

Performers seeking a particular repertory based on performance media are encouraged to consider the following performance categories.

Accompanied Song (music for one to three solo vocal parts and one or more independent instrumental parts).

The reader should be aware that although mixed ensembles of this type have been commonly employed by modern performers, recent scholarship suggests that some repertories more appropriately belong to purely vocal or to purely instrumental traditions.

The following works represent categories of music for which our "accompanied song" ensemble appears to be a historically authentic option: Examples III-5, 6, 8, 9, 10, 11, 12, 13, 14, 15, 17, 18, 21, 26, 29, and 34.

Instrumental-Ensemble Music

Consider the following: Examples III-7, 20, 22, 24, 30, 31, 32, and 33.

Vocal-Ensemble Music (A. music for one singer per part).

Consider the following: Examples III-4, 5, 6, 7, 8, 9, 10, 11, 12, 13, 15, 17, 18, 23, 26, 28, 29, and 34.

Vocal-Ensemble Music (B. choral works with or without solo sections).

Consider the following: Examples III-1, 2, 3, 9, 16, 17, 19, 27, and 35.

1. *Haec dies*
(Gregorian chant)

Haec dies is the Gradual from the Mass for Easter Sunday. This particular chant is the source of two tenors (*In seculum* and *Domino*) used frequently in medieval polyphony. Its text, from Psalm 117 (118 in Protestant Bibles), begins, "This is the day which the Lord hath made." Neither the composer nor the time of composition of this piece can be determined; however, Graduals, as a class, emerged sometime after the second half of the fifth century,[1] and *Haec dies* is one of the oldest of them.[2]

Within the structure of the Mass, the Gradual is the second item of the Proper. Graduals are the most florid and melismatic chants in the Gregorian repertory. The form consists of two sections, a respond and a verse.

Haec dies employs mode two (Hypodorian) transposed up a fifth. Such transposition occurred in the Middle Ages, at the time when chants were first written in staff notation, in order to avoid pitches that lay outside the *gamut*. The authenticity of the flat that precedes the third note has been questioned.[3] Example III–1 is the version used by the Roman Catholic Church. For an interesting edition and discussion of the Easter Mass according to the Sarum rite, consult *The Oxford Anthology of Music: Medieval Music*.[4]

The chant repertory was sung basically by male voices, the exception being convent performance. Originally, performance of Graduals involved a solo rendition of the refrain, followed by a choral repetition of the refrain; the soloist then sang the verse, and the choir again performed the refrain (A A b A). In subsequent centuries this format was abbreviated. There is some evidence to suggest that in the Middle Ages two or more "soloists" sometimes sang solo portions of chant in unison.[5]

Rhythm in this repertory is not specifically notated, and it has been the subject of much scholarly debate. Undoubtedly, rhythmic interpretation has varied over the centuries and from locale to locale. The modern Roman Catholic Church adopted the systematization provided by the Benedictines of Solesmes, a solution of synthesis. This style of interpretation groups pitches into units of two or three, and indicates points of stress and phrasing. More recent scholarship suggests that although chant may have been unmeasured in the Carolingian period, the Solesmes approach is incompatible with the measured style of chant in practice by the time of Franco of Cologne (ca. 1260) and discussed in numerous treatises of the thirteenth and fourteenth centuries.[6]

A few manuscripts from the tenth and eleventh centuries contain indications of chant rhythm.[7] Based on evidence from these centuries, modern scholars have proposed systems embracing free-rhythm, equalist, modified-equalist, and mensuralist (duple-meter, triple-meter, mixed-meter, and poetic-meter) interpretations.[8]

The authors recommend the following for a modern performance of this piece:

§ A small choir of male voices or of female voices

§ A single voice for the solo portions

§ A rendition that follows earlier practice:
solo respond—choral respond—solo verse—choral respond

§ Or one of the abbreviated forms:
solo respond, up to the asterisk—tutti conclusion of respond—solo verse, up to the asterisk—tutti conclusion of verse
solo respond—choral respond—solo verse[9]
choral respond—solo verse—choral respond
choral respond—solo verse[10]

§ A rhythmic solution decided upon after exploring several of the possibilities currently advocated

Source

The Liber Usualis, with Introduction and Rubrics in English. Edited by the Benedictines of Solesmes. Tournai: Desclée, 1952. 778–779.

Edition used

Hoppin, Richard H., ed. *Anthology of Medieval Music*. New York: Norton, 1978. 13 (no. 10).

Facsimile

Frere, Walter Howard, ed. *Graduale Sarisburiense*. London: Bernard Quaritch for the Plainsong and Mediaeval Music Society, 1894. Reprint. Farnborough, U.K.: Gregg, 1966. 117.

Other transcriptions

Davison, Archibald T., and Willi Apel, eds. *Historical Anthology of Music.* Vol. 1, *Oriental, Medieval, and Renaissance Music.* Rev. ed. Cambridge, MA: Harvard University Press, 1949. 12 (no. 12).

Marrocco, Thomas, and Nicholas Sandon, eds. *The Oxford Anthology of Music: Medieval Music.* London: Oxford University Press, 1977. 32 (no. 11 f).

Tack, Franz, ed. *Gregorian Chant.* Anthology of Music, vol. 18. Cologne: Arno Volk Verlag, 1960. 109.

Recordings

Gregorian Chant: Easter Liturgy; Christmas Cycle. La Schola des Pères du Saint-Esprit du Grand Scholasticat de Chevilly. Angel 35116.

Gregorian Chants for Lent and Easter. Choir of the Vienna Hofburgkapelle. Turnabout TV 34070S, Turnabout TV 34070, or Turnabout FSM 34070.

Gregorianische Gesänge: Anthologie des Gregorianischen Chorals. Capella Antiqua, Munich. MPS/BASF 7821985-2.

EXAMPLE III–1. *Haec dies*

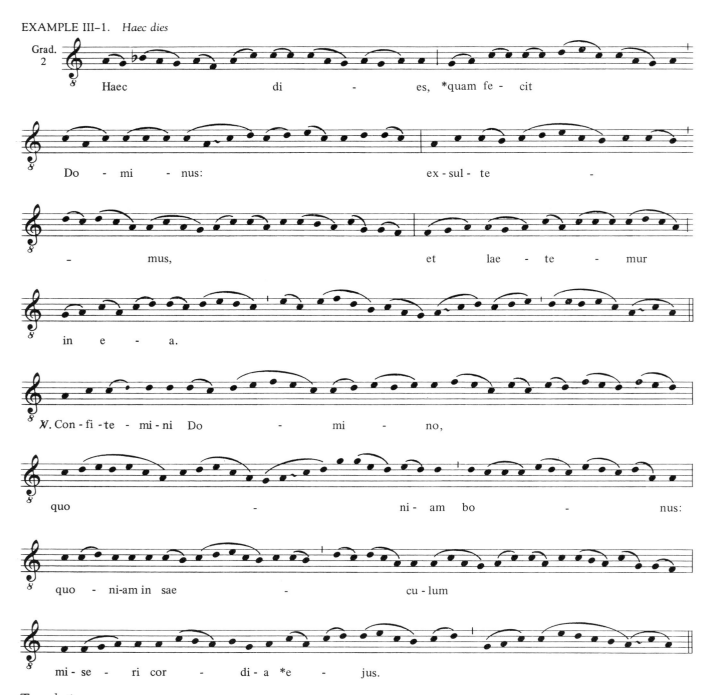

Translation

> This is the day which the Lord hath made: let us
>   be glad and rejoice therein.
> ℣. Give praise to the Lord, for he is good; for his
>   mercy endureth forever.

2. Leonin(?), *Alleluia: Nativitas* (Organum à 2)

Leonin (fl. ca. 1163–1190) was possibly the composer of this piece.[11] Almost nothing is known about Leonin's life. Attribution of this composition depends on information supplied by Anonymous IV, a treatise from the second half of the thirteenth century, regarding the *Magnus liber organi*. This book was a collection of two-part organa for the entire liturgical year of the Roman Catholic Church. It was associated with the church of Notre Dame in Paris. *Alleluia: Nativitas* is a trope on the Alleluia of the Mass for the Nativity of the Blessed Virgin Mary. The Alleluia functions as the third item of the Proper of the Mass.

This piece is an example of organum duplum, which consists of a tenor taken from plainsong and a newly composed duplum. Only certain portions of the chant receive this treatment. Thus performance of the complete Alleluia results in an alternation of two-part polyphony and plainchant. Alleluias are highly melismatic chants consisting of two parts, the word *Alleluia* and the verse.

In *Alleluia: Nativitas*, as in other organa dupla, polyphony occurs only with melismatic portions of the chant that would have been sung by a soloist. This piece contains three such sections. Two styles of composition appear in the polyphony: organum purum and clausula. The former style is characterized by unmeasured notes in the tenor supporting long melismas in the duplum. Clausulae employ modal rhythms in both parts, with a smaller ratio of notes between duplum and tenor. Clausula portions of *Alleluia: Nativitas* are cast in rhythmic mode one for the duplum and mode five for the tenor.

Rhythmic interpretation of the original notation of organa pura remains uncertain. Scholarly opinion is divided between those who endorse the application of modal rhythm to the duplum[12] and those who advocate a freer interpretation.[13]

There is no direct evidence showing that instruments other than the organ participated in the medieval liturgy.[14] In fact, instruments were frequently proscribed by the early Church Fathers,[15] with the possible exception of the organ.[16] The Council of Milan (1287) permitted only the organ to be played in church.[17] Although we cannot document the use of this instrument at Notre Dame in the time of Leonin and Perotin,[18] the organ certainly existed in other churches. Evidence suggests that on some occasions the organ reinforced the singing of tenor parts of organa dupla.[19] Some scholars have hypothesized that an organ might have performed the tenor alone,[20] but at least one authority refutes assertions that the organ participated in polyphony.[21]

The authors recommend the following for a modern performance of this piece:

§ A small choir of male voices for the chant sections

§ A solo tenor voice for the duplum of polyphonic sections

§ One to four singers for the tenor of polyphonic sections[22]

§ Perhaps adopting a freer approach to the rhythm of the duplum of organum purum sections than the essentially modal rhythm shown in the edition that follows. In general, determine the length of each note according to its relative consonance with the tenor (unison intervals longest, tritones shortest).[23] (No transcription into modern notation can capture the subtlety of such a performance.)

§ Possibly using an organ to reinforce the tenor

Source

Florence, Biblioteca Medicea Laurenziana, MS. Pluteus 29, 1, ff. 129r–130r.

Edition used

Hoppin, Richard H., ed. *Anthology of Medieval Music.* New York: Norton, 1978. 50–56 (no. 33).

Facsimile

Dittmer, Luther, ed. *Facsimile Reproduction of the Manuscript Firenze, Biblioteca Mediceo-Laurenziana, Pluteo 29, 1.* Publications of Mediaeval Musical Manuscripts, vols. 10, 11. Brooklyn: Institute of Mediaeval Music, n.d. 10: ff. 129r–130r.

Other transcription

Waite, William G. *The Rhythm of Twelfth-Century Polyphony, Its Theory and Practice.* Yale Studies in the History of Music, no. 2. New Haven: Yale University Press, 1954. 195–202 (no. M38).

EXAMPLE III–2. Leonin(?), *Alleluia: Nativitas*

S.C. (replaces mm. 55-68)

se vir - gi -

nis

S.C. (expands mm. 95-101)

Ma - ri - e

Ma - ri - e

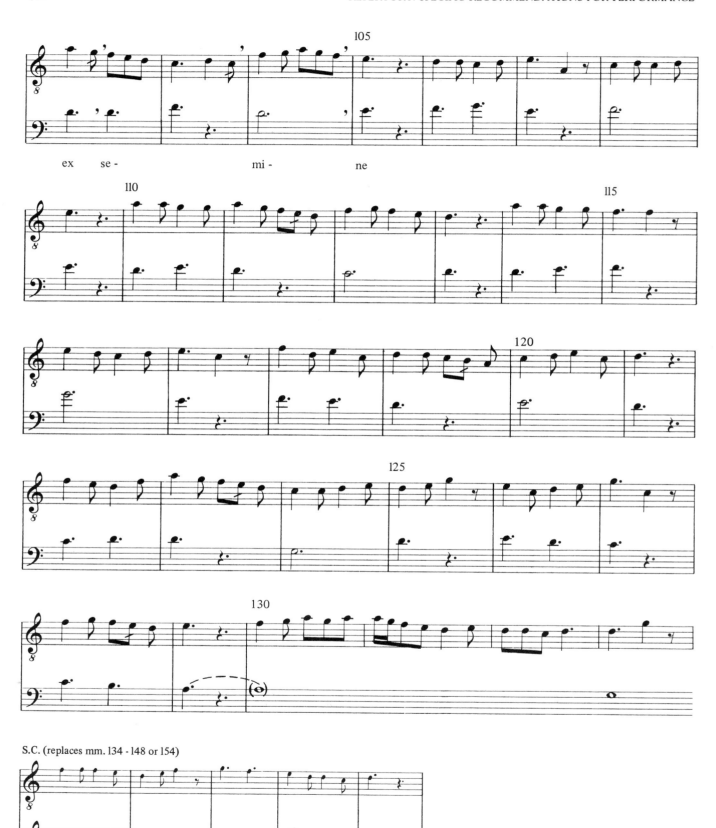

ex   se -   mi -   ne

S.C. (replaces mm. 134 - 148 or 154)

A -   bra -

A -

bra -

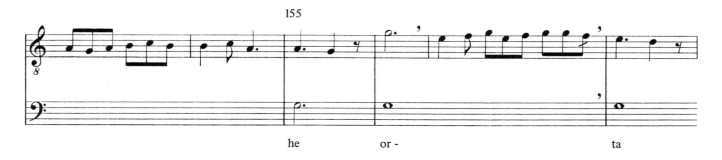

he   or -   ta

cla - ra   ex stir - pe Da   -   vid

Al -

le -   lu -

ya   Jubilus as above.

Translation

Alleluia: The birth of the glorious Virgin Mary,
from the seed of Abraham, descended from
the tribe of Judah, from the illustrious stock
of David.

3. Perotin, *Alleluia: Nativitas* (Organum à 3)

Perotin (fl. ca. 1200) was a composer of polyphony in the generation following Leonin. He was an important contributor to the revisions of the *Magnus liber organi*, supplying substitute clausulae and new compositions having as many as four parts. Compared to the organa of Leonin, Perotin's exhibit more extensive and varied use of rhythmic modes, especially in the tenor. The more compressed style of his tenors apparently suggested the need for repetition of the tenor in the same or a modified rhythmic pattern.

Alleluia: Nativitas is an organum triplum constructed on the same chant melody as that of the preceding organum duplum (see p. 68). These two pieces resemble each other in structure: Polyphony elaborates the solo sections of chant; the tenor part alternates sustained notes and measured passages. Upper parts of the organum triplum consistently employ modal rhythms. This composition and the previous one, in addition to sharing the same *cantus firmus*, are virtually identical in the duplum and tenor of the clausulae over the words *ex semine*.

The edition that follows includes only the polyphonic sections of the *Alleluia: Nativitas*. The plainsong sections that conclude the *Alleluia* and the verse may be borrowed from the previous example. The complete form is *Alleluia*, verse, repeated *Alleluia*.

The authors recommend the following for a modern performance of this piece:

§ A small choir of male voices for the chant sections

§ Two solo tenor voices for the duplum and triplum of the polyphonic sections

§ One to four voices for the tenor of polyphonic sections

§ Possibly using an organ to reinforce the tenor

Source

Montpellier, Faculté de Médicine, MS. H 196, ff. 9r–12v.

Edition used

Tischler, Hans, ed. *The Montpellier Codex*. Recent Researches in the Music of the Middle Ages and Early Renaissance, vols. 2–7. Madison: A–R Editions, 1978. Pt. 1 (vols. 2–3): 13–20 (nos. 9–10).

Facsimiles

Baxter, J. H., ed. *An Old St. Andrews Music Book (Cod. Helmst. 628)*. London: Oxford University Press, 1939. 11–14.

Besseler, Heinrich, and Peter Gülke. *Schriftbild der mehrstimmigen Musik*. Musikgeschichte in Bildern, vol. 3, pt. 5. Leipzig: Deutscher Verlag für Musik, 1973. 39 (no. 8), partial facsimile.

Dittmer, Luther, ed. *Facsimile Reproduction of the Manuscript Firenze, Biblioteca Mediceo-Laurenziana, Pluteo 29, 1*. Publications of Mediaeval Musical Manuscripts, vols. 10, 11. Brooklyn: Institute of Mediaeval Music, n.d. 10: ff. 31r–32v.

————. *Facsimile Reproduction of the Manuscript Wolfenbüttel 1099 Helmstadiensis-(1206) W²*. Publications of Mediaeval Musical Manuscripts, vol. 2. Brooklyn: Institute of Mediaeval Music, 1960. Ff. 16r–17v.

Parrish, Carl. *The Notation of Medieval Music*. New York: Norton, 1957. Reprint. New York: Pendragon, 1978. Pl. 25, partial facsimile.

Rokseth, Yvonne. *Polyphonies du XIIIᵉ siècle: Le Manuscrit H 196 de la Faculté de Médicine de Montpellier*. 4 vols. Paris: Editions de l'Oiseau-Lyre, 1935–1939. 1: ff. 9r–12v.

Other transcriptions

Husmann, Heinrich. *Die drei- und vierstimmigen Notre-Dame-Organa*. Publikationen älterer Musik, vol. 11. Leipzig: Breitkopf und Härtel, 1940. Reprint. Hildesheim: Georg Olms, 1967. 86–91.

Parrish, Carl, and John F. Ohl. *Masterpieces of Music before 1750: An Anthology of Musical Examples from Gregorian Chant to J. S. Bach*. New York: Norton, 1951. 24–25 (no. 9).

Perotin. *Works*. Edited by Ethel Thurston. New York: Kalmus, 1970. 71–83.

Rokseth, Yvonne. *Polyphonies du XIIIᵉ siècle*. 2: 16–23 (nos. 9–10).

Recording

Notre Dame Organa; Leoninus and Perotinus Magister. Russell Oberlin et al. Musical Heritage Society 676.

EXAMPLE III–3.   Perotin, *Alleluia: Nativitas*

Translation: see Example III–2.

- ya.]

- ya.]

- YA.

ex   se -   mi -   ne

ex   se -   mi -   ne

EX   SE -   MI -   NE

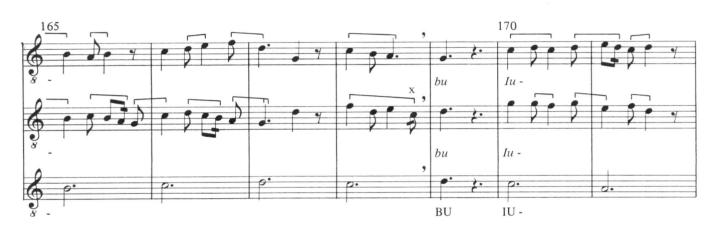

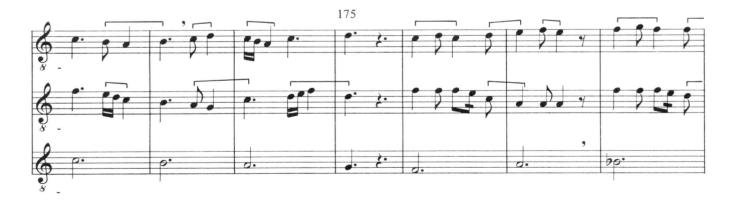

4. *Soli nitorem* (Conductus à 2)

This anonymous conductus appears in sources from the mid-thirteenth century that include music from the Notre Dame repertory. The edition that follows is based on the manuscript from which the example of organum duplum also was transcribed (Example III–2).

The conductus is both a monophonic genre and a polyphonic genre of two to four parts. The texts, in Latin, deal with a wide range of subject matter, sacred and secular. Some of these pieces could have been used in a liturgical context, perhaps as processional music.[24] Unlike other early polyphony, conducti have tenors that were not borrowed from chant, but were most often newly composed or sometimes borrowed from popular tunes. Conducti were notated in score format, with the text of the first stanza written beneath the lines of music.

Soli nitorem belongs to the group of polyphonic conducti having *caudae*, substantial sections of melisma framing sections of syllabic writing. Conducti having caudae were considered superior. These occur most often as two-part settings. Transcription of the rhythm of syllabic sections of conducti is controversial, but modal rhythm is generally adopted for the transcription of caudae.[25]

Franco of Cologne (ca. 1260) describes the compositional process for conducti as an additive procedure from the tenor up. Consecutive composition reflects the medieval attitude toward the relative independence and linear quality of each part of a polyphonic work. The organization of *Soli nitorem*, nevertheless, suggests a somewhat different approach to composition. Repetition of rhythmic and melodic figures in this piece contributes to a highly unified organization of syllabic and melismatic sections, an organization that could not have been achieved by adherance solely to a procedure of successive counterpoint.[26]

If the conductus is treated as a purely vocal genre, all voices sing the text simultaneously.[27] Opinions regarding the possible participation of instruments in polyphonic conducti are supported only by internal evidence and speculation, not by historical documentation. Some scholars have proposed that caudae sections are instrumental[28] and

that in secular situations entire conducti might have been played with or without voices.[29] Likewise, the organ might have participated in liturgical performances of conducti.[30] In spite of all these hypotheses, the authors feel that a purely vocal performance is possible and perhaps preferable. Conducti with caudae, whether sacred or secular works, were likely to have been a soloistic repertory. The ornate character of the melismatic passages substantiates this supposition.

The authors recommend the following for a modern performance of this piece:

§ Two voices of like quality, transposed if necessary

§ Or perhaps a performance involving singers and instruments, without transposition; for instance, two tenors and two vielles. (The secular and festive nature of the text suggests this piece as a possible candidate for instrumental participation.)

Source

Florence, Biblioteca Medicea Laurenziana, MS. Pluteus 29, 1, ff. 327v–328v.

Edition used

Hoppin, Richard H., ed. *Anthology of Medieval Music*. New York: Norton, 1978. 69–71 (no. 37).

Facsimile

Dittmer, Luther, ed. *Facsimile Reproduction of the Manuscript Firenze, Biblioteca Mediceo-Laurenziana, Pluteo 29, 1*. Publications of Mediaeval Musical Manuscripts, vols. 10, 11. Brooklyn: Institute of Mediaeval Music, n.d. 11: ff. 327v–328v.

Other transcriptions

Anderson, Gordon A., ed. *Two-Part Conductus, Unica in the Four Central Sources*. Pt. 5 of *Notre-Dame and Related Conductus: Opera Omnia*. Collected Works of the Institute of Mediaeval Music, vol. 10. Henryville, PA: Institute of Mediaeval Music, 1979. 23–25.

Anglès, Higini. *El Còdex musical de Las Huelgas: Música a veus del segles XIII–XIV*. 3 vols. Barcelona: Institut d'Estudis Catalans, 1931. Reprint. New York: AMS Press, 1977. 3: 324–327 (no. 149).

EXAMPLE III–4. *Soli nitorem*

pre - su - mo ti - tu - [lum]

- lum.

Translation

> I add brilliance to the sun,
> a handful of water to the sea,
> dew to spring water,
> I attach branches of fern to the oak when,
> to the leader who,
> by the illustrious star of his virtues,
> illumines the night and banishes the shadows of
>   our age,
> I presume to subjoin an inscription of praise.

5. *Laus Domino/Eius* (Motet à 3)

Laus Domino/Eius is an early-thirteenth-century motet found in one of the sources of music from the *Magnus liber organi*. Medieval motets were polyphonic works composed on tenors borrowed from other sources, usually Gregorian chant. Motets contain one to three added parts, which bear text(s) different from that of the tenor. The earliest types were perhaps clausulae for which new texts were added to the upper parts. Other motets had newly composed upper parts.

It is apparent that in order to be considered suitable for liturgical use, a motet must have a chant-derived tenor and exclusively Latin text that is appropriate to an occasion of worship. Motets that lack chant-derived tenors, incorporate the vernacular, or have texts lacking spiritual content must have served secular functions, not liturgical ones.

Laus Domino/Eius belongs to a type in which the upper voices were notated in score format and share a single text. Some authorities refer to this type as a "conductus motet." Normally the tenor part appears at the end of the score in the manuscript.

A facsimile of this piece appears as Figure 4–2. Our transcription applies rhythmic mode three to the upper parts. The tenor uses mode five. Plicas are transcribed as small notes with slashed stems.

This work could have served a liturgical function. Its tenor, *Eius*, comes from the verse of the Great Responsory *Stirps Jesse*, sung at First Vespers of the Feast of the Nativity of the Blessed Virgin. In the Office of Vespers, the Great Responsory occurred midway through the service, between the Chapter and the Hymn.[31] *Laus Domino/Eius* constitutes a polyphonic setting of the melisma on the word *eius*, and could have been performed in its place when something more elaborate than the chant alone was desired.

Texted upper parts of motets were apparently intended for soloists. Tenors in the earliest motets, especially compositions that fit a liturgical scheme, would probably have been performed by a solo voice (or perhaps by a few trained soloists) in a melismatic fashion, as in organum. The organ might have reinforced or perhaps substituted for singing on tenor parts.[32]

The authors recommend the following for a modern performance of this piece:

§ Two solo tenor voices for the duplum and triplum

§ One to four male voices for the tenor

§ Possibly using an organ to reinforce the tenor

Source

Wolfenbüttel, Herzog August Bibliothek, Cod. Guelf. 1099 Helmst., ff. 126v–127r.

Edition used

The authors' transcription.

Facsimiles

Apel, Willi. *The Notation of Polyphonic Music, 900–1600.* 5th ed., rev. Cambridge, MA: Medieval Academy of America, 1961. 275 (no. 55).

Dittmer, Luther, ed. *Facsimile Reproduction of the Manuscript Wolfenbüttel 1099 Helmstadiensis-(1206) W².* Publications of Mediaeval Musical Manuscripts, vol. 2. Brooklyn: Institute of Mediaeval Music, 1960. Ff. 126v–127r.

Figure 4–2.

Other transcriptions

Anderson, Gordon A., ed. *The Latin Compositions in Fascicules VII and VIII of the Notre Dame Manuscript Wolfenbüttel Helmstadt. 1099 (1206).* Musicological Studies, vol. 24. 2 pts. Brooklyn: Institute of Mediaeval Music, 1968–1976. 2: 12 (no. 1, 5).

Spiess, Lincoln B., "Polyphony in Theory and Practice from the Ninth Century to the Close of the Thirteenth Century." 3 vols. Ph.D. dissertation, Harvard University, 1947. 3: 188–189 (no. 46).

Tischler, Hans. *The Earliest Motets (to Circa 1270): A Complete Comparative Edition.* 3 vols. New Haven: Yale University Press, 1982. 1: 773–775 (no. 109).

EXAMPLE III–5. *Laus Domino/Eius*

Permission for transcription from Cod. Guelf. 1099 Helmst. granted by Herzog August Bibliothek, Wolfenbüttel.

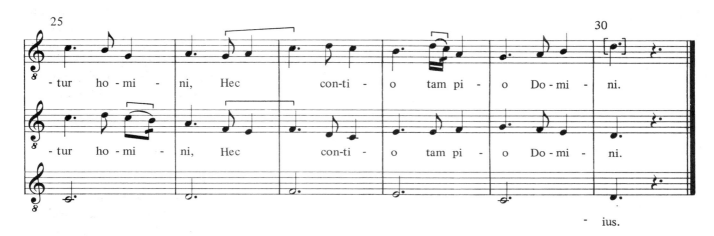

Translation

> Let the exultation of all echo the praise of God
> Who, feeling sorrow for the condemned man,
> Was born from the womb of the Virgin Mary.
> O marvel worthy of proclamation!
> The glowing red sun is arising from the resplendent
>   heaven
> And comes hither to man.
> Let therefore this glory be imparted to so just a Lord.

Translation by René Immelé.

6. *Cruci/Crux/Portare* (Motet à 3)

Cruci/Crux/Portare is an example of a poly-textual motet from the mid-thirteenth century. The manuscript in which it is located displays the shift toward completely mensural notation and relates to a system described by Johannes de Garlandia.[33]

Polytextual motets occur in three or four parts, each of which bears a different text. These motets have Latin or French texts or both. Language and subject matter of the texts must be taken into account when attempting to assign a work to a liturgical or nonliturgical function.

The two added Latin texts of *Cruci/Crux/Portare* refer to the cross of Christ as the source of our strength and deliverance. The tenor melody is taken from the verse of *Alleluia: Dulce lignum*, part of the Mass for May 3, the Feast of the Finding of the Holy Cross. The borrowed melisma is stated three times, the last statement employing a different rhythmic pattern. According to principles mentioned earlier (see p. 93), this motet could have been used in the liturgy at the point where the borrowed melisma occurs in the chant. It is also conceivable that the piece could have been performed outside the church, in which case an instrument other than the organ might have played the tenor.[34]

Several elements of stratification are apparent in this work. The tessitura of each part occupies a slightly different level, the tenor being lowest and the triplum highest. Polytextuality is an important feature of stratification. Unlike *Laus Domino/Eius*, this duplum and triplum exhibit independence of phrase relative to each other and to the tenor. The resulting avoidance of simultaneous cadence points creates a more expansive form than the previous example. Variants of rhythmic modes three and five are employed.

The authors recommend the following for a modern performance of this piece:

§ Two solo tenor voices for the duplum and triplum

§ For a liturgical style of performance, one to four male voices for the tenor, possibly with organ

§ For a nonliturgical style of performance, a solo male voice for the tenor, possibly reinforced or replaced by a bowed instrument, such as the vielle (which was said to be appropriate for every form of music)[35]

§ If the tenor part is sung, we recommend placing the second syllable on the fourth pitch and the final syllable on the final pitch of each statement of borrowed melody. (This solution assumes that singers would have been familiar with both the melody and the text underlay of the chant and might have adopted a parallel solution. In this chant, however, and in certain other motets that use the same tenor, the word *sustinere* occurs in place of *portare* to accompany the melisma. Nevertheless, the principle of placing the melisma on the penultimate syllable could still apply.)

Source

Bamberg, Staatsbibliothek, MS. Lit. 115, f. 11r.

Edition used

Anderson, Gordon A., ed. *Compositions of the Bamberg Manuscript.* Corpus Mensurabilis Musicae, vol. 75. N.p.: American Institute of Musicology, 1977. 24–25 (no. 19). Translations. 75:lxxxiv; 68: lxvii.

Facsimiles

Aubry, Pierre. *Cent motets du XIIIᵉ siècle: Publiés d'après le manuscrit Ed.IV.6 de Bamberg.* 3 vols. Paris: Rouart-Lerolle, 1908. Reprint. New York: Broude Bros., 1964. 1: f. 11r.

Parrish, Carl. *The Notation of Medieval Music.* New York: Norton, 1957. Reprint. New York: Pendragon, 1978. Pl. 35.

Seay, Albert. *Music in the Medieval World.* 2nd ed. Englewood Cliffs, NJ: Prentice-Hall, 1975. 118.

Other transcription

Aubry, Pierre. *Cent motets.* 2: 40–41 (no. 19).

EXAMPLE III–6. *Cruci/Crux/Portare*

Example and translation of triplum from Corpus Mensurabilis Musicae, volume 75, (©) copyright 1977 by American Institute of Musicology/Hänssler-Verlag, Neuhausen-Stuttgart. Translation of duplum from Corpus Mensurabilis Musicae, volume 68, (©) copyright 1975 by American Institute of Musicology/Hänssler-Verlag, Neuhausen-Stuttgart.

Translation

Duplum

O Cross, figure of penitence, key of grace, staff for the sinner, vein of pardon, tap-root of the tree of justice, way of life, banner of glory, bridegroom's nuptial couch at noontide, light of abundance, washing away the clouds of sadness, tranquil stay of the mind; let a man carry this Cross; by this Cross let him be comforted; for if you wish the joys of the true light, you must bear the Cross.

Triplum

To the Cross of Christ may praise be made at all hours, through which salvation was given to man; which held him who snatched away the sins of all by his body given over to death, when it was sacrificed on the Cross. Therefore, how honourable and praiseworthy is this tree, which alone was worthy to sustain the price of the true life!

7. *In seculum longum* (Hocket à 3)

In seculum longum might have been composed by "a certain Spaniard" referred to by Anonymous IV (second half of the thirteenth century).[36] It comes from the same source as *Cruci/Crux/Portare*, the previous example. *Hocket* is both a technique and the name of a genre based on the technique. Hocket technique is the breaking up of a melodic line so that its pitches are distributed among two or more parts of polyphony. Ours is one of several works in the source that are dominated by this principle. Like clausulae, these textless pieces are constructed over a Gregorian tenor.

The tenor of this piece comes from the verse of the Easter Gradual, *Haec dies* (Example III–1). The borrowed melody is repeated once. Although all parts of *In seculum longum* share basically the same range, distinct polarity exists between the tenor and the upper parts. The latter engage in a dialogue permeated by hocket, the rhythmic fragmentation of which contrasts with the simplicity of the tenor. This example displays rhythmic organization derived from modes three and five.

Historical evidence concerning the performance and function of hockets is scant. Some scholars have suggested that hockets are "instrumental motets," because of their lack of text, their use of hocket, and their appearance in manuscript sources of motets.[37] One authority has even specified winds as the most appropriate instruments.[38] A comment by Jerome of Moravia (second half of the thirteenth century) could be construed to support this view.[39] Such an interpretation clearly places the genre outside a liturgical context.

Other scholars, however, take the position that this is a vocal repertory, because the hocket technique appears to have developed out of an impro-

vised singing tradition.[40] Furthermore, other textless genres—for example, organum and clausula—are vocal. Also, some hockets that are textless in one source are texted elsewhere. *In seculum longum* appears in two other sources with added texts (and other differences).[41]

The authors recommend the following for a modern performance of this piece:

§ For a vocal rendition, three tenor voices (Such a performance could satisfy liturgical demands.)

§ For an alternate solution, two like instruments for the duplum and triplum and a contrasting, sustaining instrument for the tenor; for instance, two recorders and an organetto (all at four-foot pitch), or two rebecs and a vielle

§ If sung, consider possibility of vocalizing on a neutral vowel, or alternatively, applying solmization

Source

Bamberg, Staatsbibliothek, MS. Lit. 115, f. 63v.

Edition used

Anderson, Gordon A., ed. *Compositions of the Bamberg Manuscript.* Corpus Mensurabilis Musicae, vol. 75. N.p.: American Institute of Musicology, 1977. 137–138 (no. 104).

Facsimile

Aubry, Pierre. *Cent motets du XIIIe siècle: Publiés d'après le manuscrit Ed.IV.6 de Bamberg.* 3 vols. Paris: Rouart-Lerolle, 1908. Reprint. New York: Broude Bros., 1964. 1: f. 63v.

Other transcriptions

Aubry, Pierre. *Cent motets.* 2: 224–225 (no. 104).

Parrish, Carl. *A Treasury of Early Music: An Anthology of Masterworks of the Middle Ages, the Renaissance, and the Baroque Era.* New York: Norton, 1958. 59–61 (no. 11).

EXAMPLE III–7. *In seculum longum*

In seculum longum

8. *Aucun qui ne sevent/Iure tuis/Maria* (Motet à 3)

Aucun/Iure/Maria appears in fascicle eight of the Montpellier Codex, along with other motets that appear to date from the late thirteenth century. Some of these works exhibit a style that has been associated with the composer Petrus de Cruce (fl. ca. 1290). In this style, elements of stratification that were a compositional concern of earlier motet composers reach their most extreme manifestation. The vernacular texts of some Petronian motets place them outside the liturgical tradition of performance. The theory of Jacobus de Liège (early fourteenth century) is associated with the rhythmic interpretation of works in this repertory.[42]

The triplum text of the motet that follows expresses the sentiment that those who wish to enjoy love must suffer its sweet ills. The duplum offers praise and dedication to the Virgin Mary. The tenor is taken from the Marian antiphon *Salve Regina*; only the pitches associated with the last two words, *Virgo Maria*, were borrowed. Four statements of the tenor melody occur, framed by double bar lines in the edition.

Features of this motet that contribute to stratification include: multilingual text (French triplum, Latin duplum and tenor); independent text subjects (one sacred, one secular); text setting (syllabic triplum, somewhat melismatic duplum); density of notes (extremely fast-moving triplum, slower duplum, very slow tenor); range and tessitura (triplum *e–f′*, duplum *e–d′*, tenor *c–f*); independence of phrase lengths.

Some writers have suggested that tenors of polytextual motets were commonly performed by instruments alone.[43] Sustaining instruments (i.e., bowed or wind) seem preferable to plucked instruments, owing to the sustaining nature of tenor parts. If we assume that notated pitches correspond approximately to modern pitch standards, then the choices among historically available instruments are few (e.g., vielle, rebec, organ, organistrum).

The authors recommend the following for a modern performance of this piece:

§ Two solo tenor voices for the duplum and triplum

§ An instrument for the tenor (see preceding discussion)

§ For an all-vocal performance, a tenor/baritone voice for the tenor part

§ If tenor part is sung, place first four syllables under first four pitches and final syllable under final pitch of each statement of the borrowed melody (The words will thus be sung four times.)

§ The level of pulse indicated by the transcription corresponds approximately to that of the preceding motet examples. Thus triplum will require rapid articulation

Source

Montpellier, Faculté de Médicine, MS. H 196, ff. 366r–367r.

Edition used

Tischler, Hans, ed. *The Montpellier Codex*, Recent Researches in the Music of the Middle Ages and Early Renaissance, vols. 2–7. Madison: A–R Editions, 1978. Pt. 3 (vols. 6–7): 185–187 (no. 317).

Facsimile

Rokseth, Yvonne. *Polyphonies du XIIIe siècle: Le Manuscrit H 196 de la Faculté de Médicine de Montpellier.* 4 vols. Paris: Editions de l'Oiseau-Lyre, 1935–1939. 1: ff. 366r–367r.

Other transcriptions

Husmann, Heinrich, ed. *Medieval Polyphony.* Anthology of Music, vol. 9. Cologne: Arno Volk Verlag, 1962. 38–39 (no. 12).

Rokseth, Yvonne. *Polyphonies du XIIIe siècle.* 3: 217–219 (no. 317).

EXAMPLE III–8.   *Aucun qui ne sevent/Iure tuis/Maria*

[VIRGO] MARIA

Reprinted from *The Montpellier Codex*, edited by Hans Tischler, Recent Researches in the Music of the Middle Ages and Early Renaissance, vols. 2–7 (Madison: A–R Editions, 1978), pt. 3 (vols. 6–7): 185–187, by permission of A–R Editions, Inc. Copyright (©) by A–R Editions, Inc., 315 West Gorham Street, Madison, WI 53603.

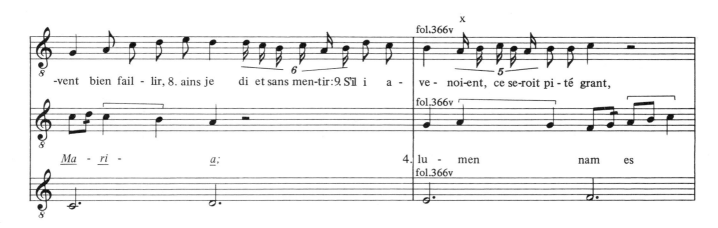

d'a-mour jo-ïr   tout er-rant 24.ne   se sont de riens en a- mer en-ten-dant,25.je le te-moing en mon chant.

9.da no - bis   pre - ce pi - a!

Translation

Duplum

With well disposed minds, we rightly
Stand by your praises, O Maria.
For you are for our hearts full of sins and baseness
The light and the road to salvation.
Eia! Do give us, through holy prayer, rest
In the celestial abode.

Triplum

Those who cannot please Love
And who are unable to keep up with its worship,
Sometimes speak ill of Love and Ladies
When, in the eagerness of their desire,
They cannot obtain the reward
Which true lovers long for.
Surely, they must fail in their endeavor;
I mean it honestly.
If they should succeed,
It would be a great pity;
For those who want to find joy in love
Must suffer heartily,
Endure the sweet pains
Love imposes on them;
They must be courteous and very discreet,
Generous and urbane with others.
They must not be afraid of quivering,
Trembling or growing pale
While they are yearning.
For Love can reward a lover
Far more than he deserves;
Such is the strength of its vigor.
Therefore, those who are too ardent in love
And want Love's joy too hastily,
Do not have any understanding of it:
My song will testify for it.

Translation by René Immelé.

9. Adam de la Halle, *Fi maris de vostre amour* (Rondeau à 3)

Adam de la Halle (b. 1245–1250, d. ?1285–1288 or after 1306) was a French trouvère poet and composer. A writer of both monophonic and polyphonic music, he is probably best known for his *Jeu de Robin et Marion*.

Fi maris is one of fourteen polyphonic rondeaux composed by Adam. These are likely to have been dance-songs, and they appear to be based on preexistent monophonic melodies.[44] The borrowed tune appears in either the lowest or the middle voice of the score. Like conductus, Adam's secular polyphony was notated in score format, with all parts sharing a single text.

Fi maris belongs to the type that has the tune in the lowest voice. It exhibits homorhythmic and concise phrases. The form of the piece is dictated by the poetic form of the rondeau, *A B a A a b A B*. (The two letters represent the two sections of music, while upper case indicates repeated text, and lower case, new text.)

Various solutions to the performance of Adam's rondeaux have been proposed, as follows:

A and B	a and b
§ Choral polyphony	Vocal monophony on the tune
§ Choral monophony on the tune	Three voices in polyphony
§ Polyphony	Polyphony[45]
§ Choral polyphony	Solo tune with instruments on other parts
§ Choral tune with instruments on other parts	Solo tune with instruments on other parts[46]

The authors recommend the following for a modern performance of this piece:

§ Three voices of similar range, polyphonically

§ A small choir, polyphonically

§ For either of foregoing, consider performing only the tune (the lowest part) for A and B or for *a* and *b*

§ Consider possibility of using instruments in a doubling capacity (The authors consider Adam's rondeaux to be too short and simple to warrant elaborate "orchestration.")

Source

Paris, Bibliothèque Nationale, MS. fr. 25566, ff. 33r–33v.

Edition used

Wilkins, Nigel, ed. *The Lyric Works of Adam de la Hale.* Corpus Mensurabilis Musicae, vol. 44. N.p.: American Institute of Musicology, 1967. 53 (no. 6 of the rondeaux).

Facsimile

Coussemaker, Edmond de, ed. *Oeuvres complètes du trouvère Adam de la Halle.* Paris: Durand et Pédone-Lauriel, 1872. Reprint. New York: Broude Bros., 1964. 217, quasi-facsimile.

Other transcriptions

Adam de la Halle. *Le Jeu de Robin et de Marion; Li Rondel Adam.* Edited by Friedrich Gennrich. Musikwissenschaftliche Studien-Bibliothek, vol. 20. Langen: n.p., 1962. 47 (no. 6).

Coussemaker, Edmond de, ed. *Oeuvres complètes.* 217–218 (no. 6 of the rondeaux).

Recordings

Adam de la Halle; Music of the Minstrels. Pro Musica Antiqua, Brussels. Archive ARC 3002.

The World of Adam de la Halle. Cambridge Consort. Turnabout TV 34439, Turnabout TV-S 34439, or Turnabout FSM 34439.

EXAMPLE III–9.   Adam de la Halle, *Fi maris de vostre amour*

Reprinted from Corpus Mensurabilis Musicae, volume 44, by permission of the publisher, American Institute of Musicology/Hänssler-Verlag, Neuhausen-Stuttgart.

Translation

> *Fie on your love, husband!*
> *For I have a lover.*
> *He is handsome and well dressed.*
> *Fie on your love, husband!*
> *He pleases me night and day*
> *For I love him so much.*
> *Fie on your love, husband!*
> *For I have a lover.*

Translation by René Immelé.

10. Philippe de Vitry, *Tuba sacre/In arboris/Virgo sum* (Motet à 3)

Philippe de Vitry (1291–1361) was not only a respected composer and theorist, but also an outstanding poet and philosopher of his day. He composed at least 10 surviving motets and wrote the treatise *Ars nova,* the name of which has been applied to the music of his age. In addition to these accomplishments, he held responsible positions in the French court and became Bishop of Meaux.

The Codex Ivrea, source of *Tuba/In arboris/ Virgo,* dates from around 1360 and contains motets, portions of the Mass, and a few French secular works. Typical of the motets is the use of isorhythm, a procedure that repeats a rhythmic pattern (*talea*) with or without correspondence to a repeated melodic pattern (*color*). The majority have Latin texts in both duplum and triplum.[47]

This piece embodies two Latin texts, together with an isorhythmic tenor written in black and red inks that have durational significance. In this edition, red ink is indicated by open brackets. A Roman numeral identifies each talea during the first statement of the color (A), and an Arabic numeral identifies each talea during the second statement of the color (B).

The triplum text is concerned with the difficulty of reconciling reason and faith. The duplum presents the same theme in a metaphor about a tree. Although the nature of these texts does not seem to preclude a liturgical function, the fact that no source of the tenor has been identified prohibits regarding this as a liturgical piece. The relationship between the upper parts is characterized by overlapping phrases and occasional hocket. Rests in each part create alternating two- and three-part textures. While the upper parts cross frequently, the tenor almost always provides the lowest-sounding pitch.

Soloists would probably have performed motets of this type.[48] The notated range of the upper parts is considerably higher than that of earlier polyphony, which leads us to consider transposition of the music downward, a solution that may also be inferred from treatises.[49] As with motets of the

thirteenth century, it is possible that tenors were played by instruments (organ, vielle, etc.), depending upon the performance situation (see comments about previous motet examples).

The authors recommend the following for a modern performance of this piece:

§ Transposing the music down a perfect fourth

§ Two solo tenor voices for the duplum and triplum

§ A vielle or organ for the tenor

§ Consider alternate solution for tenor, using tenor/baritone voice

§ If tenor is sung, place first two syllables under first two pitches, and last syllable under last pitch

Source

Ivrea, Biblioteca Capitolare, MS. without signature (Codex Ivrea), ff. 15v–16r.

Edition used

Schrade, Leo, ed. *The "Roman de Fauvel;" The Works of Philippe de Vitry; French Cycles of the "Ordinarium Missae."* Polyphonic Music of the Fourteenth Century, vol. 1. Monaco: Editions de l'Oiseau-Lyre, 1956. 88–90 (no. 10 of the motets of de Vitry).

Facsimiles

Besseler, Heinrich, and Peter Gülke. *Schriftbild der mehrstimmigen Musik.* Musikgeschichte in Bildern, vol. 3, pt. 5. Leipzig: Deutscher Verlag für Musik, 1973. 59 (no. 19 a, b).

Hoppin, Richard H. *Medieval Music.* New York: Norton, 1978. 369, partial facsimile.

Other transcriptions

Besseler, Heinrich, and Peter Gülke. *Schriftbild.* 58, partial transcription.

Hüschen, Heinrich, ed. *The Motet.* Anthology of Music, vol. 47. Cologne: Arno Volk Verlag, 1975. 29–30 (no. 5).

Recording

Missa Tournai; Motets, Circa 1320. Capella Antiqua, Munich. Telefunken AW 6.41231 or Telefunken SAWT 9517-A.

EXAMPLE III–10.   Philippe de Vitry, *Tuba sacre/In arboris/Virgo sum*

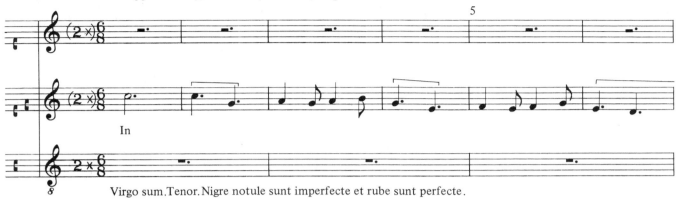

Translation

Duplum

> On top of the tree sits Faith, virgin and mediator of childbirth. In the middle, with her stump cut, Reason seeks the seven sisters who supported her sophistry; as she climbs while leaning more and more on her weak branches, she falls. Therefore, let her make a pledge to Faith or let her strive forever in error.

Triplum

> The trumpet of sacred Faith, herald of mysteries, proclaims to the world the very word of God: doubt is cast upon Reason, ground for all errors. One has to admit honestly and strongly believe—and this is essentially true—that God exists in three equal persons and that all three are one; that the Virgin Mary did not conceive by the seed of a man but by the breath of the Word; that the Virgin herself bore Man and God to the world. Since all this supernatural exists for the believers unconcerned with the nature of death, Reason, in her progressive efforts, brings forth doubt and therefore relies on prophecy; whereas Faith always follows the path which leads to divine mysteries and makes them appear more lucid.

Translation by René Immelé.

11. Guillaume de Machaut, *Dous amis* (Ballade à 2)

Guillaume de Machaut (ca. 1300–1377) was the major poetic and musical figure of fourteenth-century France. He left more music than any other composer of the century, both monophonic and polyphonic works. These include chansons, motets, a hocket, and a Mass, among others. He served as secretary to King John of Bohemia for many years and later served other high-ranking nobility. Machaut himself compiled complete collections of his own music.

The composer set music to 42 of his ballades. All but one are polyphonic settings in two to four parts. Some of these pieces are texted in all parts, while others have from one to three untexted parts. Three ballades are polytextual. All parts in Machaut's secular works are newly composed. The two forms in which he constructed his ballades may be labeled *a a b C* and *a a b b*.

Dous amis employs the latter form. In each section (*a, b*), the first line of text ends with an open cadence. The repeat of each section uses the second line of text and a closed cadence. The text follows the courtly love tradition of declaring the pain of unrequited love. *Dous amis*, like the other polyphonic music of Machaut, exhibits a style characterized by a high level of dissonance and sophisticated rhythmic subtlety.

Such intimate chamber music as *Dous amis* would probably have been performed for the pleasure of a small group of elite listeners. Recent scholarship has strengthened the position of advocates of all-vocal performance of most fourteenth-century music.[50] For vocal performance of untexted lines, singers must underlay the text or sing on a neutral vowel or solmize. Like other polyphonic music of the Middle Ages, Machaut's secular works appear to call for solo performers. The traditional view agrees with that approach but assigns untexted parts to instruments.[51] Although a decision to employ instruments on textless parts may result from a purely structural interpretation, evidence exists to show that this type of performance did occur.[52] The question of using instruments to double the sung parts has been addressed by writers who support or reject this solution.[53] Even an all-instrumental performance has some historical justification.[54]

If pitch in the sources of Machaut's music corresponds approximately to modern pitch, instruments with a range capable of playing tenors and contratenors include vielle, harp, positive organ, lute, and possibly portative organ, psaltery, douçaine, gittern, and shawm.[55] Many more instruments had a range capable of playing *cantus* parts; for example, flute, rebec, organetto, bagpipe (presumably without drones in this context), and citole. A structural interpretation might assign a sustaining instrument to tenors and a plucked instrument to contratenors, because of the generally contrasting nature of the parts.

The authors recommend the following for a modern performance of this piece:

§ A tenor/baritone voice for the *cantus*

§ A vielle or a harp for the tenor

§ For a different solution, a tenor/baritone voice for the tenor part

§ If tenor part is sung, set text, generally following underlay of the cantus; or vocalize on a neutral vowel

§ Set text of remaining stanzas, following underlay of first stanza as closely as possible

Source

Paris, Bibliothèque Nationale, MS. fr. 1584, f. 456v.

Edition used

Hoppin, Richard H., ed. *Anthology of Medieval Music*. New York: Norton, 1978. 140–142 (no. 62).

Facsimile

Apel, Willi. *The Notation of Polyphonic Music, 900–1600*. 5th ed., rev. Cambridge, MA: Medieval Academy of America, 1961. 357 (no. 69).

Other transcriptions

Guillaume de Machaut. *Works*. Edited by Leo Schrade. Polyphonic Music of the Fourteenth Century, vols. 2, 3. Monaco: Editions de l'Oiseau-Lyre, 1956. 3:77 (ballade no. 6).

Wilkins, Nigel, ed. *One Hundred Ballades, Rondeaux and Virelais from the Late Middle Ages*. Cambridge, England: Cambridge University Press, 1969. 150–151 (musical example no. 5), 26–27 (textual example no. 16).

EXAMPLE III–11.   Guillaume de Machaut, *Dous amis*

1. Dous amis, oy mon complaint:
   A toy se plaint
   Et complaint,
   Par defaut de tes secours,
   Mes cuers qu'amours si con-
   straint
   Que tiens remaint
   Dont mal maint
   Ay, quant tu ne me secours
   En mes langours,
   Car d'aillours
   N'est riens qui confort
   m'amaint.
   S'en croist mes plours
   Tous les jours,
   Quant tes cuers en moy ne maint.

2. Amis, t'amour si m'ataint
   Que mon vis taint
   Et destaint
   Souvent de pluseurs coulours,
   Et mon dolent cuer estraint;
   Si le destraint
   Qu'il estaint
   Quant en toy n'a son recours.
   S'a jours trop cours
   Se n'acours
   Pour li garir, car il creint
   Mort, qui d'amours
   Vient le cours,
   Quant tes cuers en moy ne maint.

3. Mon cuer t'amour si ensaint
   Qu'il ne se faint
   Qu'il ne t'aint
   Pour tes parfaites doucours;
   Et ta biaute qui tout vaint
   Dedens li paint
   Et empraint
   Avec tes hautes valours.
   S'en sont gringnours
   Mes dolours
   Et plus dolereus mi plaint
   Et en decours
   Mes vigours,
   Quant tes cuers en moy ne maint.

Translation:

1. Gentle friend, hear my complaint:
   To you laments
   and complains,
   for want of your succour,
   my whole self, whom love so
   constrains
   that I am held fast,
   from which I have great pain,
   when you do not succour me
   in my weakness;
   for otherwise
   there is nothing that brings me
   comfort.
   Thus my tears increase
   every day,
   when your whole self does not dwell in me.

2. Friend, your love so attacks me
   that my face flushes
   and pales
   often with several colors,
   and grips my sorrowing heart;
   so constricts it
   that it ceases to beat
   when it does not find refuge in you.
   So its days are too short
   if you do not hasten
   to cure it, for it fears
   death, which results
   from love,
   when your whole self does not dwell in me.

3. Your love so wounds my heart
   that it does not pretend
   that it does not love you
   for your perfect charms;
   and your beauty, which conquers all,
   penetrates within it
   and imprints (it)
   with your great virtues.
   So from this are my sorrows
   great
   and more dolorous my plaint
   and my strength
   in decline,
   when your whole self does not dwell in me.

12. Philipoctus de Caserta, *En remirant* (Ballade à 3)

Philipoctus de Caserta (fl. ca. 1370) was an important theorist and composer of the late fourteenth century and was active at the Papal court in Avignon. All but one or two of his compositions are ballades. Almost nothing is known about his life.

En remirant comes from a manuscript that is one of the largest sources of manneristic music. Some of its diverse collection of sacred and secular works appears to be associated with the Avignon court.[56] The manneristic style of the Ars Subtilior focused on extreme rhythmic complexity and nuance. This style depends on established systems of consonance and mensuration as points of departure for the exploration of greater dissonance and more complex rhythmic relationships than previously known.[57] Clearly this music was performed for very astute listeners by very adept musicians. Any transcription into modern score notation produces an awkward and syncopated appearance that disguises the suavity of the rhythms and phrases as originally notated. A facsimile of this work appears as Figure 4–3. (Note that the clef signs and B-flats in the superius are misplaced and should be read a perfect fifth lower; also note that red notation signifies rhythmic alteration.)

En remirant is a ballade having the form *a a b C* (see the discussion of Example 3-11). Its three stanzas deal with the usual pangs of unrequited love. Fragments of texts by Machaut appear in the third stanza: *De triste cuer* and *Se Dieus e vous ne me prenez en cure*.[58]

Options for the performance of secular music of the fourteenth century have been presented in the discussion of the previous piece. The authors feel that the Ars Subtilior repertory is less suited to the all-vocal option. Furthermore, instrumental doubling of the *cantus* seems particularly inappropriate, due to the extravagant complexities of that part.

The authors recommend the following for a modern performance of this piece:

§ If the piece is performed at the notated pitch level, a countertenor voice or a female voice for the *cantus*

§ A lute or harp for the contratenor

§ A vielle for the tenor

§ Consider possibility of transposition down a perfect fourth, in order to permit a tenor voice to sing the *cantus* (see p. 110).

§ Set text of remaining stanzas, following underlay of first stanza as closely as possible

Sources

Modena, Biblioteca Estense, MS. αM.5.24 (formerly Lat. 568), f. 35v, with one stanza.

Chantilly, Musée Condé, MS. 564, f. 39r, remaining stanzas.

Edition used

Apel, Willi, ed. *French Secular Music of the Late Fourteenth Century.* Cambridge, MA: Medieval Academy of America, 1950. Section 2, pp. 98–99 (no. 59).

Facsimiles

Apel, Willi, ed. *French Secular Music of the Late Fourteenth Century.* Pl. 3.

Figure 4–3.

EXAMPLE III–12. Philipoctus de Caserta, *En remirant*

Copied, by permission, from *French Secular Music of the Late Fourteenth Century*, ed. Willi Apel (Cambridge, MA.: Medieval Academy of America, 1950), pp. 98–99.

da - me sans per, Se vo

doul - çour ne me va se - cour - rant!

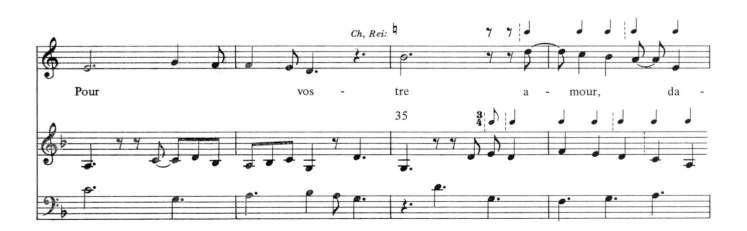

Pour vos - tre a - mour, da -

Translation

When I glanced at your lovely picture,
Which reflects your sweet image,
Love touched me with such ardent desire
That, alas! my heart is unable to bear it,
Sweet Lady without peer,
If your graciousness does not come to my rescue.
For your love, Lady, I go pining.

He, bel acueillir, ou je prens noureture,
Vo cuer vueilliez de m'amor alumer,
Car se mon cuer devoit en grant ardure
Ardre, brunir a tous jorns sans finer,
Si ne lairay que ne vous doie amer,
Mes vo cuer meyme va trop detriant:
Pour vostre amour, dame, vois languissant.

Gracious Lady, source of my nourishment,
Let my love warm up your heart,
For, if my heart is to burn ardently
And glow without respite,
I shall not stop loving you,
Even if your heart keeps me away from you.
For your love, Lady, I go pining.

A vous me plains, car sui en aventure
De toust mourir pour loyalment amer,
Se Dieus e vous ne me prenez en cure,
En face amour le dur en doulz muer.
Telz mauls ne puis longuement endurer.
De triste cuer dire puis en plourant:
Pour vostre amour, dame, vois languissant.

I am complaining to you, for I am
About to die because of my honest love
If God and you do not take care of me
And if Love does not change from harsh to sweet.
I can no longer endure such a suffering.
Sadly, I can only say while crying:
For your love, Lady, I go pining.

Translation by René Immelé.

13. Giovanni da Firenze, *Nascoso el viso* (Madrigal à 2)

Giovanni da Firenze (fl. 1340–1350) was an Italian composer from the early trecento. Also known as Giovanni da Cascia, he apparently came from the village of Cascia, near Florence. Little is known for certain about his life. Fewer than two dozen works survive, all but three of them being madrigals. His works appear in nine manuscript sources.[59]

The madrigal (not to be confused with the sixteenth-century genre of the same name) is a form cultivated by the first generation of trecento composers. This form comprises two or three stanzas, usually set to the same music, followed by a final stanza set to new music usually in a different meter. Most madrigals are composed in two parts. The music has a treble-dominated texture, characterized by melismas in the upper part, and is more consonant than contemporaneous French compositions.

Nascoso el viso appears in three manuscripts, as indicated by the following edition. These sources reveal differences in pitch, rhythm, and floridity; particularly curious is the appearance of the ritornello a whole step lower in one source. This madrigal exhibits the musical form *a a b*. Alternation of syllabic and melismatic passages appears in both parts, the *cantus* displaying more florid writing.

Compositions of this genre make us aware of the high level of vocal art that must have prevailed in fourteenth-century Italy. Evidence that has been used to support all-vocal performance of the works of Machaut has also been applied to the performance of trecento music.[60] Tenors and contratenors have sometimes been considered instrumental,[61] even when texted.[62] Information from writings of the period suggests all-instrumental performance of this repertory,[63] or mixed voices and instruments.[64] There is reason to suppose, however, that Italian references to the use of instruments and voices together describe the practice in monophonic repertories.[65] Whatever the case, trecento polyphony is likely a soloistic repertory, however meager the documentary evidence.[66]

The authors recommend the following for a modern performance of this piece:

§ Using the version from Codex Rossi (*Rs*)

§ A countertenor/tenor voice for the upper part

§ A tenor/baritone voice for the lower part

§ For another solution, play lower part on a vielle

§ Set text of second stanza to the *a* section of music, following underlay of first stanza as closely as possible

Sources

Florence, Biblioteca Nazionale, MS. Panciatichi 26, ff. 49v–50r. (*FP*).

Florence, Biblioteca Medicea Laurenziana, MS. Palatino 87 (Squarcialupi Codex), ff. 3v–4r. (*FL*).

Rome, Biblioteca Vaticana, MS. Rossi 215, ff. 18v–19r. (*RS*).

Edition used

Pirrotta, Nino, ed. *Bartholus de Florentia, Johannes de Florentia, Gherardellus de Florentia.* Pt. 1 of *The Music of Fourteenth-Century Italy.* Corpus Mensurabilis Musicae, vol. 8. Amsterdam: American Institute of Musicology, 1954. 20–24 (no. 9 of the works of Johannes de Florentia), vii (additional stanzas).

Facsimiles

Apel, Willi. *The Notation of Polyphonic Music, 900–1600.* 5th ed., rev. Cambridge, MA: Medieval Academy of America, 1961. 387, with first stanza of text.

Besseler, Heinrich, and Peter Gülke. *Schriftbild der mehrstimmigen Musik.* Musikgeschichte in Bildern, vol. 3, pt. 5. Leipzig: Deutscher Verlag für Musik, 1973. 71 (no. 25 a, b), with first stanza of text.

Other transcriptions

Besseler, Heinrich, and Peter Gülke. *Schriftbild der mehrstimmigen Musik.* 70, partial transcription.

Marrocco, W. Thomas, ed. *Italian Secular Music by Magister Piero, Giovanni da Firenze, Jacopo da Bologna.* Polyphonic Music of the Fourteenth Century, vol. 6. Monaco: Editions de l'Oiseau-Lyre, 1967. 42–43 (no. 9 of the works of Giovanni da Firenze).

Wolf, Johannes, ed. *Der Squarcialupi-Codex, Pal. 87, der Biblioteca Medicea Laurenziana zu Florenz.* Lippstadt: Kistner und Siegel, 1955. 8 (no. 6 of the works of Jouannes de Cascia), with partial text.

Recording

Madrigale e Caccie from the Codex of Antonio Squarcialupi; Guillaume Dufay, Sacred Songs. Pro Musica Antiqua. Archive ARC 3003.

EXAMPLE III–13.   Giovanni da Firenze, *Nascoso el viso*

Reprinted from Corpus Mensurabilis Musicae, volume 8, by permission of the publisher, American Institute of Musicology/Hänssler-Verlag, Neuhausen-Stuttgart.

Nascoso el viso, stava fra le fronde
D' un bel çardino: apresso a mi guardava
Sopra una fonte dove se pescava;

E vedea donne vermigliete e bionde,
Liçadre al modo che solea le Euguane,
Trovarse al bosco e quando a le fontane.

Qual era scalça e qual com' ela naque;
Piu non vo' dir quanto quel di me piaque.

Translation

With my face hidden, I stood among the branches
Of a lovely garden; I spied into a
Spring nearby, where people fished.

There I saw ladies, rosy and blonde,
Graceful as were the water-nymphs,
Finding themselves in the woods or at the springs.

One was barefoot and one was as she was born.
More I'd rather not say how much I was pleased
        that day.

Translation by Margaret Israel, in collaboration with Lucy Cross.

14. *Or qua, compagni*
(Caccia à 3)

Although *Or qua, compagni* bears no attribution in its source, the work has tentatively been ascribed to Maestro Piero, the composer of two other pieces in the Codex Rossi.[67] Piero (fl. 1340–1350) left eight known works, four of which make use of canon.

The caccia is a fourteenth-century Italian canonic genre that usually employs two texted, canonic parts over a free, untexted tenor. The other examples bear text in all three parts or differ in the number or placement of canonic parts. With few exceptions, the caccia, like the madrigal, has two sections, the second being a ritornello. The texts of most cacce concern the hunt.

Or qua, compagni is the earliest known caccia.[68] It is unusual in having no ritornello. This piece represents the type of caccia that has canonic parts over a free tenor. The canonic voices present an interplay of melisma and syllabic declamation.

Many scholars view cacce as appropriate for performance by two singers, with an instrument playing the tenor.[69] Although various authorities have suggested an all-vocal rendition of all polyphony of the fourteenth century, the authors have not found any research or conjecture favoring this solution specifically for the caccia.

The authors recommend the following for a modern performance of this piece:

§ If the piece is performed at the notated pitch, two solo countertenor voices for the canonic parts

§ A vielle or organ for the tenor

§ Consider possibility of transposition down a perfect fourth in order to permit tenor voices to sing canonic parts. (This suggestion by the authors derives from a hypothesis that fourteenth-century French polyphony should be transposed. See p. 110.)

See p. 110.

Source

Rome, Biblioteca Vaticana, MS. Rossi 215, ff. 19v–20r.

Edition used

Pirrotta, Nino, ed. *Maestro Piero; Codex Vatican Rossi 215; Anonymous Madrigals and Cacce from Other Manuscripts.* Pt. 2 of *The Music of Fourteenth-Century Italy.* Corpus Mensurabilis Musicae, vol. 8. N.p.: American Institute of Musicology, 1960. 37–39 (no. 28).

Facsimiles

Apel, Willi. *The Notation of Polyphonic Music, 900–1600.* 5th ed., rev. Cambridge, MA: Medieval Academy of America, 1961. 383 (no. 76), with first stanza of text.

Hoppin, Richard H. *Medieval Music.* New York: Norton, 1978. 445.

Marrocco, W. Thomas, ed. *Fourteenth-Century Italian Cacce.* 2nd ed. Cambridge, MA: Medieval Academy of America, 1961. Pl. 5.

Die Musik in Geschichte und Gegenwart. 1: cols. 719–720.

Other transcriptions

Husmann, Heinrich, ed. *Medieval Polyphony.* Anthology of Music, vol. 9. Cologne: Arno Volk Verlag, 1962. 44–45 (no. 15).

Marrocco, W. Thomas, ed. *Fourteenth-Century Italian Cacce.* 2nd ed. 64–66 (no. 18).

———, ed. *Italian Secular Music: Anonymous Madrigals and Cacce and the Works of Niccolò da Perugia.* Polyphonic Music of the Fourteenth Century, vol. 8. Monaco: Editions de l'Oiseau-Lyre, 1972. 72–74 (anon. madrigals and cacce, no. 31).

EXAMPLE III–14.   *Or qua, compagni*

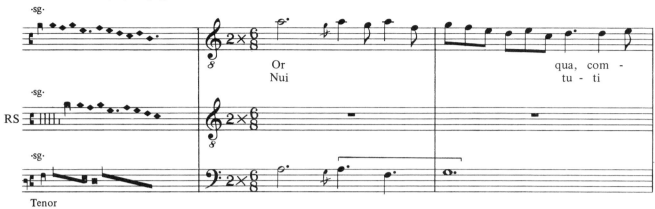

Reprinted from *Corpus Mensurabilis Musicae*, volume 8, by permission of the publisher, American Institute of Musicology/Hänssler-Verlag, Neuhausen-Stuttgart.

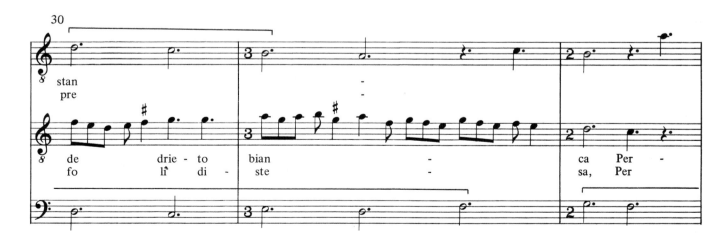

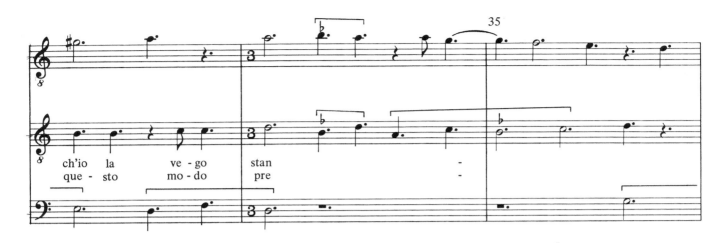

Translation

"Here now, companions, here with great pleasure,
Call the dogs here at once!"
"Black mouth, here!
White fur, stay here, stay,
For I think I see a chamois!"
"Where does she go? This way, this way!
Which path does she take?"
"Through that forest fearfully watching, hidden!"
"Molton, Molton! Who are you, who are you?"
"I am the guard."
"What do you want, what do you want?"
"She goes this way!"
"Don't you see there are many?
Take one!" "Which do you want?"
"The one with the white backside,
Because I see she is tired."

We are all following her with firm resolve,
Helping each other.

"Grab it, go on!
Run hard, that way!"
For seeing the lair, she goes almost with delight!
She cannot flee, she can't, she can't,
For the dog is holding her.
Nor can she move, don't you know, since she is
        bewildered.
"Oaf, tie her up!
See how she scares you off!"
"Go on if you want!
That'll do it!
I'm afraid she'll bite me,
Because she's a wild animal!" "She won't, she
        won't!"
So I leave her lying there,
Captured in this way.

Translation by Margaret Israel, in collaboration with Lucy Cross and
Paul Olson.

15. Francesco Landini, *Partesi con dolore* (Ballata à 3.)

The works of Francesco Landini (ca. 1325–1397) constitute the most significant body of music by a single Italian composer of the fourteenth century. He was a poet as well as a composer, and was active as an organist, despite being blind from childhood. His compositions include madrigals, cacce, and ballate, the last category being the largest.

The source used for the following edition of *Partesi con dolore* is a large collection of secular vocal polyphony from fourteenth-century Italy. It includes approximately 150 items: madrigals, ballate, cacce, and a few French works. The first part of the manuscript seems to represent an effort to collect Landini's known works.[70]

Like many trecento works, *Partesi con dolore* expresses the poetic conceit of unfulfilled love. Although the poem appears to be a ballata minore,[71] the musical setting does not follow the usual form of the ballata (A b b a A). In this piece, the two *piedi* of the poem are set to through-composed music (*b*, not *b b*), a type of setting rarely found.[72] Johannes Wolf interpreted this piece to have the form *a a b*, based on information found in the music as it appears in the manuscript sources. Leo Schrade has found French features in the form of the text and the rhythm.[73] It is interesting to note that both sections of this piece conclude with identical music, a characteristic more closely identified with the French ballade.

Landini's three-part music exhibits diverse texting practices: text in all three parts; text in cantus and tenor; or text in the cantus only. Some pieces show more than one practice among concordant sources.[74] The varied habits of different scribes may account for the diversity of trecento texting practices.[75] Scholars have long puzzled over possible relationships between texting practices and performance practices. Some think that texted parts are vocal and textless parts are instrumental.[76] The possibility that the presence or absence of text in a source does not necessarily relate to performance practice has also been suggested.[77] If that is the case, then an all-instrumental performance becomes an option. Instrumental arrangements of fourteenth-century secular polyphony appear in the Robertsbridge and Faenza Codices. Additional discussion of options appears in the commentary provided for the previous examples of fourteenth-century music. No easy solution exists for performing the trecento repertory.

The authors recommend the following for a modern performance of this piece:

§ A countertenor/tenor voice for the *cantus*

§ Two vielles for the contratenor and tenor

§ Alternatively, lute or harp for contratenor and vielle for tenor. (This suggestion follows iconographic evidence that instrumental ensembles were usually made up of contrasting instruments.)[78]

§ For all-vocal solution, tenor voice for contratenor and tenor/baritone voice for tenor part. Set text, closely following underlay of *cantus*

Source

Florence, Biblioteca Nazionale, MS. Panciatichi 26, ff. 27v–28r.

Edition used

Landini, Francesco. *Works*. Edited by Leo Schrade. Polyphonic Music of the Fourteenth Century, vol. 4. Monaco: Editions de l'Oiseau-Lyre, 1958. 136–137 (no. 108).

Facsimile

Besseler, Heinrich, and Peter Gülke. *Schriftbild der mehrstimmigen Musik*. Musikgeschichte in Bildern, vol. 3, pt. 5. Leipzig: Deutscher Verlag für Musik, 1973. 73 (no. 26).

Other transcriptions

Besseler, Heinrich, and Peter Gülke. *Schriftbild*. 72, partial transcription.

Wolf, Johannes, ed. *Der Squarcialupi-Codex, Pal. 87, der Biblioteca Medicea Laurenziana zu Florenz*. Lippstadt: Kistner und Siegel, 1955. 276–277 (no. 95 of the works of Landini).

EXAMPLE III–15.   Francesco Landini, *Partesi con dolore*

From *Polyphonic Music of the Fourteenth Century,* vol. 4 (Monaco: Editions de l'Oiseau-Lyre, 1958). Copyright © Margarita M. Hanson 1974, Editions de l'Oiseau-Lyre, Monaco.

Translation

> *My body and my life*
> *Part ways in sorrow.*
>
> *My grieving eyes cry*
> *For they are distant from you.*
>
> *They do not hope to live happy,*
> *But to be tormented.*
>
> *But my heart and my soul*
> *Remain in your power.*
>
> *My body and my life*
> *Part ways in sorrow.*

Translation by Margaret Israel, in collaboration with Lucy Cross.

16. John Dunstaple, *Ave Regina celorum* (Motet à 3)

John Dunstaple (ca. 1390–1453) was the best-known English composer of his time. Although the spelling *Dunstable* is better known today, the first version is supported by more historical evidence.[79] In addition to his musical activities, he was a mathematician and astronomer. He wrote motets, Mass movements, and a few secular songs. Most of these works appear in manuscripts of Continental provenance, very few in English sources. It is agreed that he likely was in the employ of the Duke of Bedford, who served in France (1422–1435). Dunstaple's possible presence on the Continent would account for the locations of his works in manuscripts and also for his historically acknowledged influence on Burgundian composers.[80]

Ave Regina celorum appears in several manuscripts. The Modena source includes the words *chorus* and *duo*. *Chorus* appears at the beginning of the chant incipit, in the contratenor part; *duo* appears in each part (superius and contratenor) at the word *Gaude* (*Ave*). This source is also the only one fully texted in all parts.

Motets of Dunstaple's time are works generally in three or four parts. Some are based on *cantus firmi*, while others are newly composed in all parts. Treble-dominated texture is an important aspect of many motets. Other stylistic features that sometimes occur are isorhythm, fauxbourdon style, and a euphonious sonority.

Ave Regina celorum is a motet based on the well-known Marian antiphon. The antiphon hails Mary as Queen of Heaven and Lady of Angels. Dunstaple has freely paraphrased the chant melody in the superius part. This work may have been performed as part of an Office, replacing the chant or the text that it incorporates. Because its text is familiar and not limited to a specific Feast, Dunstaple's motet might also have been sung for diverse ceremonial occasions. Its expansive treble melody, consonant harmonies, and relative rhythmic simplicity ally it more closely to Italian style of the previous century than to the manneristic style of the Avignon court.

This motet appears to be an early example of choral polyphony, based on the indications in the Modena source. If this is the case, the choir would sing the sections *Regina . . . orta* and *Et pro nobis . . . exora*; soloists would perform the middle section, first a duo between superius and contratenor, then one between superius and tenor. Although this manuscript contains the word *chorus* next to the incipit, the authors point out that in the context of the chant, this portion would have been sung by a soloist or a few solo singers. The other sources of this motet bear complete text in only the superius part. One authority has suggested that singers perhaps vocalized the untexted parts of Dunstaple's sacred works.[81]

The work might also have been performed by a solo vocalist with two instruments, in a nonliturgical context. Some sacred English polyphony of the early fifteenth century seems to indicate a tradition of unison choral singing of a single part. Such a practice implies rendition of the other parts by solo voices or instruments.[82] A French document mentions the use of *bas* instruments in the Mass, along with organ and singers.[83] Instruments are also mentioned in connection with an English choir attending the Council of Constance in 1416.[84]

The authors recommend the following for a modern performance of this piece:

§ A countertenor voice for the incipit and the superius

§ A countertenor voice for the contratenor

§ A tenor voice for the tenor

§ A small choir of male voices for the three-part sections only

§ Alternatively, consider transposition down a perfect fourth, using tenor and baritone voices (see p. 110 regarding transposition)

Source

Modena, Biblioteca Estense, MS. αX I, II (Lat. 471), ff. 102v–103r.

Edition used

Dunstable, John. *Complete Works.* Edited by Manfred Bukofzer. Revised by Margaret Bent, Ian Bent, and Brian Trowell. Musica Britannica, vol. 8. 2nd ed. London: Stainer & Bell Ltd., 1970. 99–100 (no. 37).

Facsimiles

Codex Tridentinus 92. Rome: Bibliopola, 1970. 184–185.

Dunstable, John. *Complete Works*. xxii, partial facsimile.

Other transcription

Ficker, Rudolf von, et al., eds. *Sechs (Sieben) Trienter Codices*. Denkmäler der Tonkunst in Österreich, vols. 14, 15, 22, 38, 53, 61, 76. Vienna: Artaria, and Universal Edition A. G., 1900–1933. Reprint. Graz: Akademische Druck- u. Verlagsanstalt, 1959–1960. 76 (Jg. 40): 50–51.

Recording

Dunstable: Motets. Pro Musica Antiqua. Archive ARC 3052.

EXAMPLE III–16.   John Dunstaple, *Ave Regina celorum*

Reprinted from John Dunstable, *Complete Works*, edited by Manfred Bukofzer and revised by Margaret Bent, Ian Bent, and Brian Trowell, Musica Britannica, vol. 8, 2nd ed. (London: Stainer & Bell Ltd., 1970), 99–100, by permission of the publisher.

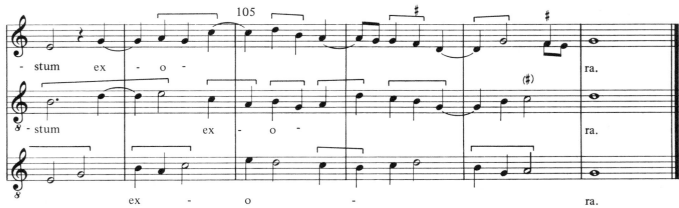

Translation

    Hail, Queen of Heaven,
    Hail, Mistress of the Angels
    Hail, holy root
    From whom the light of the world has come.
    Hail, glorious one,
    Loveliest of women.
    Hail, most illustrious one,
    And for us always
    Pray to Christ.

17. *Tibi laus, tibi gloria* (Carol à 2)

Tibi laus comes from a manuscript that dates from circa 1450 or earlier and contains a Mass, hymns, carols, and other works.[85] Carols constitute a genre of long ancestry. Early carols were monophonic dance-songs composed of alternating choral and solo sections (burden and verse); fifteenth-century carols had lost all dance connotations, and were set polyphonically in two, three, or four parts. The carol repertory perhaps served as processional music in liturgical, courtly, and civic ceremonies.[86] Texts, which appear in Latin, English, or macaronic settings, are concerned with a variety of sacred and secular subjects. *Tibi laus* is a song of praise celebrating the birth of Christ. This piece appears in score format in its source, with text under the lower voice.

The performance of early polyphonic carols apparently employed soloists for the verses and a chorus for the burden. Some later carols involve both groups of performers in both sections of the music.[87] The manuscript source of *Tibi laus* contains a number of repeat signs. These suggest that each of the indicated passages, in both the burden and the verse, is sung first by soloists, then by choir.[88] It appears in some cases that only the immediately preceding phrase is to be repeated. The burden precedes each verse and closes the piece.

The tessituras of this piece accommodate tenor- and countertenor-range voices. Secular functions could conceivably have involved instruments doubling or replacing voices.[89] The editor has interpreted repetition signs as applying to short phrases.

The authors recommend the following for a modern performance of this piece:

§ A countertenor voice for the upper part

§ A tenor voice for the tenor part

§ A small choir of male voices for the burden

§ Alternatively, as a practical solution, an alto voice for the upper part, a tenor voice for the tenor part, and a small, mixed choir for the burden

Source

London, British Library, MS. Egerton 3307, f. 49r.

Edition used

Stevens, John, ed. *Medieval Carols.* Musica Britannica, vol. 4. 2nd ed. London: Stainer & Bell Ltd., 1970. 33 (no. 44). Translation. 143.

Facsimile

Stevens, John, ed. *Medieval Carols.* xviii.

EXAMPLE III–17.   *Tibi laus, tibi gloria*

ORDER: B V₁ B V₂ . . . B; soloists throughout
Chorus may repeat m. 1–7, 20–26, 35–41, 45–49.

Music and translation reprinted from *Medieval Carols*, edited by John Stevens, *Musica Britannica*, vol. 4, 2nd ed.
(London: Stainer & Bell Ltd., 1970), 33 and 143, by permission of the publisher.

Translation

To thee be praise, to thee be glory, to thee the giving of thanks / 1. Glory to thee, O Lord, who wast born of a virgin, cleansing us of our guilt; to thee be praise, to thee be glory, and all reverence / 2. From the rising-point of the sun thou wast born to us today, redeeming the guilty from blood; to thee be praise. . . . who dost marvellous things / 3. Now, the star of light being risen, let us gladly adore thee, O Lord, with consecrated song; to thee be praise. . . . throughout the confines of the world.

18. Guillaume Dufay, *Ce moys de may* (Rondeau à 3)

Guillaume Dufay (ca. 1400–1474) was the principal exponent of the new harmonic language of the early fifteenth century. He was active in many musical centers of France and Italy. Important as a composer of both sacred and secular music, he left many chansons, motets, and Masses.

The source of *Ce moys de may* contains more than 300 sacred and secular works from the late fourteenth and early fifteenth centuries.[90] Among Dufay's more than 70 chansons are found works in the standard forms and in numerous variants thereof. Two common settings employ either one texted and two untexted parts or two texted and one untexted. The tenor and *cantus* exhibit sustaining qualities, while the contratenor seems more fragmented. Some three-part chansons bear text in all parts. There are also a few chansons in four parts.

Ce moys de may is an example of the rondeau form (see Example III–9). Its text celebrates the joy of spring, in a poem that includes the composer's name. The name *Perinet* could be that of the poet.[91] *Ce moys de may* has been described as rhythmically distinctive among Dufay's chansons.[92] Its original notation combines white and black note forms. The edition that follows indicates white notes (coloration) by means of open brackets. Its manuscript source is texted in all parts; textless passages occur at the beginning, middle, and end. In another source only the *cantus* and tenor are fully texted.

Current research suggests a number of solutions to the problem of dealing with untexted parts and portions of parts in performing Burgundian chansons.[93] Most authorities assume that this is a repertory intended for soloists. Some of their proposals follow:

1. An all-vocal solution.[94] This would require setting text to untexted parts. Textless passages could be vocalized on neutral vowel or nearest syllable of text; or words could be repeated on untexted pitches
2. An all-male vocal solution, necessitating transposition downward[95]
3. A mixed male-female vocal solution[96]
4. Voices for texted parts and instruments for completely untexted parts[97]
5. Instruments on tenors and contratenors, perhaps even when texted[98]
6. An all-instrumental solution (*haut* or *bas* ensemble)[99]
7. An all-instrumental solution (chordal instrument)[100]
8. *Cantus* and tenor played or sung, and contratenor omitted from three-part pieces[101]
9. *Cantus* sung and lower parts played on a chordal instrument, in three-part pieces[102]
10. *Cantus* played on a melody instrument, with lower parts on a chordal instrument, in three-part pieces[103]
11. When instruments are employed for parts other than principal melody, preference should be given to plucked or struck string instruments[104]
12. When multiple instruments have been employed in some modern performances, one solution has been to use contrasting *bas* instruments, such as woodwind or organetto for the *cantus*, plucked instrument for the contratenor, and sustaining instrument for the tenor (This essentially structural interpretation is one that the authors have found musically convincing in their experience.)

The repetition pattern of the rondeau form changed over the centuries. Although later literary sources fail to repeat the complete refrain, performance practice in the fifteenth century remains uncertain, and some musical settings perhaps employed a curtailed refrain.[105]

The authors recommend the following for a modern performance of this piece:

§ An alto voice for texted portions of *cantus* part, doubled by organetto, which plays both the textless and texted passages (Both the range of the melody and the nature of the poem are appropriate for a female singer. Furthermore, iconographic and other evidence suggests that women took an active role in performance of courtly music of this type; see p. 6.)

§ A tenor voice for texted portions of contratenor part, doubled by a lute or harp that plays both textless and texted passages

§ A tenor voice for texted portions of tenor part, doubled by a vielle that plays both textless and texted passages

§ Alternatively, consider employing similar rather than contrasting instruments with voices; that is, all bowed or all plucked instruments

Source

Oxford, Bodleian Library, MS. Canonici misc. 213, no. 23.

Edition used

Dufay, Guillaume. *Cantiones*. Edited by Heinrich Besseler. Pt. 1 of *Opera Omnia*. Corpus Mensurabilis Musicae, vol. 1. Rome: American Institute of Musicology, 1964. 59 (no. 39).

Facsimile

Dufay, Guillaume. *Cantiones*. First facsimile following lxix.

Other transcription

Stainer, J. F. R., and Cecie Stainer, eds. *Dufay and His Contemporaries*. Early Bodleian Music, without series number. London: Novello, 1898. Reprint. Amsterdam: Frits Knuf, 1963. 105–107.

Recordings

The Art of Courtly Love. Early Music Consort of London. Seraphim SIC-6092, Seraphim S-6092, EMI SLS 863, or EMI HMV 86301.

Dufay: Complete Secular Music. Medieval Ensemble of London. L'Oiseau-Lyre Florilegium D237 D6.

Guillaume Dufay: Adieu m'amour. Studio der frühen Musik. EMI Reflexe 1C 063-30 124; also in a set, EMI Reflexe 1C 163-30119/24.

Music at the Court of Burgundy. Early Music Consort of London. EMI ASD 3643.

EXAMPLE III–18. Guillaume Dufay, *Ce moys de may*

Reprinted from Corpus Mensurabilis Musicae, volume 1, by permission of the publisher, American Institute of Musicology/Hänssler-Verlag, Neuhausen-Stuttgart.

161

Translation

> In this month of May, let us be joyous and gay,
> And remove melancholy from our hearts.
> Let us sing, dance, and make merry
> In order to defy the treacherous, jealous ones.
> More than ever, let everyone be eager
> To please his pretty mistress.
> In this month of May, let us be joyous and gay,
> And remove melancholy from our hearts.
> For this season urges every lover to do so;
> Therefore, let us not miss the chance.
> Dearest, Dufay begs you to
> And Perinet will say it even better.
> In this month of May, let us be joyous and gay,
> And remove melancholy from our hearts.
> Let us sing, dance, and make merry
> In order to defy the treacherous, jealous ones.

Translation by René Immelé.

19. Johannes Ockeghem, *Kyrie* from the *Missa Sine nomine* (Mass movement à 3)

Johannes Ockeghem (ca. 1410–1497), an eminent Franco-Flemish composer, served three French kings in various musical capacities. In addition he was for a time treasurer of the royal Abbey of St. Martin, Tours. Upon his death, he was honored by a number of musical and poetic laments. His relatively small output includes Masses, Mass fragments, motets, chansons, and the earliest-known polyphonic Requiem.

By Ockeghem's time the common polyphonic setting of the Mass included all five movements of the Ordinary. Several types of composition can be distinguished: the plainsong Mass, the *cantus firmus* Mass, the motto Mass, the parody Mass, and the freely invented Mass. They incorporate three to five parts.

The *Missa Sine nomine* is probably one of the composer's earlier works in this genre. The Mass appears to be freely composed, not based on chant or other borrowed material. All three parts function as equals and are governed by a style of nonimitative counterpoint, unified by a recurring motto.[106]

Our example is the Kyrie movement, typically the first section of the Ordinary to be set polyphonically. Its Greek text beseeches the Lord to grant mercy. The manuscript indicates the main divisions of the movement (Kyrie, Christe, Kyrie), within each of which the text must be sung thrice to conform to liturgical practice.

Performance of this work at the notated pitch level requires a small ensemble of soprano- and alto-range male voices: falsettists and countertenors, boy sopranos and altos, boy sopranos and countertenors, or combined boys' and adult voices on all parts. While *a cappella* singing is probably the ideal,[107] instruments could have doubled the voices on special occasions.[108]

The authors recommend the following for a modern performance of this piece:

§ A choir of male voices

§ Alternatively, as a practical solution, a choir of female voices

§ Consider transposition downward by perfect fourth in order to suit male choir of countertenors and tenors

§ Consider adjusting underlay of the two Kyrie sections to permit three complete statements of text

§ Consider adding a *musica ficta c'♯* to contratenor at each of the three principal cadences

§ Apply proportion Kyrie I ♩ = Christe ○ = Kyrie II ○

Source

Verona, Biblioteca Capitolare, Cod. DCCLIX, ff. 2v–3r.

Edition used

Ockeghem, Johannes. *Collected Works.* Edited by Dragan Plamenac. American Musicological Society Studies and Documents, no. 3, vol. 1. 2nd ed. New York: Galaxy Music Corp. for the American Musicological Society, 1959. 15–16.

Facsimile

Ockeghem, Johannes. *Collected Works*, vol. 1: pl. 2.

EXAMPLE III–19.   Johannes Ockeghem, *Kyrie* from the *Missa Sine nomine*

Reprinted, with changes in clefs and note values, from Johannes Ockeghem, *Collected Works*, edited by Dragan Plamenac, American Musicological Society Studies and Documents, no. 3, vol. 1, 2nd ed. (New York: Galaxy Music Corp. for the American Musicological Society, 1959), 15–16, by permission of the American Musicological Society.

Translation

       Lord, have mercy upon us.
       Christ, have mercy upon us.
       Lord, have mercy upon us.

20. Loyset Compère, *Ung franc archier* (Chanson à 4)

Loyset Compère (ca. 1445–1518) was a significant French composer of chansons and motets. Before entering the service of Charles VIII in Paris, he worked briefly in Milan. His compositions include chansons, motets, and a few Masses.

Compère's chansons were composed in three or four parts. The usual number of parts in the Franco-Flemish chanson is four, although three-part works continued to appear early in this period, and five-part composition became common near the end. Many three-part works retain the functional characteristics of Burgundian chansons, whereas others reflect the emerging imitative technique. Within the four- and five-part settings, parts are functionally equal, and their contrapuntal relationship ranges from melodic independence to pervading imitation or homophony. Parts are separated in range, with resulting infrequency of voice-crossing.

The Franco-Flemish repertory exhibits inconsistency in texting practices, ranging from untexted sources to those with texts in all parts. Recent research suggests that the variety of texting practices parallels a variety of performance practices relating to time and place. According to one study, the earlier French sources of three-part Franco-Flemish chansons show only the highest voice texted, suggesting a performance practice involving one singer either with instruments or with wordless vocalise. The later French sources, generally texted in all three parts, imply vocal performance. The later Italian sources of three- and four-part chansons, many of which are untexted, seem to reflect a purely instrumental performance practice.[109] Yet chansons bearing texts were also apparently known and performed in late fifteenth-century Italy.[110]

A structural interpretation for the treatment of untexted lines suggests that three-part pieces in conservative style be performed in a manner described for the Burgundian chanson (see the discussion preceding Example III–18). In the later four- and five-part repertory, structural interpretation assumes that a part should be sung if completely texted in the original source, and otherwise played on an instrument. Works with functional equality and melodic independence of parts seem to suggest unlike, blending instruments. Compositions based on imitative and homophonic techniques might imply like instruments. However, if the part-writing exhibits polarity (e.g., superius-and-altus versus tenor-and-bassus; or tenor versus superius-and-altus-and-bassus), the choice of instruments could reflect this dichotomy.

Ung franc archier and several other chansons by Compère are included in *Harmonice musices Odhecaton A*, the first collection of part-songs printed from movable type, issued in 1501 by Petrucci, in Venice. The *Odhecaton* provides text incipits for each part, whereas the edition that follows places the text of the popular song *Ung franc archier* beneath its borrowed melody.[111]

The structure of this work incorporates imitative writing in all parts. *Cantus* and *altus* exhibit strict canon at the interval of a fifth, with entrances occurring at varying intervals of time. Tenor and bassus share motives of the canon with the upper parts, intermingled with independent melodic material.

The authors recommend the following for a modern performance of this piece:

§ An instrumental performance using pairs of like instruments to emphasize the polarity between canonic and free parts; for instance, soprano and alto crumhorns for the *cantus* and *altus*, and tenor and bass viols for the *tenor* and *bassus*. (An instrumental solution assumes an Italian performance practice contemporary with the source.)

Source

Petrucci, Ottaviano. *Harmonice musices Odhecaton A.* Venice: 1503 or 1504 (RISM 1503² or 1504²). Ff. 24v–25r.

Edition used

Hewitt, Helen, ed. *Harmonice musices Odhecaton A.* Cambridge, MA: Medieval Academy of America, 1942. Reprint. New York: Da Capo, 1978. 279–280 (no. 28).

Facsimile

Petrucci, Ottaviano. *Harmonice musices Odhecaton A* (Venice, 1504). Monuments of Music and Music Literature in Facsimile, 1st ser., vol. 10. New York: Broude Bros., 1973. Ff. 24v–25r.

Other transcription

Compère, Loyset. [*Motet-Chansons, Chansons, Frottole, Opera Dubia*]. Edited by Ludwig Finscher. Pt. 5 of *Opera Omnia*. Corpus Mensurabilis Musicae, vol. 15. N.p.: American Institute of Musicology, 1972. 57.

EXAMPLE III–20. Loyset Compère, *Ung franc archier*

[1]The text derives from a collection of songs published by Severin Cornet (1581) where the music is not that of the Odh.

Copied, by permission, from *Harmonice Musices Odhecaton*, ed. Helen Hewitt, literary texts ed. Isabel Pope (Cambridge, MA: Medieval Academy of America, 1942), pp. 279–280.

Translation

A noble archer goes to war.
He made his testament as a Christian should.
He entrusted his wife to the care of the curate.
To the priest he left the key of his house.
Viragon, vignette sur vignon.

Le franc archer une arquebuse avoit,
Laqelle estoit de sablon blanc chargée,
Et si avoit un foureau sans espée,
Encore plus les mules, aux talons:
Viragon, vignette sur vignon.

The noble archer had an archebus
Which was loaded with white sand.
He had also a sheath without a sword
And was, moreover, ravenously hungry.
Viragon, vignette sur vignon.

Le franc archer à son hoste disoit:
Sangoy! morgoy! Je renigoy! je te tue!
Tout beau, monsieur, nos oies sont en mue,
Et l'appaisa d'une soupe a l'ognon:
Viragon, vignette sur vignon.

The noble archer said to his host:
"Bleed, die! I renounce you! I kill you!"
"Patience, Sir, we are cooping our geese!"
And he calmed him down with an onion soup.
Viragon, vignette sur vignon.

Translation by René Immelé.

21. Bartolomeo Tromboncino, *Ben ch'amor me facci*, arranged by Franciscus Bossinensis (Frottola for voice and lute, with a ricercare for lute by Bossinensis)

Bartolomeo Tromboncino (ca. 1470–ca. 1535) composed a great number of frottole and a relatively small number of other works, including motets and laude. Among his patrons were Isabella d'Este and Francesco Gonzaga, Lucrezia Borgia and Alfonso d'Este, and perhaps Lorenzo de' Medici.

Franciscus Bossinensis (fl. 1510) is known only for two publications, which contain his arrangements of four-part frottole written by other composers. Each publication concludes with a group of ricercare in lute tablature.

The majority of works in the frottola idiom (Petrucci published 11 books of frottole) display treble-dominated, somewhat homophonic texture. Their texts are often satirical or amorous, the present example being about the torments of love. Despite the apparent simplicity of these works, they were considered sophisticated court music.

The following edition of *Ben ch'amor me facci* is an arrangement by Bossinensis of an earlier version of the work published by Petrucci in *Frottole, libro primo* (Venice, 1504). This arrangement casts the original four-part work in a three-part setting for voice and lute that omits the altus part. Bossinensis designated several ricercari as suitable preludes (or possibly postludes)[112] for the piece, from which one has been selected by the authors. Bossinensis's arrangement requires a six-course lute in normal A tuning.

It appears that the composers of frottole in Petrucci's prints intended the music to be performed by one singer accompanied by instruments.[113] The most likely choices for accompaniment would have been a plucked chordal instrument or a group of like instruments; for example, viols. Other possible performance solutions are one singer accompanied by mixed instruments, an all-vocal ensemble, or an instrumental realization (solo or ensemble).[114] Ornamentation is apparently appropriate for the performance of the melody line.[115] The form of the poem, a *barzelletta*, requires repetitions of the first phrase of music.

The authors recommend the following for a modern performance of this piece:

§ The ricercare as a prelude

§ A soprano voice

§ A six-course lute

§ Set remainder of poem, following as nearly as possible underlay provided[116]

Source

Bossinensis, Franciscus. *Tenori e contrabassi intabulati col sopran in canto figurato per cantar e sonar col lauto. Libro primo.* Venice: Petrucci, 1509 (RISM 1509³). Ff. 36v–37r (frottola), f. 51r (ricercare).

Edition used

The authors' transcriptions.

Facsimiles

Bossinensis, Franciscus. *Tenori e contrabassi.* Geneva: Minkoff Reprint, 1977. Ff. 36v–37r, 51r.

Noske, Frits, ed. *The Solo Song outside German Speaking Countries.* Anthology of Music, vol. 16. Cologne: Arno Volk Verlag, 1958. 11 (frottola only).

Other transcriptions

Disertori, Benvenuto, ed. *Le Frottole per canto e liuto intabulate da Franciscus Bossinensis.* Istituzioni e Monumenti dell'Arte Musicale Italiana, new ser., vol. 3. Milan: Ricordi, 1964. 398–399 (no. 51, frottola), 438 (no. 7, ricercare).

Noske, Frits, ed. *The Solo Song.* 17 (no. 1), frottola only, with partial text.

EXAMPLE III–21a.   Franciscus Bossinensis, *Ricercare*

EXAMPLE III–21b. Bartolomeo Tromboncino, *Ben ch'amor me facci*, arranged by Franciscus Bossinensis

Translation

Although love has wronged me
I do not yet want to leave this venture
For to serve with inflamed desire
I am prepared in life and death.
Although love has wronged me
I do not yet want to leave this venture.

Se ben hor me contra el cielo
Et offeso damor sia
Cangiar voglio prima el pelo
Che mia ferma fantasia
Et se pato oltraggio a torto
Non pero lascio l'impresa (measures 1–7, 3 times)
Che servir con voglia accesa
Me dispongo vivo e morto (measures 8–13)

Even if Heaven is against me now
And is offended by love
I would first change myself
Than my steadfast fantasy.
And if I wrongfully suffer outrage
Still I do not want to leave this venture
For to serve with inflamed desire
I am prepared in life and death.

Ben ch'amor me sia crudele
Spero uscir pero daffanno
Per che spesso un hom fidele
Con sua fe vince ogni inganno
E pero non mi sconforto
A seguir mia dolce impresa
Che servir con voglia accesa
Me dispongo vivo e morto

Though love be cruel to me
Yet I hope to escape suffering
For a faithful man often
Conquers deceit with his faith.
And still I am not discouraged
From following my sweet venture
For to serve with inflamed desire
I am prepared in life and death.

Ben ch'in foco el cor se stempre
Con mortal cieco tormento
Io staro constante sempre
Come fa loro alargento
E se pena amando porto
Non pero lascio l'impresa
Che servir con voglia accesa
Me dispongo vivo e morto

Although the heart melts in fire
In blind mortal torment
I shall remain always constant
As gold does to silver.
And if I bear the pain in loving
Still I do not want to leave this venture
For to serve with inflamed desire
I am prepared in life and death.

Poi chio son intrato in campo
Io non vo morir fugendo
Che le biasmo poi far scampo
Si che saldo star intendo

Since I have taken the field
I don't want to die fleeing
For its is blameworthy to attempt escape
And I intend to remain steadfast.

Pur amando io me conforto
A seguir questa mia impresa
Che servir con voglia accesa
Restero vivo e non morto
Ben [. . .]
(measures 14–24)

Still, loving comforts me
In following this venture of mine
For in serving with inflamed desire
I shall remain alive and not dead.
Although [love has wronged me
I do not yet want to leave this venture.]

Translation by Margaret Israel, in collaboration with Lucy Cross and Paul Olson.

22. Eustachio Romano, *Cantus cum Tenore* (Instrumental duo)

Eustachio Romano (fl. 1500–1525) was an Italian composer of duos and frottole. Almost nothing is known about his life, and his compositional output is minimal. Nevertheless, he is credited with being the first known composer of instrumental duets. His *Musica duorum* is the earliest publication of instrumental ensemble music.[117]

Numerous instrumental duos appeared in print during the course of the sixteenth century. They exhibit the new, imitative style of the Franco-Flemish school. These pieces are relatively short, cast in a through-composed, sectional form. Their rhythm shifts between duple and triple groupings. Some duos call for instruments of like range; others have contrasting ranges. Like bicinia, these pieces might have been used for teaching.[118]

The authors recommend the following for a modern performance of this piece.

§ Two like instruments of alto and tenor ranges; for example, viols, or recorders at four-foot pitch.

Source

Romano, Eustachio. *Musica di Eustachio Romano. Liber primus.* Rome: G. G. Pasoti, 1521 (RISM E889). Ff. 25v–26r.

Edition used

Romano, Eustachio. *Musica Duorum.* Edited by Hans T. David, Howard Mayer Brown, and Edward E. Lowinsky. Monuments of Renaissance Music, vol. 6. Chicago: University of Chicago Press, 1975. 94 (no. 24).

Facsimile

Romano, Eustachio. *Musica Duorum.* Edited by Hans T. David et al. 53.

EXAMPLE III–22. Eustachio Romano, *Cantus cum Tenore*

Reprinted from Eustachio Romano, *Musica Duorum*, edited by Hans T. David, Howard Mayer Brown, and Edward E. Lowinsky, Monuments of Renaissance Music, vol. 6 (Chicago: University of Chicago Press, 1975), 53, by permission of the publisher.

23. Robert Cooper, *I have been a foster* (Part-song à 3)

Robert Cooper (Cowper) (b. ca. 1474, d. 1535–1540) was an English composer and priest. A few sacred and secular works by him have survived in manuscript. The following example occurs in a source that contains music principally by Henry VIII (see the commentary for Example III–24).

Part-songs in Cooper's time were compositions in three or four parts with homophonic texture. The melody lies in the highest part. These songs were likely performed at court for the entertainment of royalty.[119]

I have been a foster is a three-part work texted in all parts. Its humorous text decries age taking its toll on lovers. The poetry consists of a refrain and six verses, each of which has a different scansion.

The authors recommend the following for a modern performance of this piece:

§ A tenor voice for the highest part
§ A baritone voice for the middle part
§ A bass voice for the lowest part
§ Set remaining stanzas, following as nearly as possible underlay of first stanza. In opening passage, adopt uniform text underlay within each stanza. (The somewhat more contrapuntal sections of the piece permit performers more flexibility in underlaying the subsequent stanzas.)

Source
London, British Library, Additional MS. 31922, ff. 65v–66r.

Edition used
Stevens, John, ed. *Music at the Court of Henry VIII.* Musica Britannica, vol. 18. 2nd ed. London: Stainer & Bell Ltd., 1969. 48 (no. 62).

Facsimile
Stevens, John, ed. *Music at the Court of Henry VIII,* xxvii.

Other transcription
Davison, Archibald T., and Willi Apel, eds. *Historical Anthology of Music.* Vol. 1, *Oriental, Medieval, and Renaissance Music.* Rev. ed. Cambridge, MA: Harvard University Press, 1949. 90 (no. 86b), with partial text.

Recordings
Courtly Pastimes of Sixteenth Century England. St. Georges Canzona. L'Oiseau-Lyre SOL 329.

The King's Musick. Ricercare Ensemble für alte Musik, Zurich. EMI Reflexe 1C 063-30 119; also in a set, EMI Reflexe 1C 163-30119/24.

EXAMPLE III–23.   Robert Cooper, *I have been a foster*

Reprinted from *Music at the Court of Henry VIII*, edited by John Stevens, Musica Britannica, vol. 18, 2nd ed. (London: Stainer & Bell Ltd., 1969), 48, by permission of the publisher.

Hang I will my noble bow
Upon the greenwood bough,
For I cannot shoot in plain
Nor yet in rough;
Yet have I been a foster.

Every bow for me is too big;
Mine arrow nigh worn is;
The glue is slipp'd from the nick;
When I should shoot I miss;
Yet have I been a foster.

Lady Venus hath commanded me
Out of her court to go;
Right plainly she sheweth me
That beauty is my foe;
Yet have I been a foster.

My beard is so hard, God wot,
When I should maidens kiss,
They stand aback and make it strange;
Lo, age is cause of this;
Yet have I been a foster.

Now will I take to me my beads
For and my psalter-book,
And pray I will for them that may,
For I may nought but look;
Yet have I been a foster.

24. Henry VIII, [*Consort IV*] (Instrumental trio)

Henry VIII (1491–1547) needs no introduction. In addition to his royal duties, he played the lute and composed a number of songs and instrumental works.

The size and diversity of his royal instrument collection testifies to the keen interest in instrumental music displayed by the English court in Henry's time. That collection included examples of the principal string, wind, brass, keyboard, and percussion instruments of the period.[120]

The source of Henry's consort music is the earliest sizable collection of English music for instrumental ensembles.[121] The king is represented by a dozen or more pieces in this genre. Compared to the vocal music found in this manuscript, the "consorts" appear more polyphonic and more florid.[122] The following example exhibits a dance-like quality, a somewhat florid treble part, and a brevity common in the repertory. This piece, like many other three- and four-part English works of the period, seems suited to like instruments. The ranges in this repertory are frequently narrow enough to accommodate winds.

The authors recommend the following for a modern performance of this piece:

§ For an ensemble of like instruments, one tenor viol and two bass viols

§ For a mixed ensemble, an alto recorder for the highest part, a lute for the middle part, and a bass viol for the lowest part. (Stylistic characteristics of Tudor consorts seem to suggest sustaining instruments, but the overall simplicity of the repertory affords many possible solutions. This particular example could accommodate instruments of one or more families.)

Source

London, British Library, Additional MS. 31922, ff. 59v–60r.

Edition used

Stevens, John, ed. *Music at the Court of Henry VIII.* Musica Britannica, vol. 18. 2nd ed. London: Stainer & Bell Ltd., 1969. 44 (no. 55).

Facsimile

Not available in print.

EXAMPLE III–24.   Henry VIII [*Consort IV*]

Reprinted from *Music at the Court of Henry VIII*, edited by John Stevens, Musica Britannica, vol. 18, 2nd ed.
(London: Stainer & Bell Ltd., 1969), 44, by permission of the publisher.

25. Claude Gervaise (?), *Branle [simple]* (Dance à 4)

Claude Gervaise (fl. 1540–1560) was a French composer and arranger who also worked as an editor for the publishing firm of Pierre Attaingnant in Paris. Evidence for assigning the source of this example (book two) to Gervaise is based on information that he edited books three through five of the series and composed the music in book six.[123] Attaingnant (ca. 1494–late 1551 or 1552) published vast quantities of secular and sacred vocal music as well as solo and ensemble instrumental music.

The dances that appear in Attaingnant's second book include *branles*, *pavanes*, *gaillardes*, *basses dances*, and *tourdions*. These four- and five-part dances are strongly homophonic. Their step patterns are reasonably well documented. Most dances comprise several repeated strains. Similar dances appear in many other sixteenth-century collections, some of the dances occurring in pairs and other sets.

This branle appears to be a piece intended for actual dancing, owing to its straightforward harmonic and rhythmic construction. Branles were danced by couples in a circle or a line.[124] Arbeau's description of the *branle simple* fits this piece perfectly. The step patterns operate in six-measure phrases:

m. 1—left foot steps to left
   2—right foot closes
   3—left foot steps to left again
   4—right foot closes
   5—right foot steps to right
   6—left foot closes
or 5—left foot kicks, right foot kicks
   6—left foot kicks, rest[125]

Clearly, execution of these patterns requires a lively tempo (pulse by the measure in the example that follows). Homophonic music of this type suggests the use of like instruments.

In the authors' opinion, the ensemble chosen for a single dance should be maintained within the piece and may be continued throughout a set having close musical relationships. The existence in the sixteenth century of sets of homogeneous instruments suggests that the basic ensemble was one of these sets. However, the makeup of an ensemble might have varied according to such factors as the available forces and the importance of an occasion. Thus the most festive occasion perhaps called for a great number of instruments, including percussion and perhaps involving reinforcement by chordal instruments and doubling.

The authors recommend the following for a modern performance of this piece:

§ A quartet of crumhorns (soprano, two altos, and bass)

§ Alternatively, a quartet of recorders (soprano, alto, alto/tenor, and bass) accompanied by a small drum

§ The possibility of a mixed ensemble of soft winds and strings, perhaps reinforced by a chordal instrument

§ If a one-on-a-part solution is chosen, consider ornamenting the melody, particularly in repetitions, according to sixteenth-century diminution practices (see Chapter 8)

Source

Gervaise, Claude (?). *Second livre contenant trois Gaillardes. . . .* Paris: Attaingnant, 1547 (RISM G1673). Ff. 9v–10r.

Edition used

Attaingnant, Pierre. *Second Livre de Danceries, 1547, for Four Instruments.* Edited by Bernard Thomas. The Attaingnant Dance Prints, vol. 2. London: London Pro Musica Edition, 1976. 14 (no. 14).

Facsimile

Gervaise, Claude. *Six livres de danseries.* Introduction by François Lesure. Geneva: Minkoff Reprint, 1977. Bk. 2: ff. 9v–10r.

Other transcription

Attaingnant, Pierre. *Danseries à 4 parties.* Edited by Raymond Meylan. Le Pupitre, vol. 9. Paris: Heugel, 1969. 16 (no. 14).

Dance step-patterns

Arbeau, Thoinot [Jehan Tabourot]. *Orchesographie, et traicte en forme de dialogue.* Lengres: Iehan des Preyz, 1589(?). Ff. 71r–71v.

Ibid. Facsimile edited by Laure Fonta. Geneva: Slatkine Reprints, 1970. Ff. 71r–71v.

Arbeau. *Orchesography.* Translated by Mary Stewart Evans and revised by Julia Sutton. 2nd ed. New York: Dover, 1967. 132–133.

EXAMPLE III–25.   Claude Gervaise (?), *Branle [simple]*

Reprinted from Pierre Attaingnant, *Second Livre de Danceries, 1547, for Four Instruments*, edited by Bernard Thomas, The Attaingnant Dance Prints, vol. 2 (AD2) (London: London Pro Musica Edition, 1976), 14, by permission of the publisher.

26. Ludwig Senfl, *Ewiger Gott* (Tenorlied à 4)

Ludwig Senfl (ca. 1486–1542 or 1543), who probably studied under Heinrich Isaac, was an important Swiss composer. He was associated with the chapel of Emperor Maximilian I (see frontispiece), and later with the Bavarian court in Munich. In addition to a large number of polyphonic lieder, his music consists mainly of sacred works for the Roman Catholic Church.

Ewiger Gott was published in Hans Ott's *Liederbuch* of 1534, which was printed by Hieronymus Formschneider in Nuremberg.[126] Senfl is one of only three known composers whose works appear in this volume.

The tenorlied was an important form of German polyphonic lied from the mid-fifteenth to the mid-sixteenth century. Its texture consists of a *cantus firmus* and two or three independent parts. Whereas in the earliest examples of this genre the *cantus firmus* often appears in the highest part, four-part works from the sixteenth century generally place the borrowed melody in the tenor part. In texted sources before 1536, complete text appears only in the tenor. Works in this genre have texts in German, whether secular or related to sacred (Protestant) subjects.

Ewiger Gott is an example of the latter type. Senfl, like several other composers known or presumed to be Catholic, contributed works to Lutheran collections.[127] (Ten years after its initial publication, *Ewiger Gott* was reprinted in a Lutheran songbook, with text under each part.) In Ott's original partbooks, the text of this piece appears only with the tenor. Some scholars interpret the more animated, textless parts of tenorlieder as being instrumental,[128] but because later sources are texted throughout, an all-vocal performance is also a possibility. One scholar states that this repertory was meant for trained singers,[129] while another points out that German schoolboys used the anthology in which *Ewiger Gott* was reprinted fully texted.[130] The style of this piece is basically imitative, and the rhythm of the added parts is only slightly more active than that of the tenor.

A structural approach to the selection of instruments for tenorlieder suggests that—

§ a highly imitative piece points to instruments of one family;

§ a piece constructed with nonimitative but functionally equal parts favors an accompanying ensemble of mixed, blending instruments;

§ a piece with functionally dissimilar parts is more appropriately treated like a fifteenth-century secular piece.

The authors recommend the following for a modern performance of this piece:

§ A tenor voice for the tenor part

§ Three like instruments; for instance, treble, tenor, and bass viols

§ Alternatively, tenor voice and three mixed, blending instruments; for example, alto flute (transposing an octave higher), tenor viol, and bass curtal

§ For an all-vocal performance, an ensemble of soprano, two tenors, and bass, with or without instruments

Source

Ott, Hans. *Der erst Teil. Hundert und ainundzweinzig newe Lieder.* Nuremberg: Formschneider, 1534 (RISM 1534[17]). No. 21.

Edition used

Senfl, Ludwig. *Deutsche Lieder*, pt. 2. Edited by Arnold Geering and Wilhelm Altwegg. Vol. 4 of *Sämtliche Werke.* Wolfenbüttel: Möseler, 1962. 3–4 (no. 1).

Facsimile

Senfl, Ludwig. *Deutsche Lieder*, pt. 2. xii.

Other transcriptions

Schering, Arnold. *Geschichte der Musik in Beispielen.* Leipzig: Breitkopf und Härtel, 1931. Reprint. New York: Broude Bros., 1950. 79–80 (no. 84).

Wolf, Johannes, ed. *Newe deudsche geistliche Gesenge für die gemeinen Schulen* (Wittemberg: Georg Rhau, 1544). Denkmäler der deutscher Tonkunst, vol. 34. Wiesbaden: Breitkopf und Härtel, 1958. 178–180 (no. 67).

EXAMPLE III–26.   Ludwig Senfl, *Ewiger Gott*

1) = Sohn

Reprinted from Ludwig Senfl, *Sämtliche Werke*, vol. 4, edited by Arnold Geering and Wilhelm Altwegg (Wolfenbüttel: Möseler, 1962), 3–4, by permission of the publisher.

1) = Prahlen, Grosstun 2) = Sohnes 3) 𝅝 = 𝅗𝅥𝅗𝅥

1) = am Leben erhalten, bewahren

Translation

> *Eternal God, at whose command the Son came here on earth to obey the counsel of the Trinity by becoming man, through thy goodness, I beseech Thee, keep pure from sin Thy Christian congregation; may Thy grace be imparted, so that they will not be deceitfully overtaken by the power of the Devil's boasting. Impart, O Lord, Thy Son's intercession, so that they may each day take sustenance in true belief without sinful lamentation, and keep their souls from torment.*

Translation by Douglas Hilt.

27. Nicolas Gombert. *Et exultavit* from *Magnificat septimi toni* (Magnificat verse à 4)

Nicolas Gombert (ca. 1495–ca. 1560) was one of the greatest Flemish composers of the generation after Josquin, who was apparently Gombert's teacher.[131] The German theorist Hermann Finck (1556) refers to Gombert as showing others the way to create a new, seamless style filled with harmony and imitation.[132] A member of the chapel of Emperor Charles V, Gombert traveled to Spain, Italy, Austria, and Germany. His compositions include Masses, motets, chansons, and other secular genres.

The source of this Magnificat is a manuscript in Madrid that is dated 1552. The copyist was Robertus Quercentius, working in Liège. This manuscript contains Gombert's eight Magnificat.[133]

The Magnificat, which occurs near the close of the Office of Vespers, is a canticle of the Virgin consisting of twelve verses.[134] Vespers is the only Office to allow music other than plainsong.[135] The principle of antiphonal choral performance of plainsong Magnificat is retained in polyphonic compositions by alternating verses of chant with polyphonic verses.[136]

Gombert followed common practice in his Magnificat by setting the even-numbered verses polyphonically. The odd-numbered verses were intended for plainsong performance. The composer based his setting of each Magnificat on the plainsong melody of the corresponding mode, sometimes placing the *cantus firmus* in long notes, sometimes weaving it into the polyphonic fabric.[137]

Et exultavit is the second verse of the Magnificat, thus the first to be set polyphonically. Like Gombert's motets, it is imitative in style.

An *a cappella* performance of this work is clearly a historical option, one perhaps most appropriate to Gombert's homeland. However, the presence of this work in a Spanish source together with Gombert's presence in Spain could point to the more elaborate style of performance practiced in Spanish musical centers at that time. In the major cathedrals, a large number of instruments were regularly employed; organs, shawms, sackbuts, cornetti, recorders, bassoons, *rabels*, *cascabeles*, portative organ, and cymbals have been documented at Seville.[138] Choral forces included *moços de coro* (boys who sang only plainchant and *seises*), *cantorçicos* (boys who sang polyphony), adult male sopranos, altos, tenors, and basses.[139] Choirs ranged in size from sixteen to twenty adults and from twelve to sixteen boys.[140] One scholar has suggested that instrumental usage in Spanish churches may have occurred in *alternatim* fashion,[141] although doubling of voices is also a possibility.

The authors recommend the following for a modern performance of this piece:

§ In keeping with a Spanish performance practice, a male choir of about two dozen voices (boys and men), supplemented by organ and mixed instruments

§ Alternatively, an *a cappella* performance by the same type of choir

§ For a practical solution or study purposes, a mixed choir, with or without instruments

§ A public performance should present all 12 verses, alternating plainsong and polyphony.

Source

Madrid, Biblioteca Nacional, MS. M 2433, f. 40r, f.

Edition used

Gombert, Nicolai. *Magnificat*. Edited by Joseph Schmidt-Görg. Pt. 4 of *Opera Omnia*. Corpus Mensurabilis Musicae, vol. 6. N.p.: American Institute of Musicology, 1957. 70–72.

Facsimile

Die Musik in Geschichte und Gegenwart. 5: pl. 22.

EXAMPLE III–27.   Nicolas Gombert, *Et exultavit* from *Magnificat septimi toni*

Reprinted from Corpus Mensurabilis Musicae, volume 6, by permission of the publisher, American Institute of Musicology/Hänssler-Verlag, Neuhausen-Stuttgart.

Translation

    And my spirit rejoices in God, my Savior.

28. Pierre Certon, *Ce n'est a vous* (Chanson à 4)

Pierre Certon (d. 1572) was one of the principal composers of Parisian chansons in the second quarter of the sixteenth century. His known works belong to sacred and secular genres and include nearly 200 chansons. The reader will note that Attaingnant published the source of this piece a few years before the publication of his second book of dances (see Example III–25).

Chansons of this period were nurtured in courtly circles and subsequently were disseminated widely via numerous printed editions. Small partbooks were issued for the convenience of one or two singers; for instance, soprano with tenor (see Figure 4–4 a, b). *Ce n'est a vous* represents this category well, with its four-part setting, its textual and musical brevity, its characteristic opening rhythmic motive (♩ ♪ ♪), its extremely diatonic harmony, and its alternation of homophonic and succinct imitative passages. While this piece is not composed in a fixed form, the element of refrain is suggested by the use of identical music in the opening and closing sections of the piece (*a b a' a'*). The text of this work concerns a lover's pledge to be his beloved's servant forever.

There is general agreement today that Parisian chansons of this type were intended to be sung by one voice per part. It seems plausible to the authors that men and women sometimes sang together in the performance of these chansons, although an all-male ensemble might have been the preferred group.

The authors recommend the following for a modern performance of this piece:

§ A quartet of male voices (countertenor, two tenors, and baritone)
§ Alternatively, a mixed quartet (mezzo-soprano, two tenors, and baritone)

Source

Attaingnant, Pierre, and Hubert Jullet. *Tiers livre contenant xxviii chansons.* Paris, 1538 (RISM 1538[12]). Two partbooks: superius/tenor; contratenor/bassus, f. 16v.

Edition used

Certon, Pierre. *Chansons polyphoniques publiées par Pierre Attaingnant.* Edited by Henry Expert and Aimé Agnel. Maîtres Anciens de la Musique Française, vols. 2–4. Paris: Heugel, 1967–1968. 2: 64–65 (no. 30).

Facsimile

Certon, Pierre. *Chansons polyphoniques.* 2: iv.
Figure 4–4 a, b.

EXAMPLE III–28.   Pierre Certon, *Ce n'est a vous*

Reprinted from Pierre Certon, *Chansons polyphoniques publiées par Pierre Attaingnant*, edited by Henry Expert and Aimé Agnel, Maîtres Anciens de la Musique Française, vols. 2–4 (Paris: Heugel, 1967–1968), 2: 64–65. Avec l'autorisation de Heugel et Cie Editeurs-Propriétaires pour tous pays.

Translation

    It is not you I shall choose
    If you and I, if you and I
    Do not live together.
    I do not mind, I do not mind;
    And you are willing too, I presume,
    And you are willing too, I presume.
    Therefore, I shall be your servant forever.

Translation by René Immelé.

29. Jacobus Arcadelt, *O felic' occhi miei* (Madrigal à 4)

Jacobus Arcadelt (?1505–1568), although born a Northerner, became a leading representative of the early Italian madrigalists and was admired in Italy for works such as this example. Active in both Italy and France, he also wrote chansons, motets, and Masses. Most of his madrigals were composed in four parts.

The sixteenth-century madrigal as a musical form is quite different from the fourteenth-century genre (see Example III–13), although their poetry is related. Arcadelt's examples belong to the early period in the development of the sixteenth-century madrigal (before ca. 1550). During this period the genre exhibited a predominantly homophonic texture of three or four parts. Diatonic harmony prevails.

O felic' occhi miei employs a text that expresses the torments of love. The *Recercada primera* by Ortiz (Example III–30) draws upon this madrigal to illustrate improvisatory techniques. Arcadelt's piece, a through-composed work, exhibits shifting textures of imitation and homophony in two, three, or four parts. Its stylistic features (harmony, melody, rhythm) owe much to the simplicity and directness of the Italian frottola and the Parisian chanson.

Madrigals were cultivated by and performed within aristocratic circles. Their normal mode of performance probably involved one singer per part, unaccompanied, but evidence shows that instruments sometimes participated, either doubling voices or substituting for them.[142] Although modern performances often feature small choirs, the authors feel that the intimacy of the madrigal style dictates the use of solo singers, with or without instruments. Unlike sacred polyphony of the period, which employed male voices exclusively, secular works such as the present example are likely to have involved mixed ensembles of men and women.

Vocal ornamentation in the style described in the writings of dalla Casa, Bovicelli, Bassano, and Conforto would be appropriate in this repertory. Ornamentation could be confined to a single part or applied to more than one part (but not simultaneously). Likewise, when an instrument doubles a voice, only one of them may ornament at any given moment.[143]

The authors recommend the following for a modern performance of this piece:

§ A mixed quartet of voices (mezzo-soprano, alto, tenor, and baritone)

§ Alternatively, an ensemble suited to a lavish occasion: the preceding vocal quartet, doubled by a treble viol for the superius, a tenor viol and an alto flute in *g* (at four-foot pitch) for the altus, a bass viol and a tenor recorder (at four-foot pitch) for the tenor, and a tenor sackbut for the bassus, all reinforced by a lute and a harpsichord. (This ensemble is patterned after one that performed for a Medici wedding in 1565.)[144]

§ For either of foregoing recommendations, consider adding ornamentation (see Chapter 8)

Source

Arcadelt, Jacobus. *Il primo libro di madrigali.* Venice: Gardane, 1539 (RISM 1539[22]; RISM A1314). No. 52.

Edition used

Arcadelt, Jacobus. *Madrigali, libro primo.* Edited by Albert Seay. Pt. 2 of *Opera Omnia.* Corpus Mensurabilis Musicae, vol. 31. N.p.: American Institute of Musicology and American Musicological Society, 1970. 82–83 (no. 37).

Facsimile

Ortiz, Diego. *Tratado de glosas.* Edited by Max Schneider. Kassel: Bärenreiter, 1967. xxii–xxiii, partial facsimile.

Other transcription

Ortiz, Diego. *Tratado de glosas.* 69–72.

EXAMPLE III–29   Jacobus Arcadelt, *O felic' occhi miei*

Reprinted from Corpus Mensurabilis Musicae, volume 31, by permission of the publisher, American Institute of Musicology/Hänssler-Verlag, Neuhausen-Stuttgart.

Translation

> Oh, my happy eyes, how fortunate you are,
> For you are dear to my beloved
> Because you resemble
> The eyes which to her were both dear and cruel.
> You, yes, you—you, you are happy; you are, and I,
> I am not, for to calm your desire,
> I run to gaze, there where I am in torment.

Translation by Margaret Israel, in collaboration with Lucy Cross and Paul Olson.

30. Diego Ortiz, *Recercada primera sobre O felici occhi miei* (Ricercare for viola da gamba and harpsichord)

Diego Ortiz (ca. 1510–ca. 1570) was a Spanish composer and theorist who served in the chapel of Spanish viceroys in Naples. His fame rests almost entirely on his *Trattado de glosas* (1553), which was published simultaneously in Spanish and Italian.[145]

Trattado de glosas serves the purpose of instructing viol players in the art of improvised embellishment. Ortiz's manual systematizes basic ornamental procedures and incorporates these patterns into solo compositions of several types: unaccompanied ricercari; variations on ground basses; and divisions on polyphonic vocal works, both French and Italian. This tutor, one of the first of its kind, presents an approach to instrumental performance that continues in ornamentation treatises and compositional practices of later generations.

The *Recercada primera* is one of four that Ortiz composed on Arcadelt's madrigal (Example III–29). In this setting, the solo viol ornaments the bassus voice part, while the *cimbalo* (harpsichord, virginal) plays all four parts of the madrigal without embellishment. Ortiz suggests that the viol player perform two or three such *differentias*, or more. While this example is a composed piece, it is intended to serve as a model for similar improvisations on *O felici occhi* and other madrigals. The performer who studies this ricercare will discover that its ornamental formulae are applied in an idiomatic manner,

creating a florid line that remains true to the musical structure of the original work.

The authors recommend the following for a modern performance of this piece:

§ A bass viola da gamba and an Italian-style harpsichord (1 × 8′, 1 × 4′; or 2 × 8′)

Source

Ortiz, Diego. *Trattado de glosas* (RISM O136). Rome: Valerio and Luis Dorico, 1553. Ff. 37v–38r.

Edition used

Ortiz, Diego. *Tratado de glosas*. Edited by Max Schneider. Kassel: Bärenreiter, 1967. 73–75.

Facsimiles

Besseler, Heinrich, and Peter Gülke. *Schriftbild der mehrstimmigen Musik*. Musikgeschichte in Bildern, vol. 3, pt. 5. Leipzig: Deutscher Verlag für Musik, 1973. 131 (no. 69a), partial facsimile.

Ortiz, Diego. *Tratado de glosas*. Edited by Max Schneider. xxiv, partial facsimile.

Other transcriptions

Besseler, Heinrich, and Peter Gülke. *Schriftbild*. 130, partial transcription.

Roy, Otto, ed. *Musik des Mittelalters und der Renaissance*. Musikalische Formen in historischen Reihen. New ser. Wolfenbüttel: Möseler, 1960. 40.

Recording

Diego Ortiz, "Recercadas" from the Tratado de glosas. Jordi Savall and Genoveva Galvez. Musical Heritage Society MHS 1888.

EXAMPLE III–30.   Diego Ortiz, *Recercada primera sobre O felici occhi miei*

Reprinted from Diego Ortiz, *Tratado de glosas*, edited by Max Schneider (Kassel: Bärenreiter, 1967), 73–75, by permission of the publisher.

31. Fiorenzo Maschera, *Canzona prima . . . detta la capriola* (Canzona à 4)

Fiorenzo Maschera (ca. 1540–ca. 1584) was an Italian composer, organist, and player of the viola da braccio and violin. His 23 surviving works are all instrumental canzonas in four parts.[146] The present example appeared in his *Libro primo de canzoni da sonare*, printed in 1584 (apparently a reprint of an earlier publication now lost).

Maschera's works are among the earliest purely instrumental ensemble canzonas. The earlier practice of performing vocal chansons and motets instrumentally led to the development of an independent repertory of chanson- and motet-like instrumental works with such labels as *canzona*, *ricercare*, and *carmen*. The Venetian school around the turn of the century produced works labeled *canzona*, *ricercare*, or *sonata*, many of which require antiphonal ensembles. Instrumentation is sometimes specified. This category, transitional to the Baroque period, may involve the emerging violin family along with standard Renaissance instruments. Sometimes organ accompaniment in a quasi-continuo fashion is appropriate.[147]

La capriola shows many features typical of canzone of this period: the dactylic rhythmic pattern of the French chanson, sectional structure, and imitation in the Flemish style. This piece represents a specialized type in which monothematic organization generates the form (*a a a′ a′ a″*). The work exhibits voice pairing as well as textures of three and four parts; textural density increases toward the end of the piece.

Although derived from a secular genre, canzone of Maschera's time might have been performed in churches; certainly, later works of this type by Giovanni Gabrieli and others were heard in the church of St. Mark, Venice. Following a structural interpretation, the performer might conclude that canzone based on imitative and homophonic techniques are best performed by like instruments. Compositions that exhibit more melodic independence suggest the use of unlike, blending instruments.

The authors recommend the following for a modern performance of this piece:

§ Two cornetts for the upper parts
§ Two sackbuts for the lower parts
§ Alternatively, consider string ensemble of violin-family or viol-family instruments

Source

Maschera, Fiorenzo. *Libro primo de canzoni da sonare a quattro voci* (RISM M1205). Brescia: Sabbio, 1584. 1.

Edition used

Maschera, Fiorenzo. *Five Canzonas for Four Instruments SATB*. Edited by Bernard Thomas. Venetian Instrumental Music c. 1600, vol. 7. London: London Pro Musica Edition, 1977. 4–5 (no. 1).

Facsimile

Besseler, Heinrich, and Peter Gülke. *Schriftbild der mehrstimmigen Musik*. Musikgeschichte in Bildern, vol. 3, pt. 5. Leipzig: Deutscher Verlag für Musik, 1973. 157 (no. 94), partial facsimile.

Other transcriptions

Besseler, Heinrich, and Peter Gülke. *Schriftbild*. 156, partial transcription.

Wasielewski, Joseph Wilhelm von, ed. *Instrumentalsätze vom Ende des XVI. bis Ende des XVII. Jahrhunderts*. Bonn: M. Cohen und Sohn, 1874. Reprint. *Anthology of Instrumental Music from the End of the Sixteenth to the End of the Seventeenth Century*. Edited by John Suess. New York: Da Capo, 1974. 1 (no. 1).

EXAMPLE III–31. Fiorenzo Maschera, *Canzona prima . . . detta la capriola*

32. Richard Alison, *The Batchelars delight* (Consort lesson à 6)

Richard Alison (fl. 1592–1606) is perhaps best known for his *The Psalmes of David in Meter* (1599). Thomas Morley (1557 or 1558–1602) arranged works of several composers for broken consort, among them compositions by Richard Alison.

Morley's *The First Booke of Consort Lessons* contains settings of popular dances and vocal music in a variety of styles, treated with varying degrees of ornamentation. The type of music contained in this publication functioned as household music in aristocratic circles and also enjoyed success in the theater.[148] Thus it was both an amateur and a professional repertory.

The earliest standardized ensemble of specified mixed instruments, the English "consort" comprised treble viol or violin, recorder or flute, lute, cittern, pandora, and bass viol. Although the woodwind part of some pieces is notated in a range that appears to require a bass recorder or bass flute, pictorial evidence and musical considerations suggest an octave transposition upward and the use of a smaller instrument.[149]

The Batchelars delight comprises four strains, each varied (*a a′ b b′ c c′ d d′*). Its title may refer to Daniel Batchelar, another composer of works for broken consort. Changes of meter appear in the last two strains, indicated in the sources by inconsistently applied proportion signs. The authors recommend the following solutions:

a) ¢ o = ¢ o·   b) ¢ ♩ = ♪ ♦·
   ($\frac{2}{4}$ ♩ = $\frac{3}{4}$ ♩·)   ($\frac{3}{4}$ ♩ = $\frac{6}{8}$ ♩·)

In order to realize the tablatures, the plucked string instruments require the following tunings: lute *g′ d′ a f c G*; cittern *e′ d′ g b*; and pandora *a′ e′ c′ g d c*.

The recorder/flute part requires a decision with regard to range and size of instrument. Morley's employment of the alto clef for this part is likely to have suggested the use of an alto instrument to flautists of the time. Furthermore, other musical considerations, particularly balance, seem to require an instrument in the higher octave. Choices between recorder or flute, and between treble viol or violin, perhaps reflected differences in taste and practice between amateurs and professionals.

Stylized dance pieces in this repertory might require somewhat slower tempi than genuine dance music, in order to permit clear execution of the highly ornamented sections. The level of pulse, the authors feel, should still convey the sense of the original dance.

The authors recommend the following for a modern performance of this piece:

§ An ensemble consisting of treble viol, alto recorder (transposing an octave higher), bass viol, six-course lute, cittern, and pandora

Sources

Cambridge, University Library, MS. Dd.3.18, ff. 44v–45r (lute); MS. Dd.5.20, f. 2v (bass viol).

Morley, Thomas. *The First Booke of Consort Lessons.* 2nd ed. (RISM 1611²¹). London: Thomas Snodham, 1611. No. 24 (treble viol, flute, and pandora part books).

Oakland, Mills College Library, Mills Cittern Part-book, no. 13 (cittern).

Edition used

Morley, Thomas. *The First Book of Consort Lessons, 1599 and 1611.* Edited by Sydney Beck. New York: C. F. Peters for the New York Public Library, 1959. 161–169 (no. 24), together with corrections supplied by the editor.

Facsimiles

Morley, Thomas. *The First Book of Consort Lessons, 1599 and 1611.* Edited by Sydney Beck. 33–36.

Recordings

Altenglische Consortmusik. Linde-Consort. EMI Reflexe 1C 063-30 105; also in a set, EMI Reflexe 1C 163-30101/6.

An Evening of Elizabethan Music. Julian Bream Consort. RCA SER 5687/8, RCA DX26.35045, or RCA Victor LD-2656.

EXAMPLE III-32. Richard Alison, *The Batchelars delight*

From Thomas Morley, *The First Book of Consort Lessons, 1599 and 1611*, ed. Sydney Beck (New York: C. F. Peters, 1959), pp. 161–169 (no. 24). Copyright 1959 by C. F. Peters Corporation. Reconstructed from the scattered parts, transcribed and edited by Sydney Beck. By kind permission of the publishers.

216

33. John Ward, *In nomine* (Instrumental quartet)

John Ward (1571–1638) was an English composer who left instrumental works, madrigals, and sacred music. His instrumental ensemble music appears in many sources and is generally considered to be intended for viols, perhaps with organ. These works range from short pieces in two parts to fantasias in six parts.[150]

The unique source of the following example is a manuscript that contains 26 four-part compositions attributed to "J. Ward." Because 6 of them appear in several sources and seem to differ in style from the others, the authorship of the remainder (including our example) has been questioned.[151]

The type of fantasia that Ward composed was an essentially sectional form comprising contrapuntal and imitative sections alternating with short, dance-like passages. The *In nomine* is a uniquely English contribution to the fantasia genre. Its hallmark is the use of the *In nomine* passage from the Benedictus of John Taverner's *Missa Gloria tibi Trinitas* as the basis for fantasia composition. This slow-moving *cantus firmus* may appear in any single part, or may wander among the various voices. Our example places the *cantus firmus* in the alto part. The work is cast in three sections, all displaying highly imitative textures.

Pieces of this type were written for solo chordal instruments or for ensembles. The performance of viol fantasias was cultivated by members of the English gentry, usually in informal settings. English music for viols was perhaps performed a fourth lower than its notation implies (see information in Appendix B relevant to Figure B-19).

The authors recommend the following for a modern performance of this piece:

§ For performance at the notated pitch, a quartet of viols (one treble, two tenors, and bass)

§ Consider possibility of transposition downward by a perfect fourth, using ensemble of two tenor viols and two basses

Source

Paris, Bibliothèque Nationale, Bibliothèque du Conservatoire, MS. Rés. F.770, p. 270 ff.

Edition used

Dart, Thurston, and William Coates, eds. *Jacobean Consort Music.* Musica Britannica, vol. 9. 2nd ed. London: Stainer & Bell Ltd., 1971. 44–46 (no. 29).

Facsimile

Dart, Thurston, and William Coates, eds. *Jacobean Consort Music.* xxi, partial facsimile.

EXAMPLE III–33.   John Ward, *In nomine*

Reprinted from *Jacobean Consort Music*, edited by Thurston Dart and William Coates, Musica Britannica, vol. 9, 2nd ed. (London: Stainer & Bell Ltd., 1971), 44–46, by permission of the publisher.

34. John Wilbye, *Weep, O mine eyes* (Madrigal à 5)

John Wilbye (1574–1638) was one of the most gifted composers of English madrigals. Most of his compositions belong to this genre. Two books of madrigals by Wilbye were published in his lifetime.

Weep, O mine eyes is an example of the English madrigal at its best. As in the five-part madrigals of Italian masters such as Marenzio, Wilbye shows great sensitivity in setting poetry with melodic and rhythmic subtlety and expressive word-painting. This lament is cast in two sections, the second being repeated (*a B B*). Wilbye explores a wide range of homophonic and contrapuntal techniques within three-, four-, and five-part textures.

Works such as this undoubtedly enjoyed skilled performances at court and in patrician households. As indicated previously (see the discussion preceding Example III–29), the authors believe madrigals to be a soloistic repertory. The intimacy of late Italian and English examples make them particularly unsuited to choral forces. Although instrumental doubling of voices in madrigals and related forms was a historically authentic option in Italy, and possibly elsewhere, the authors feel that the intimate and expressive nature of this particular piece precludes the use of doubling instruments, with the possible exception of viols.

The authors recommend the following for a modern performance of this piece:

§ A vocal quintet (two sopranos, alto/countertenor, tenor/baritone, and bass)

§ Consider the possibility of an all-instrumental performance on viols, in accordance with the title of Wilbye's publication
(Scholars have observed that titles of this sort, indicating optional use of instruments in vocal repertoires, might have been a marketing ploy, rather than the composer's intention.)

§ Note that tempo and dynamic markings and the pianoforte part are editorial

Source

Wilbye, John. *The Second Set of Madrigales to 3. 4. 5. and 6. parts, apt both for Voyals and Voyces* (RISM W1066). London: Thomas Este, 1609. Five partbooks: cantus, altus, bassus, p. 30; quintus, p. 12; tenor, p. 22 (no. 23).

Edition used

Wilbye, John. *Second Set of Madrigals to Three, Four, Five, and Six Voices.* Edited by E. H. Fellowes and revised by Thurston Dart. The English Madrigalists, vol. 7. 2nd ed. London: Stainer & Bell Ltd., 1966. 138–144 (no. 23).

Facsimiles

Wilbye, John. *The Second Set of Madrigales to 3. 4. 5. and 6 parts.* The English Experience, no. 633. New York: Da Capo, 1973. Cantus, altus, bassus, p. 30; quintus, p. 12; tenor, p. 22 (no. 23).

Microfilm. Ann Arbor: University Microfilms, STC reel 980, Pollard and Redgrave 25619a.

Other transcription

Engel, Hans, ed. *The Sixteenth-Century Part Song in Italy, France, England and Spain.* Anthology of Music, vol. 3. Cologne: Arno Volk Verlag, 1961. 52–55 (no. 19).

Recordings

English Madrigals. Pro Cantione Antiqua. Peters International PLE 133/4.

Madrigals by John Wilbye. Wilbye Consort. London STS 51562.

EXAMPLE III-34.   John Wilbye, *Weep, O mine eyes*

35. Thomas Tomkins, *O Lord, rebuke me not* (Anthem à 3)

Thomas Tomkins (1572–1656), an English composer well known for his keyboard works, wrote a large amount of music for use in the Anglican Church and other compositions belonging to genres of secular vocal music. He was an organist associated with Worcester Cathedral and the Chapel Royal.

Most of Tomkins's sacred works were published posthumously in *Musica Deo Sacra* (1668). This collection contains mainly anthems, along with Services and a few other works. It was issued in five partbooks: medius, contratenor, tenor, bassus, and organ.

O Lord, rebuke me not is a full anthem based on verses one and two of Psalm 6 (as numbered in the *Book of Common Prayer*), a Penitential Psalm. Such a piece, the English equivalent of the Latin motet, would have been performed as part of an Anglican church service.[152] Despite the fact that this example was composed and published well into the seventeenth century, its conservative style is firmly rooted in Renaissance compositional practices, which persisted longer in England than on the Continent.

O Lord, rebuke me not requires a small choir of male voices, perhaps 6 to 10 boys and 6 to 12 men.[153] As mentioned in Part I, current scholarship and practical considerations of tessitura suggest that English sacred music of the sixteenth and early seventeenth centuries should be transposed higher than its apparent pitch. Upward transposition by a minor third, the interval generally advocated, will permit this anthem to be sung by boys on the highest part and by men (countertenors and tenors) on the lower parts. This degree of transposition is sup-ported by a note in one copy of the organ book regarding the length of an organ pipe.[154] (The organ part, however, does not contain music for the three-part anthems.)[155] If high voices are appropriate, it seems curious that the partbooks in which the anthem appears are medius, tenor, and bassus, rather than medius, contratenor, and tenor. One authority states, however, that Tomkins's three-part anthems were intended for a small choir not necessarily made up of adult singers.[156]

The authors recommend the following for a modern performance of this piece:

§ A male choir (boy sopranos for the highest part, countertenors for the middle part, tenors for the lowest part), transposing upward by a minor third

§ Alternatively, for a practical solution or study purposes, a mixed choir at the notated pitch level

Source

Tomkins, Thomas. *Musica Deo Sacra* (RISM T950). London: William Godbid, 1668. Three partbooks: medius, pp. 157–158; tenor, p. 136; bassus, pp. 145–146.

Edition used

Tomkins, Thomas. *Thirteen Anthems*. Edited by Robert Cavanaugh. Recent Researches in the Music of the Renaissance, vol. 4. New Haven: A-R Editions, 1968. 1–3.

Facsimile

Tomkins, Thomas. *Thirteen Anthems*. Pl. 2, tenor part.

Other transcription

Tomkins, Thomas. *Musica Deo Sacra, IV*. Edited by Bernard Rose. Early English Church Music, vol. 27. London: Stainer & Bell Ltd., 1982. 7–9.

EXAMPLE III–35. Thomas Tomkins, *O Lord, rebuke me not*

PROJECTS FOR PART III

Projects for medieval motets

1. Locate two complete examples of each type of motet illustrated in Examples III–5, 6, 8, and 10. Compare and contrast each pair of examples. Study the text(s), the features of stratification, the structure of the tenor, etc.

2. Compose the opening phrases of four motets in the styles of Examples III–5, 6, 8, and 10. Organize the tenor from a melody of your choice. Select two English texts (poems, popular songs, etc.), and set one or both as the style of the model indicates.

3. To examine the levels of stratification in motets that you have chosen to perform, have the singers recite the texts together in rhythm, without music. Also, play all the parts together on instruments, without words.

Projects for fourteenth-century polyphonic secular song

1. Find an example of each general type of work illustrated in Examples III–11 to III–15. Consider the similarities and differences among your selections. Determine a suitable performing ensemble for each piece.

2. Locate a transcription and a facsimile of its source, for a work in this category. Compare the two, and discover what changes and decisions the editor has made (e.g., text underlay, *musica ficta*, correction of wrong notes, etc.).

3. In order to become thoroughly familiar with a fourteenth-century piece that you choose to perform, each member of your ensemble should learn each part of the piece and should be prepared to perform any part independently and in any combination.

Projects for accompanied Renaissance song

1. Locate two complete examples of each type of song (Burgundian, frottola, and tenorlied) illustrated in Examples III–18, 21, and 26. Compare and contrast each pair of examples. Determine a likely ensemble for the performance of each piece.

2. Obtain a readable copy of an original source of an accompanied Renaissance song, and attempt a performance from this source. (Performers will find sixteenth-century prints more approachable than fifteenth-century manuscripts.)

3. In sixteenth-century works, determine the rhythmic groupings within each part, as described in Chapter 5. For any work in this category that you choose to perform, consider text underlay and *musica ficta*.

Projects for vocal-ensemble music

1. Select one category of vocal-ensemble music (polyphonic conductus or rondel, trecento madrigal, Flemish or French chanson, Tudor part-song, Italian or English madrigal, or villancico). In order to become familiar with your chosen repertory, study several examples in modern editions and, if possible, in facsimiles. Examine the relationships of the various voice parts within each piece and from one piece to the next. Is the subject matter of the texts varied within your repertory? If so, how is this variety reflected in musical settings?

2. Obtain several facsimiles in each of three or more categories listed in the previous Project, and determine the general problems and solutions of text underlay as they apply to each category.

3. Compare a facsimile and transcription of a piece of vocal-ensemble music. Discover what decisions the editor has made.

4. Obtain a facsimile of a simple printed French chanson. Make your own score edition and have it performed.

Projects for choral music

1. Choose one of the types of choral music discussed in Examples III-1, 2, 3, 9, 16, 17, 19, 27, and 35. Obtain several examples and familiarize yourself with their similarities and differences; for instance, number and range of parts, use of soloists, etc.

2. Obtain a facsimile and complete transcription of a sixteenth-century Mass movement. Develop your own text underlay, based on principles of underlay and rhythmic groupings discussed in Chapters 5 and 7.

3. If you have a choir or if you can assemble a group of twelve or more singers of various ranges, experiment with several possible choral sounds. For example, mix men and women on alto parts; have men sing falsetto on alto or even on soprano parts, with or without women; have boys sing upper parts, alone or with women; vary the number of singers per part from three to six; use different numbers of singers per part; transpose an *a cappella* piece to several different pitch levels.

Projects for instrumental-ensemble music

1. Choose one of the types of instrumental music discussed with Examples III-7, 20, 22, 24, 25, and 30–33. Obtain several examples and familiarize yourself with their similarities and differences.

2. Obtain a facsimile and complete transcription of an instrumental work. Determine what the editor has done with the piece. Decide on an appropriate performing ensemble, unless specified in the original source.

3. Choose a sixteenth-century dance that appears to be intended for dancing (Attaingnant, Susato, etc.). Consult Arbeau's treatise for information on step patterns, and determine appropriate tempo and accent patterns (see citations for Example III–25).

4. Choose a fantasia. Determine the duple and triple rhythmic groupings in each part.

5. Select a mid-sixteenth-century vocal-ensemble work. Compose diminutions first on the treble part, then on the bass line. Consult one of the period treatises on ornamentation and endeavor to stay within its guidelines. After gaining some familiarity with embellishment procedures, attempt to improvise on one of the parts of the work selected.

Appendices

APPENDIX A

Other Genres of Medieval and Renaissance Music

1. MEDIEVAL MONOPHONIC SECULAR MUSIC

a. Song

Performance traditions in this category are almost completely undocumented. Manuscript sources of this literature reveal next to nothing about performance, and indeed matters of rhythm, meter, and form are not precisely discernible. Even pitches often show variants among multiple sources.[1] Studies of the musico-poetic oral traditions of modern European cultures suggest that flexibility may be a characteristic of such music.[2]

In an effort to bring to life this most obscure category of early Western art music, at least two styles of modern performance have been promoted. One incorporates a heterophonic approach reliant upon Andalusian Arabic folk traditions.[3] Another adheres to the simplicity implied by the sources. Further, some performers have associated the former style with music of the Mediterranean area, and the latter style with the music of Northern Europe. Thus minnesinger, trouvère, and British song that does not in some way suggest the South or the Near East has sometimes been seen to belong to the simpler type. Conversely, cantigas and other literature originating in Moorish areas have been thought of more in terms of the heterophonic style, while troubadour and goliard song have been performed in both ways.

All of this literature can be sung without accompaniment, but often it is accompanied in modern performances. Such accompaniment is improvisatory, ranging from simple drone to complex heterophony. Although historical performance practices might have encompassed both unaccompanied and accompanied procedures, no definitive documentation exists to allow the performer to proceed with any degree of confidence, let alone certainty.

b. Dance

Only a small number of monophonic dances have survived. Information about their step patterns is minimal. This repertory of music belonged to an oral tradition that was improvisatory, thus rarely notated. Little is known about the dance-song of the type that Grocheo mentions. Likewise a dance-song of unknown character is thought to have been the precursor of the trecento ballata.

Some modern performers have applied to monophonic dances the principles of "Northern" and "Southern" styles already mentioned.[4] The latter approach sometimes uses such percussion instruments as nakers, darabuka, tabor, tambourine, and cymbals.

After lengthy consideration, the authors decided not to include secular monophonic music within the body of this text, both because it may not represent ensemble music and because the current state of knowledge does not permit a meaningful exposition of its performance practice.

We can only hope that future research will provide more evidence relating to rhythmic interpretation of the sources of monophonic music and to performance of this repertory.

2. POLYPHONIC DANCE BEFORE 1500

a. Early Dance

Only four "dances," all from thirteenth-century English sources, are composed in two or more parts. Scholars have assumed that these untitled, textless works are dances, of the type called *estampie*, but their similarity to conducti cannot be overlooked.[5] Three of the pieces have two-part texture throughout; the other begins monophonically and ends with a section in three parts. The multi-part writing in these works is essentially homophonic. Because the pieces are brief, they perhaps do not constitute complete settings such as might have been used for dancing.

b. Basse Danse

The *basse danse* was an important French dance in the fifteenth century.[6] Most fifteenth-century *basse danse* music consists of monophonic tunes written in undifferentiated, long note values. Some of these tunes also serve as tenors of polyphonic pieces dating from the same period. Considerable information survives relating step patterns to *basse danse* melodies,[7] but performance of the music is less certain. One approach involves improvising two upper parts over the slow-moving tenor, in a style resembling the polyphonic examples.[8] Based on pictorial evidence, an ensemble of two or three shawms and a slide trumpet has been suggested.[9] A contrasting theory suggests solo performance of diminutions on the tenor melody, using flute or pipe and tabor.[10] Perhaps differing types of ensembles performed this repertory, depending on the occasion, using either improvised or composed settings.[11] Pictorial evidence exists showing instruments in conjunction with dancing (not necessarily the *basse danse*).[12] These instrumental groups are either *haut* (loud) or *bas* (soft).[13]

3. SOLO INSTRUMENTAL MUSIC

This important repertory burgeoned in the sixteenth century. It includes the following genres: preludes and similar works in improvisatory style, dances, variation sets, ricercari, canzone, fantasias, *cantus firmus*-based pieces, and intabulations of vocal music. The principal instruments for which this music was composed are organ, harpsichord, virginal, lute, vihuela, and viola da gamba.

4. DRAMATIC MUSIC

Throughout history, music has been employed in the context of dramatic presentations, both sacred and secular. Evidence that dramatic music flourished in the Middle Ages and Renaissance is abundant, although much of the actual music has not survived. Extant compositions that are known or surmised to have served a dramatic function resemble music categorized earlier in this book. Some of these compositions were conceived for specific presentations, while others were borrowed from various sources.

General categories of dramatic music include the following:

a.   Liturgical drama

b.   Secular monophonic music drama

c.   Incidental music for miracle plays and related dramas

d.   Incidental music for secular Renaissance theater

e.   Court entertainments

Information about performance practice of dramatic music is in many cases nonexistent and in others extremely complex. However generous or sparse the informative detail, reconstruction of works in the foregoing categories remains problematic and often controversial. Specific recommendations for performance, therefore, lie beyond the scope of this book. The remainder of this section provides a brief introduction to the kinds of music used in medieval and Renaissance dramatic presentations.

a. Liturgical Drama

An outgrowth of the medieval practice of troping, the liturgical drama developed from an enactment of a brief portion of chant into fully staged independent plays, performed within the context of the liturgy. These dramas are entirely sung, with Latin texts set to monophonic music, utilizing both borrowed chant and newly composed material. Evidence exists for the use of organ and bells in some liturgical dramas. Because these works were not officially sanctioned as part of the liturgy, instruments that were otherwise proscribed for use in the church might have participated.[14]

The dimensions of liturgical drama range from the three-line *Quem queritis* trope to extended plays such as the Daniel and Herod dramas. Performance of the larger works requires considerable resources.

b. Secular Monophonic Music Drama

The existence of secular music theater throughout the early Middle Ages is affirmed by frequent admonitions of the Church against such pagan influences. Complete extant examples survive only from the later Middle Ages, and these are few in number. The paucity of surviving works may not accurately reflect the original extent of this repertory.

Generalizations may be drawn from the best-known example of secular monophonic music drama, Adam de la Halle's *Li Gieus de Robin et de Marion*. This work, which is based on borrowed chansons of popular character, contains both sung and spoken text, all in the vernacular. The use of instruments is likely; the text even mentions one instrument.

Compositions having dialogue characteristics occur in the monophonic song repertory; for instance, the planctus *Samson dux fortissime*. Such works suggest the possibility of independent dramatized performance, although no documentation exists to support this conjecture. Dramatized planctus, however, were included in Good Friday religious ceremonies.

c. Incidental Music for Miracle Plays and Related Dramas

The adoption of the vernacular for the presentation of plays of a religious nature brought about the rise in the fourteenth century of cycles of miracle and mystery plays. Rubrics prescribe musical interpolations of plainsong, motets, chansons, and instrumental pieces. Little actual music survives, probably owing to its incidental function. Similar to the aforementioned dramas were *moralities*, fifteenth-century plays of an allegorical character, in which music may have played a part. These three kinds of dramatic presentation occurred principally in England and France.

Italy developed a vernacular religious drama, the *sacra rappresentazione*, in the fifteenth and sixteenth centuries. Plays in this category were elaborately staged, and involved the participation of instrumental ensembles and the singing of laude and other forms. These spectacles, performed in church or out of doors, were patronized by both the clergy and the nobility. Complete incidental music is lacking for any of these plays; however, certain examples may be conjectured from information supplied by rubrics. Spain and Portugal produced plays similar to the *sacra rappresentazione*, called *autos*. Italian religious drama in the vernacular also included *devozioni* and *Maggi*, both of which incorporated music.

d. Incidental Music for Secular Renaissance Theater

Renaissance secular theater frequently incorporated music as an incidental component.

French plays of the fifteenth and early sixteenth centuries included numerous chansons, some borrowed and others newly composed. These simple pieces vary in setting from one to five parts, three being the norm. A variety of instruments participated in the productions, probably in an independent rather than accompanying capacity.

Spanish plays by such noted authors as Juan del Encina, Gil Vicente, and Lope de Vega called for both vocal and instrumental incidental music. Encina composed many villancicos for his own dramas.

Public and private theater flourished in sixteenth-century England, affording many opportunities for musical participation. Incidental music, such as ayres, ballads, and catches, was largely borrowed. Types of plays ranged from early Tudor court productions to professional playhouse repertory of the Elizabethan period and included lesser forms such as academic dramas and precursors of ballad opera. Instrumental ensembles participated in some of these productions, an example being the broken consort (see Example III–32). The plays themselves were sometimes preceded or followed by brief musical entertainments.

An important development in connection with Renaissance secular theater was the *interlude*. This form of entertainment took place between the acts of a larger dramatic conception. It frequently utilized vocal and instrumental performance. The early interlude was the ancestor of elaborate court entertainments of the late sixteenth century, to be discussed next.

e. Court Entertainments

Wealthy noble patrons in sixteenth-century England, France, and Italy produced extravagant celebrations of unprecedented scope. These lavish and sometimes lengthy affairs, generally created for royal weddings or visits, involved processions, banquets, and plays with elaborate interludes, all staged in a grandiose manner. Music was often newly composed for such events, and much of it survives, along with detailed descriptions of some productions.

Under the heading of court entertainments we include the *masque, ballet de cour,* and *intermedio.* Common to all of these spectacles was a blend of drama, music, and dance. Such entertainments ranged in complexity from the simpler Tudor *disguisings* to the *intermedii* for the 1589 Medici wedding, which involved at least 30 singers and 20 instruments. Music for this set of interludes included such types as aria, madrigal, canzonetta, villanella, sinfonia, and ballo, in settings for accompanied solo voice, one or more vocal ensembles, or various instrumental ensembles.

Fifteenth-century examples of works that may be appropriately included here are Burgundian banquets, such as the "Feast of the Oath of the Pheasant," and Florentine carnivals incorporating frottola-like *canti carnascialeschi.*

APPENDIX B
Principal Instruments of the Middle Ages and Renaissance

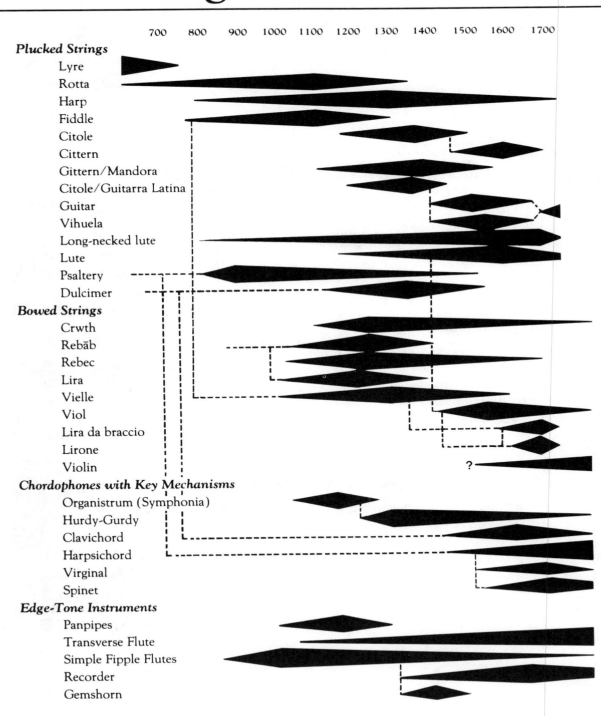

700 800 900 1000 1100 1200 1300 1400 1500 1600 1700

Plucked Strings
Lyre
Rotta
Harp
Fiddle
Citole
Cittern
Gittern/Mandora
Citole/Guitarra Latina
Guitar
Vihuela
Long-necked lute
Lute
Psaltery
Dulcimer

Bowed Strings
Crwth
Rebāb
Rebec
Lira
Vielle
Viol
Lira da braccio
Lirone
Violin

Chordophones with Key Mechanisms
Organistrum (Symphonia)
Hurdy-Gurdy
Clavichord
Harpsichord
Virginal
Spinet

Edge-Tone Instruments
Panpipes
Transverse Flute
Simple Fipple Flutes
Recorder
Gemshorn

256

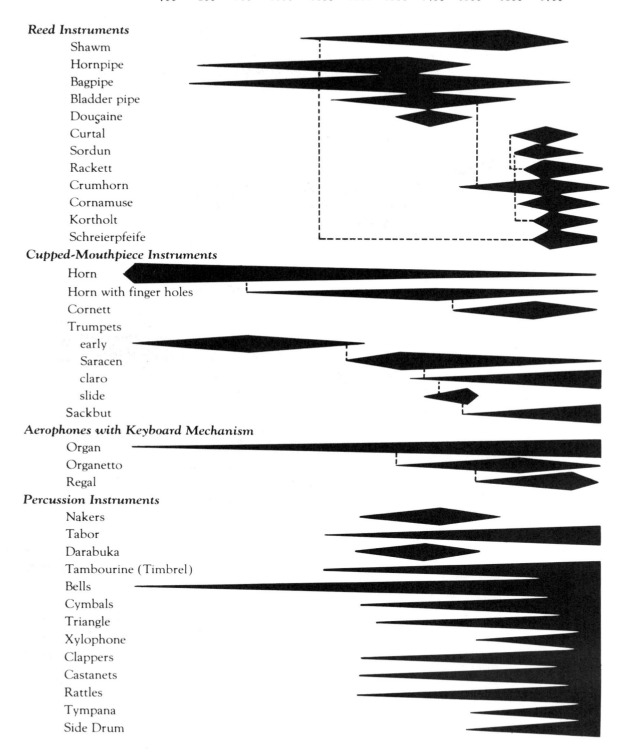

	700	800	900	1000	1100	1200	1300	1400	1500	1600	1700

Reed Instruments
- Shawm
- Hornpipe
- Bagpipe
- Bladder pipe
- Douçaine
- Curtal
- Sordun
- Rackett
- Crumhorn
- Cornamuse
- Kortholt
- Schreierpfeife

Cupped-Mouthpiece Instruments
- Horn
- Horn with finger holes
- Cornett
- Trumpets
  - early
  - Saracen
  - claro
  - slide
- Sackbut

Aerophones with Keyboard Mechanism
- Organ
- Organetto
- Regal

Percussion Instruments
- Nakers
- Tabor
- Darabuka
- Tambourine (Timbrel)
- Bells
- Cymbals
- Triangle
- Xylophone
- Clappers
- Castanets
- Rattles
- Tympana
- Side Drum

The preceding chart shows the approximate time-spans of various instruments and reflects European iconographic evidence. Origins of many instruments surely predate their appearance in works of art. The study of early musical instruments is complex and problematic owing to our imperfect state of knowledge. The brief survey that follows will introduce the reader to the principal instruments of the Middle Ages and Renaissance in a very general way. For more complete information, consult the Bibliography.[1]

PLUCKED STRINGS

Among the earliest plucked forms important for our study are those derived from the classical *lyre* (Figure B–1); that is, instruments with strings attached to a yoke that lies in the same plane as the resonator and that consists of two arms and a crossbar.

The *rotta* (*cruit, rota, rote, rotte, chrotta, hruzza, cithara*) is, according to one interpretation, not a true box lyre like the ancient Greek kithara, but rather an instrument of triangular shape with approximately thirty strings, more closely related to the harp.[2] The rotta has also been identified with the classical lyre, which eventually developed into a bowed instrument[3] (see *crwth*). It appears in literary sources from the seventh century to the fourteenth century.

The *harp* (Figure B–2) is an instrument with parallel strings running in a plane perpendicular to the resonator; that is, between the resonator and the neck. European instruments have, in addition, a pillar that connects resonator and neck; that is, the frame harp. Irish stone crosses from the ninth century depict the earliest known classical harp-like instruments. Irish harps had metal strings attached to tuning pins inserted in the neck at the top of the instrument. The pins were operated by a tuning key. Another early type of harp, the *telyn* (Welsh harp), was fitted with horsehair strings from the tenth century until the fourteenth century, when it acquired gut strings. All early harps were rather squat instruments with outcurving pillars. The "Gothic" harp of the fifteenth century adopted a more slender appearance, with an almost straight pillar, and retained the gut strings preferred for Welsh harps. The tuning for all harps was basically diatonic, though Renaissance forms were semi-chromatic.

Fiddle is a generic name for a bowed instrument with a neck. This and related terms (*fidel, vielle, vihuela*) may have referred in the early Middle Ages to more specific instruments with necks and flat backs that were bowed and/or plucked. The diversity of shape and size is astonishing, though all forms do have a flat peg-disk with front or rear pegs. Earliest evidence of this instrument seems to be from the ninth or tenth century (see *vielle* as a bowed instrument, Figure B–18).

The *citole* (Figure B–3) was first mentioned in French literature in about 1200. It was described much later by Tinctoris as having a flat body, a short, fretted neck, front pegs in a peg-disk, a frontal string fastener, and four metal strings plucked with a quill. It was eventually modified and transformed into the sixteenth-century *cittern* (Figure B–10). The true citole apparently had a variety of shapes (see Figure B–5). This accounts in part for the confusion surrounding the instruments

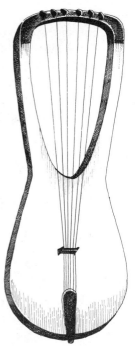

FIGURE B–1.   Lyre.

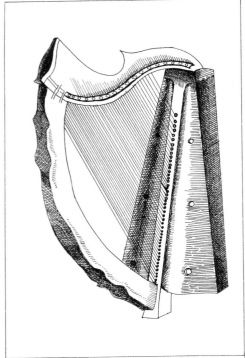

FIGURE B–3. Citole.

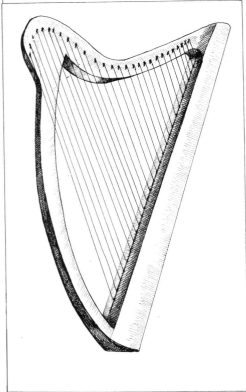

FIGURE B–2. Harps.

in B–3, B–4, and B–5, and for the erroneous labeling of some citoles as "gitterns" by investigators.[4]

The true medieval *gittern* (Figure B–4) (formerly called *mandora*) was a small, lute-like instrument with rounded back and sickle-shaped pegbox, which carried generally three or four single or double courses of strings. The standard four-course tuning was fourth-third-fourth. Although similar in appearance, the Renaissance *mandora* (*mandola, testudo minor*) adopted a standard tuning of fifth-fourth-fifth.

The instrument pictured in Figure B–5 (formerly called *guitarra latina* or *gittern*) is now considered to be a type of citole.

The *long-necked lute* (*tanbura, colascione*) (Figure B–6) is an instrument with an oval body, rounded back, and large peg-disk. (Figs. B–4, 5, and 6 are illustrated in an important Spanish manuscript of the thirteenth century: Biblioteca Escorial, MS. j.b. 2.)

The *lute* (Figure B–7) is today probably the most familiar of medieval and Renaissance plucked

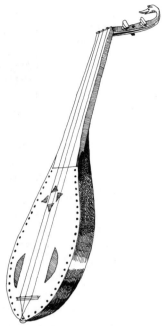

FIGURE B–4.   Gittern.

FIGURE B–6.   Long-necked lute.

string instruments, and it was certainly one of the most important during these periods. Western lutes probably originated in the vicinity of the Caucasus and then spread to Northwest Africa and

throughout the Near East. Lutes of both the long- and short-neck varieties, with peg-disk or pegbox, occurred in medieval Europe from the thirteenth century onward. The differences in these instruments may reflect different routes of arrival into

FIGURE B–5.   Citole/Guitarra latina.

FIGURE B–7.   Lute.

Europe. Early types are shown to have a rounded body with a vaulted back. Arabic instruments (*al'ūd*) had a short neck, peg-disk, frontal fastener, and approximately four gut strings. They were unfretted and were played with a plectrum. Such instruments survive today in Near Eastern cultures. European descendants were similar, featuring a short neck, but a bent-back pegbox and lateral pegs. Fifteenth-century instruments had five or occasionally six gut strings, sometimes in courses, and gut frets. They were played either with a plectrum or with bare fingers. The sixteenth-century instrument, also fretted, had a large piriform body with a flat wooden top and a bulging back composed of thin ribs. Its courses of gut strings were plucked with bare-finger technique. The most common tuning for the six-course instrument was G c f a d' g'. Instruments of both smaller and larger sizes existed, though they are of less importance from the standpoint of repertory.

Psaltery (Figure B–8) is a general term for plucked box zithers (any simple chordophones consisting solely of a string bearer and soundboard), which occurred in considerable variety and number in medieval Europe. These instruments were usually wire-strung and were played with bare fingers, nails, or a plectrum. The prototype for European instruments is the Arabic *qānūn*, with its trapeze or half-trapeze shape. The *qānūn* was held vertically, with its soundboard against the player's chest, and was played with one hand. It was first depicted in Europe in tenth-century Spain, with ten strings; later depictions show more strings. Tunings were highly variable, ranging from diatonic to semichromatic. By the twelfth century, it had spread to non-Moorish Europe and had assumed a variety of shapes, among them trapezoidal, wing-shaped, harp-shaped, rectangular, etc. The names for these instruments are legion, among them: (Latin) *ala, canale, canon, demi-canon, media ala, medicinale, medius canon, meo canno, micanon*; (German) *kanon, salmaharpha, salmsang, saltersanch*; (French) *ele, decorde, sautier*; (Italian) *canone, mezzocanone, salterio*; (Spanish) *cano, medio cano*; and (English) *salterium, saltere*.

The *dulcimer* (*dulcema, dulce melos, doucemelle, tympanon*) (Figure B–9) is a box zither whose strings are struck by curved beaters, rather than plucked by fingers or plectra (see psaltery). The instrument is of Near Eastern origin and was introduced to Europe in Moorish Spain by the twelfth century.

The *cittern* (Figure B–10) evolved at the end of the fifteenth century from the citole (Figures B–3 and B–5). The new instrument had a rib string fastener and a bridge, a piriform body, a flat back, a short neck with metal frets, a central sound hole with a rosette, various numbers of strings (not to mention tunings), and was plucked with a plectrum. By the end of the sixteenth century, several related instruments of different sizes were being made, bearing such names as *ceterone, pandora, bandora*, and *orpharion*.

Vihuela (Figure B–11), a generic term for chordophones in Spain, is also used to designate the classical plucked instrument of Spanish Renaissance society. The general shape was similar to the modern guitar, but with much shallower sides, five to seven courses of gut strings (most commonly five pairs of strings and a single chanterelle, tuned like those of the lute), and gut frets. Somewhat similar in appearance was the Italian *viola da mano*.

Of great similarity to the vihuela was the Renaissance *guitar* (Figure B–12), the principal differences

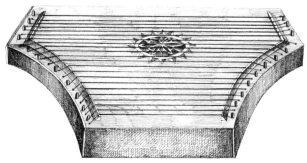

FIGURE B–8. Psaltery.

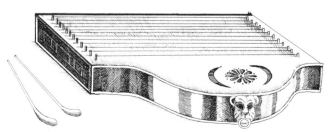

FIGURE B–9. Dulcimer and beaters.

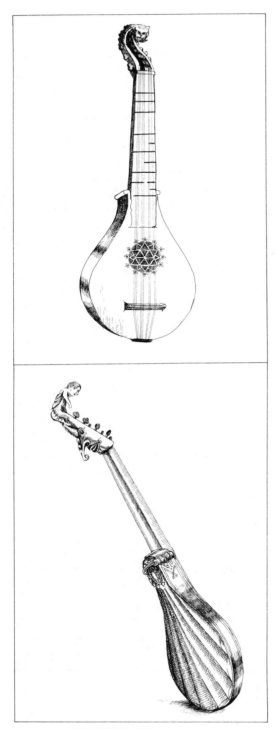

FIGURE B-10. Cittern.

FIGURE B-11. Vihuela.

century. Guitars were also made with five courses of strings; eventually the distinctions between vihuela and guitar blurred to the extent that the two instruments merged in the seventeenth century.

BOWED STRINGS

As might be expected, the early stages of bow development exhibit a great variety of shapes (Figure B-13), some of which approach the bizarre. The two basic forms that emerge are the strongly arched *round bow* and the so-called *flat bow*, in which the stick is more nearly parallel to the hair, and which features a stub at one end, actually a rudimentary frog.

Medieval bows were usually strung with horsehair, though less densely than modern bows. Bow grip was close-fisted and situated toward the middle of the bow in round bows (popular in the East), and near the stub end of the bow in flat bows. The latter type of bow and bow grip became

being the guitar's smaller size, fewer strings (generally four courses), and flat or vaulted back. This instrument was frequently (and confusingly) referred to by the old term *gittern* in the sixteenth

FIGURE B–12.   Guitar.

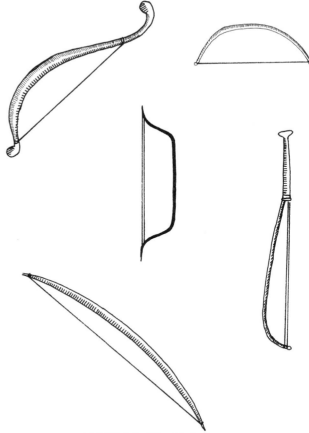

FIGURE B–13.   Early bows.

predominant in Europe. Underhand grip was possible for instruments played in the knee position.

As they are today, instruments were nearly always held in the left hand, with the bow in the right hand. In the East, the vertical playing position (i.e., supported on the knee or lap) was almost invariably adopted, whereas in Europe this position was generally reserved for waisted instruments; others were laid against the body or held out to one side (i.e., in a sort of shoulder position).

Renaissance bows represented a natural extension of the flat-bow type, with a more fully developed frog and a more highly stylized grip, as in, for example, the viola da gamba underhand grip.

The *crwth* (*chorus, crouth*) (Figure B–14) was a form of lyre illustrated particularly in English manuscripts from about the eleventh century. In the Middle Ages it had three to five strings. As with the rotta, the addition of fingerboard, bridge, and tailpiece transformed the crwth into a bowed

instrument. Sometimes strings occurred both over the fingerboard and alongside it in paired courses. Bridges appear to have been flat, implying drone playing technique. Welsh tunings of the eighteenth century were *g g′ c″ c′ d′ d″* and *a a′ e′ e″ b′ b″*. No earlier tunings are known.

The Arabic *rebāb* (Figure B–15) formed the prototype for several bowed instruments in use in Europe during the Middle Ages. Today this instrument has a body of wood, with straight sides and rounded back, and its belly is partially or wholly covered with skin. There are two metal strings of copper or brass, lateral pegs, and a very high bridge. A nail-playing technique is sometimes used, and pitch can be expressively raised by altering the degree of pressure used to stop the string.

The wooden, "Byzantine" *lira* (Figure B–16), calling for a similar playing technique, survives to-

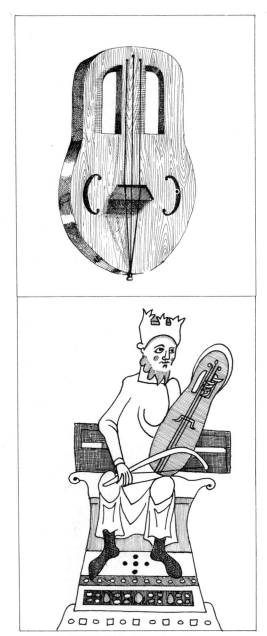

FIGURE B–14.   Crwths.

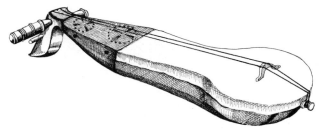

FIGURE B–15.   Rebāb.

The closely related *rebec* (*rubebe*) (Figure B–17) had a small piriform body of wood, short neck, lateral pegs, rib string fastener, and three strings. Earliest evidence of this instrument is from the eleventh century. In the Renaissance, several sizes were made. Strings were tuned in fifths. The instruments depicted in Figures B–15 through B–17 represent only three of the many variations on this theme.

Vielle (*fidula, viella, vihuela*) (Figure B–18) is here employed to refer to the medieval bowed instruments that occurred in a variety of shapes and sizes but shared these characteristics: flat back, more or less distinct neck, and three to five gut strings. As bowed instruments, these types occurred from the eleventh century through the fifteenth century. After the twelfth century there was a developmental tendency toward waisted sides, five strings, curved bridge, and (in the late thirteenth century) frets. As with all medieval bowed instruments, the flat bridges of some early examples imply considerable use of drone-playing techniques. The tunings mentioned by Jerome of Moravia (late thirteenth century) have been the subject of recent research suggesting the following relative pitches: *d G g d′ d′*, *d G g d′ g′*, and *G G d c′ c′*.[6] The lowest string was often a burden drone for

day as a three-stringed instrument in Greece and Bulgaria. Since it has no nut, its middle string is treated as a drone. The modern lira is probably the same basic instrument that medieval Europe acquired from Byzantium. It should be noted that the term *lira* (*lyra*) also has broadly generic applications and has been used as synonymous with harp, Germanic lyre, hurdy-gurdy, citole, gittern, lute, etc.[5]

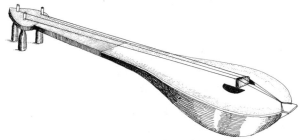

FIGURE B–16.   Lira.

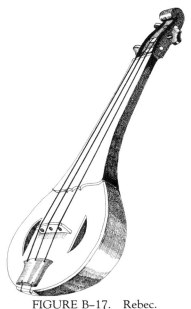

FIGURE B–17.   Rebec.

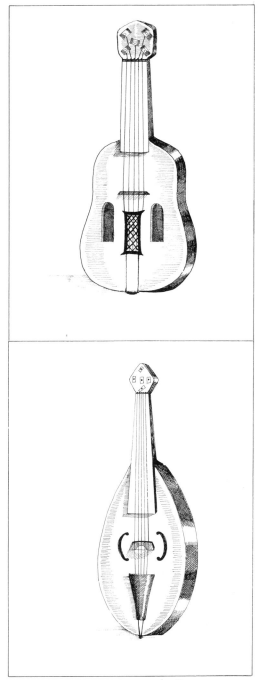

FIGURE B–18.   Vielles.

bowing or plucking. The vielle was the most important and respected bowed instrument of the Middle Ages, being suitable for any sort of music.

Just as the vielle was the principal bowed string instrument of the Middle Ages, so were the *viols* (*violas da gamba*) (Figure B–19) the principal bowed strings of the Renaissance. The exact origin of the viol is not clear, but the best evidence seems to suggest that it evolved in Spain during the second half of the fifteenth century, probably from plucked instruments such as the vihuela, the shape and constructional features of which it originally resembled.[7] As with most Renaissance instruments, viols were made in several "family" sizes that share these features: four to six gut strings tuned in fourths around a central third, frets, lateral pegs, tailpiece, deep ribs, sloping shoulders, flat back, C-holes, a vertical playing position, and an under-hand bow grip. Viols today are commonly tuned as follows:

bass: *D G c e a d'*
tenor: *G c f a d' g'*
treble: *d g c' e' a' d''*

However, it has been shown that sixteenth-century tunings and sizes sometimes differed from modern usage.[8] Recent research on the structural character-istics of viols made earlier than the type illustrated suggests that their tone might have been reedier, softer, or more blending.[9]

The *lira da braccio* (Figure B–20) represents Renaissance experimentation with the old vielle

FIGURE B–19.   Viols.

FIGURE B–20.   Lira da braccio.

type of instrument and was born of the humanist interest in antiquity and in such instruments as the lyre. The lira da braccio was approximately the size of a modern viola. It had seven strings, two of which were drones off the fingerboard, and it was unfretted until after 1600.

Of similar nature was the *lirone* (Figure B–21), a hybrid between the lira da braccio and the viola da gamba. It had a variable outline, S-holes, a broad neck, frontal pegs, flattish bridge, a number of drone strings off the fingerboard, and from nine to fourteen stopped strings, which were tuned in fourths, fifths, and octaves.

The *violin* (Figure B–22) emerged in the second half of the sixteenth century, first as a three-stringed instrument, and soon thereafter as a four-stringed instrument in three sizes. Quite different from the modern instrument, violins of this period had a smaller bass bar, a straight neck, a wider and shorter fingerboard, and gut strings. In the Renaissance, violins were played by professionals rather than by gentlemen, and their principal repertory was dance music.[10]

FIGURE B–21.   Lirone.

CHORDOPHONES WITH KEY MECHANISMS

The *organistrum, symphonia,* and *hurdy-gurdy* form an interesting group of bowed instruments that emerged in Europe in the twelfth century. During the twelfth and thirteenth centuries, this type of instrument was known as either *organistrum* or *symphonia* (Figure B–23). It had three strings attached to a figure-eight body and was sounded by a disklike wheel, the rim of which was coated with pitch or resin. The wheel was operated by a crank. Thick gut strings were used, stopped by tangent-like keys. All strings were sounded simultaneously and, during this period, the tangents probably stopped all the strings. The result, of course, is a sort of parallel organum and is analogous to the "mixture" on medieval organs. The organistrum required two performers to operate, and it was capable of only rather slow, sustained playing.

After the thirteenth century, this basic type of instrument was called the *hurdy-gurdy* (Figures B–24 a and b). It was a one-man instrument of smaller size and more facile key mechanism. Tangents probably stopped only one string, the two other strings sounding in continuous drone. The tuning was likely *g d′ c′,* though different tunings might have been adopted for different pieces. At this stage, the instrument was capable of playing rapid passages in a limited range, and it represented a technological accomplishment parallel to the development of the organetto.

The application of tangents against a string occurred in another instrument, the *clavichord* (*manichord*) (Figure B–25). This instrument, which derived its principles from the monochord, was a rectangular box with metal strings running diagonally from hitch pins on the left, over a bridge on the right, to more pins on the extreme right.

FIGURE B–22.   Violin and bow.

FIGURE B–23.   Organistrum or symphonia.

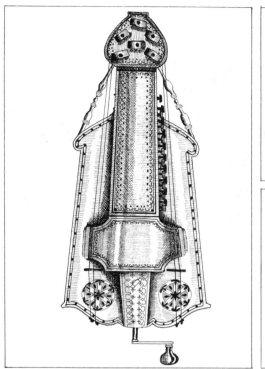

FIGURE B–24a. Hurdy-gurdies.

Pitches were produced by metal tangents activated by a keyboard. A tangent striking a string would act as a new nut and set the string between this point and the bridge into motion. The earliest clavichords were "fretted"; that is, one string (or pair) served for several pitches, and was therefore capable of being struck by several tangents (one at a time, of course). The instrument certainly dates from as early as the fifteenth century. The mysterious *chekker,* once considered to be an early type of clavichord, has recently been dismissed as a myth.[11]

The *harpsichord* (Figure B–26) began its development in the fifteenth century. It is essentially a mechanized psaltery (it even retains the qānūn shape!) in which each key activates a jack whose plectrum plucks the string, then bounces out of the

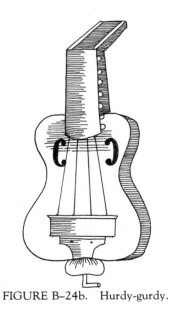

FIGURE B–24b. Hurdy-gurdy.

FIGURE B–25. Clavichord.

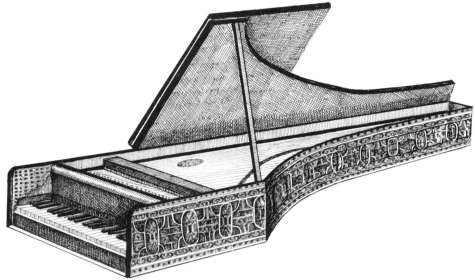

FIGURE B–26.   Harpsichord.

way as the jack falls when the key is released. Renaissance harpsichords were single-manual instruments with paired strings at eight-foot pitch or with eight-foot and four-foot registers.[12] Variants were made such as the upright *clavicytherium*, the pentagonal *spinet*, and the rather distinctive rectangular *virginal* (Figure B–27), which was made in both eight-foot and four-foot pitch sizes, and featured two bridges on the soundboard.

EDGE-TONE INSTRUMENTS

The familiar *panpipes* (Figure B–28) of classical times seem to have existed in medieval Europe as a practical instrument from the eleventh through the thirteenth centuries. Thereafter, depiction of panpipes in art is probably purely allegorical. In Europe, panpipes were made from cane, stone, metal, clay, or wood in the form of a set of tuned tubes joined together in a raft. The lower end of each tube was stopped, and sound was produced by blowing across the top, open end.

In the Middle Ages and Renaissance, the *transverse flute* (Figure B–29) was cylindrical in bore, with six finger holes and a small, round embouchure hole. The instrument was first depicted in the twelfth century in Germanic sources and was later illustrated both as a military instrument

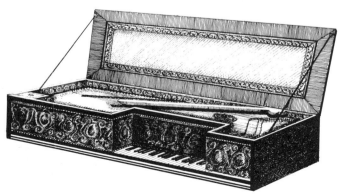

FIGURE B–27.   Virginal.

FIGURE B–28.   Panpipes.

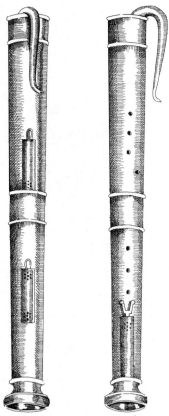
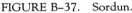

FIGURE B-37.   Sordun.

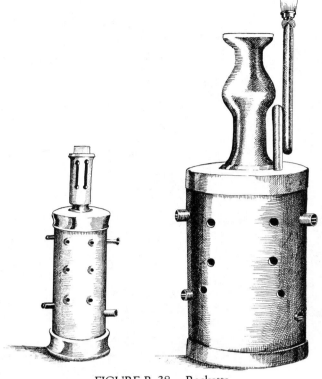

FIGURE B-38.   Racketts.

holes. As on the sordun, these were covered by the middle finger joints, and as is usually the case with medieval and Renaissance woodwinds, the instrument could be played either right- or left-handed.

The most peculiar of Renaissance multibore instruments must surely be the *rackett* (Figure B-38). It consisted of no fewer than nine connected, parallel, cylindrical channels, and it was played with a widely flared double reed inserted into a pirouette. The instrument appeared in around 1576. Praetorius lists four sizes, each having the compass of a twelfth. Later racketts were limited to the bass size and utilized a crook.

Possibly developing from the bladder-pipe concept, the *crumhorn* (*tournabout, krummhorn, storto, piva torto, orlo*) (Figure B-39) was the earliest and is the most familiar today of the many capped double-reed instruments of the late Renaissance. The crumhorn appeared in the late fifteenth cen-

tury as an instrument hooked at the lower end, with a double reed enclosed by a wooden cap, and with a very narrow cylindrical bore, the range therefore being limited to a ninth. Early writers mention four sizes (no soprano), and Praetorius mentions five.

There may have been an instrument similar to the crumhorn called the *cornamuse*. Praetorius described (without illustration) a capped double-reed instrument with cylindrical, straight bore and a perforated cap for the bell end to mute the tone. Confusion arises from the fact that in Italian usage, *cornamusa* may mean crumhorn, and *cornemuse* has also been used to refer to a type of bagpipe. Our illustration (Figure B-40) is of a modern, conjectural reproduction.[17]

The application of the capped-reed idea to cylindrical double-bore instruments resulted in the *kortholt* (Figure B-41), essentially a capped sordun. Praetorius illustrates only a bass size, though modern makers have extrapolated a family of instruments.

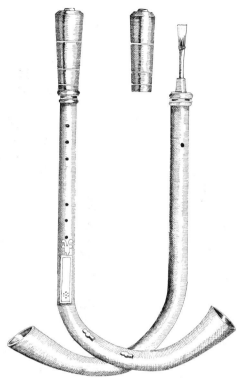

FIGURE B–39.   Crumhorn.

FIGURE B–40.   Cornamuse.

The *schreierpfeife* (Figure B–42) represented the natural extension of the reed cap to instruments with a conical bore; that is, the shawm family. Thus these instruments were suitable for *haut* (loud) music and were capable of a range extending into the second octave.

CUPPED-MOUTHPIECE INSTRUMENTS

Trumpets (*trompe*) of various sizes were important for ceremonial and court functions. Probably limited to notes of the lower harmonic series, these instruments were confined to the playing of fanfares and pedal points during the Middle Ages. Renaissance trumpeters, however, did utilize the upper harmonic series. *Claro* (*clairon, clarion*) was used from the twelfth century onward to denote various forms of trumpet. *Buisine* (*buccina*) referred originally to a long, curved horn, but after the twelfth century, it denoted the long, straight Sara-

cen trumpet. All of these trumpets had basically cylindrical bores with a flared bell. In the fifteenth century, the so-called *slide trumpet* (Figure B–43) was developed.[18]

Its limited flexibility may have influenced the development of the slide mechanism and lower range of the *sackbut* (Figure B–44), which was capable of more agile playing. This instrument also can be traced from the fifteenth century. Praetorius illustrates four sizes of sackbut. The instrument was capable of participating in either *haut* (loud) or *bas* (soft) ensembles.

Since the early Middle Ages, *horns* (Figure B–45) were used as martial instruments or as splendidly decorated symbols of royalty (the *oliphant*). By adding finger holes (often three), these cow or goat horns could be made to produce a rudimentary scale of about a sixth. The desire for a more perfect

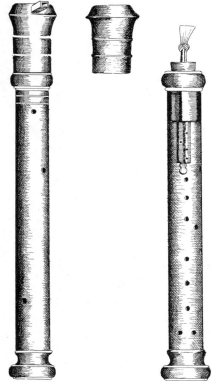

FIGURE B–41.   Kortholt.

FIGURE B–42.   Schreierpfeife.

scale led to the production of finger-hole "horns" made of wood.

The sixteenth-century, conically bored *cornett* (Figure B–46) was the result. This most versatile of cupped-mouthpiece instruments was made in both straight and curved forms. In addition, a "mute" type was produced, whose mouthpiece was not separate, but carved into the top of the instrument. Cornetts came to be made in several sizes, including the curious bass version, the *serpent*. Skilled players of the cornett were capable of considerable feats of virtuosity, and might fit into either *haut* or *bas* ensembles.

AEROPHONES WITH KEYBOARD MECHANISM

The *organ* is certainly the oldest of all keyboard instruments. By the fourth century (perhaps second or third century), the pneumatic organ had ap-
peared in Europe, replacing the ancient *hydraulis*. Early pneumatic organs were operated by a bellows mechanism requiring from one to four men to activate. Instead of a true keyboard, the instrument had a series of *linguae* (tongues), which had to be manually pulled and pushed, thus requiring two players. Its pipes were of the fipple-flute type, and each fundamental pitch was often sounded with an unalterable mixture (octaves and fifths) of pipes. Though clumsy, these instruments would have been ideal for the sustained tenors of early organum and might have served that function.

During the fifteenth century, large ("great") organs underwent considerable modification in their constructional features. Keyboards with agile action were installed, like those added to the organetto (Figure B–47) and hurdy-gurdy (Figures B–24a and b) in previous centuries. Varied registra-

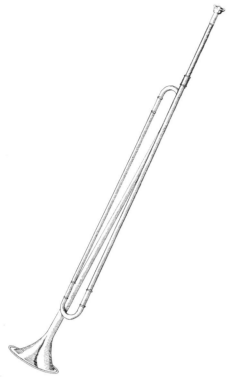

FIGURE B–43.   Slide trumpet.

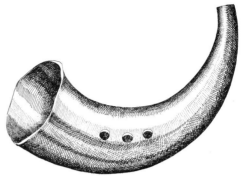

FIGURE B–45.   Horn.

tion became possible by the addition of *stops.* Reed pipes activated by metal vibrators were added to the existing ranks of flute pipes, and stops of both types were designed to imitate the sounds of vari-

ous contemporary instruments (e.g., gemshorn, crumhorn, rackett, recorder, flute, and dulcian). A pedal board, multiple manuals, and coupler mechanisms were other additions.

The *organetto* (Figure B–47) was a small portable organ played and pumped simultaneously by a single performer, and was regularly illustrated from the thirteenth through the sixteenth centuries. It was a monophonic instrument of treble range, incorporating usually two rows of flute pipes and occasionally a couple of drone pipes at a lower pitch. As with larger organs, the keyboard was diatonic at first (about two octaves) and chromatic by the beginning of the fifteenth century (up to three octaves).

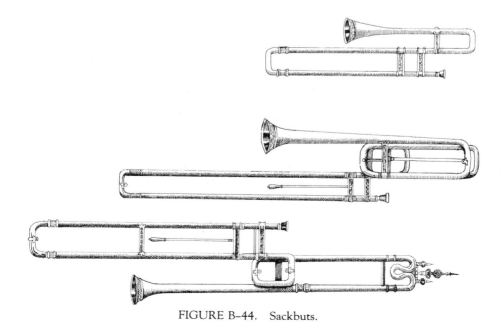

FIGURE B–44.   Sackbuts.

FIGURE B-46.   Cornett and mouthpiece.

The *positive organ* was smaller than the great organ and larger than the organetto. It combined some of the virtues of both and survives as an independent instrument (choir organ, chamber organ) and as an incorporated part of the great church organ (i.e., in one of its manuals).

The *regal* was a small portative organ containing exclusively reed pipes and was probably a sixteenth-century development. The term has also been used from the mid-fifteenth century to the present to denote a reed stop of larger organs.

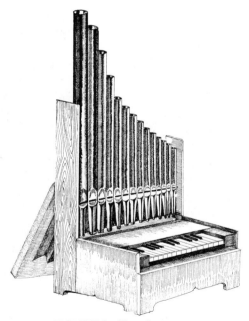

FIGURE B-47.   Organetto.

PERCUSSION INSTRUMENTS

Numerous percussion instruments (Figure B–48) existed during the Middle Ages and Renaissance. Important among them were the following.

Naqqāra (*nakers, nacaires, neccheroni*) were small, bowl-shaped copper drums, which were introduced into Europe by the Arabs in the thirteenth century. These usually occurred in pairs, played with a pair of sticks.

The *tabor* occurred in many sizes, but its essential features were a cylindrical shape, two drumheads, a snare on the upper head, and a single-stick playing technique, which freed the other hand for playing the three-holed tabor pipe, a simple fipple flute.

The constructional principles of the nakers and the tabor, respectively, are seen in larger sixteenth-century military instruments such as the *tympana* and *side drum*.

Other percussion instruments of Eastern origin are the hourglass hand drum of the Arabs called *darabuka*, as well as *cymbals, clappers, castanets, tambourines, rattles,* and *triangles. Bells* and the *xylophone* (first pictured in 1525) may be indigenous European products.

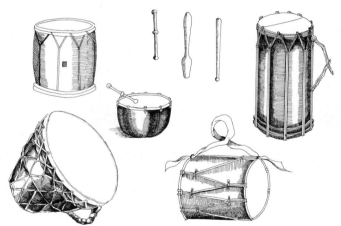

FIGURE B-48.   Percussion instruments.

APPENDIX C
Ranges of Medieval and Renaissance Instruments

Instrument	Tessitura	Tuning	Approximate Playing Range
Plucked Strings			
Lyre	intermediate	diatonic	variable; one octave
Rotta	intermediate	diatonic	variable; one to two octaves
Harp	soprano–tenor or bass, inclusive	diatonic to chromatic	variable; *F–a″* on 16th-century harps
Citole	soprano	reentrant	*c′–g″*?
Cittern	intermediate	courses; variable, reentrant	*c–e″(a″)*
Gittern	soprano/alto	4th-3rd-4th	*g–g″*
Mandora	soprano/alto	5th-4th-5th	*g–g″*
Guitar	intermediate	courses; variable, 4ths & 3rds	*g(A)–e″(a″)*
Vihuela	soprano–bass inclusive	courses; 4ths with a central 3rd	*G–g″*
Long-necked lute	intermediate	5ths and 4ths	?
Lute	soprano–bass inclusive; also smaller & larger sizes	courses; 4ths with a central 3rd	*c–d″(g″)*; *G–g″*
Psaltery	many sizes: soprano to bass	diatonic to semichromatic	highly variable; one to two octaves
Dulcimer	intermediate	diatonic to semichromatic	variable; one to two octaves
Bowed Strings			
Crwth	high/intermediate	courses: 4ths & 5ths	?*g–g″*

278

Instrument	Tessitura	Tuning	Approximate Playing Range
Rebāb	high/intermediate	5ths	two octaves above lowest open string
Rebec	sizes: soprano to tenor	5ths	two octaves above lowest open string
Lira	intermediate	4th & 5th above central drone	10th above drone
Vielle	wide/ intermediate	5ths & 4ths (7th); some-times with drones	G–d″(c″)
Viol	family: soprano to great bass, with wide range	standard: 4ths with a central 3rd; special tunings also	three octaves above lowest open string, on GG, D, G, d
Lira da braccio	soprano–tenor inclusive	8ves, 4ths, & 5ths	d–d‴
Lirone	soprano–bass inclusive	8ves, 4ths, & 5ths	G–g″
Violin	wide: soprano/ alto	5ths	g–e‴ (later much higher)

Chordophones with Key Mechanisms

Instrument	Tessitura	Tuning	Approximate Playing Range
Organistrum	intermediate	diatonic; strings in 5ths & 8ves	about one and a half octaves; drones
Hurdy-gurdy	high	semi-chromatic; strings in 5ths & 8ves	one to two octaves; drones
Clavichord	wide: soprano–bass inclusive	semi-chromatic to chromatic	three to four octaves
Harpsichord	wide: soprano–bass inclusive	chromatic with "short octave"	C–f‴
Virginal	wide: soprano–bass inclusive	chromatic with "short octave"; also at 4′ pitch	C–f‴

Edge-Tone Instruments

Instrument	Tessitura	Tuning	Approximate Playing Range
Panpipes	high, at 4′ pitch	diatonic	about two octaves

Instrument	Tessitura	Tuning	Approximate Playing Range
Transverse flute	family: soprano to bass, 4' pitch	more or less chromatic	two octaves above fundamentals on g, d', g'(a'), d"
Recorder	large family: sopranino to great bass, at 4' pitch	chromatic	13th above fundamentals on F, c, f, c', f', c", f", c"'
Gemshorn	sizes: soprano to tenor, at 4' pitch	more or less chromatic	9th above fundamentals on c', f', c"
Reed Instruments			
Shawm	family: soprano to great bass	basically chromatic	13th above fundamentals on FF, C, G, c, g, d'
Hornpipe	high	diatonic	one octave +
Bagpipe	high/intermediate	basically diatonic	one octave +; drones
Bladder pipe	intermediate	basically diatonic	9th above fundamental?
Doucaine	intermediate?	semi-chromatic?	restricted?
Curtal	family: soprano to great bass	basically chromatic	within two octaves above fundamentals on FF, GG, C, G, c, g
Sordun	family: tenor to great bass	chromatic	13th above fundamentals on FF, BB♭, C, E♭, B♭
Rackett	family: tenor to great bass	chromatic	12th above fundamentals on DD(CC), FF, C, G
Crumhorn	family: soprano to great bass	basically chromatic	9th above fundamentals on BB♭(C), F, c, g, c'

Instrument	Tessitura	Tuning	Approximate Playing Range
Cornamuse (modern)	family: soprano to bass	basically chromatic	9th above fundamentals on F, Bb(c), d, bb
Kortholt	bass	basically chromatic	within two octaves above fundamental on C?
Schreierpfeife	family: alto to bass	basically chromatic	13th above fundamentals on F, c, g

Cupped-Mouthpiece Instruments

Horn	intermediate	diatonic	6th above fundamental
Cornett	family: soprano to tenor	chromatic	about two octaves above fundamentals on c, a(g), e'
Trumpet	high	harmonic series	g upward
Sackbut	family: alto to great bass	basically chromatic	over two octaves above fundamentals on EE(CC), AA(FF), E(C), B

Aerophones with Keyboard Mechanisms

Organ	wide: soprano–bass inclusive, with many registrations at 4', 8', or 16' possible	diatonic to chromatic	8': C–f'''
Organetto	soprano/alto, at 4' pitch	diatonic to chromatic	c'(g)–c'''
Regal	intermediate; basically 8', with occasional 4' and 16' stops	chromatic	about three octaves

APPENDIX D
Selected Journals Dealing with Early Music

The American Recorder (Quarterly)
The American Recorder Society, Inc.
596 Broadway, #902
New York, NY 10012

Chelys (Journal of the Viola da Gamba Society of
Great Britain) (Annual)
Mrs. Caroline Wood
93a Sutton Road
London N10 1HH
England

The Consort (Journal of the Dolmetsch Foundation)
(Annual)
Mrs. P. Dutton
Derwen
Star Hill, Churt
Surrey GU10 2HS
England

Early Music (Quarterly)
Journals Subscriptions
Oxford University Press
Walton Street
Oxford OX2 6DP
England

The Galpin Society Journal (Annual)
Miss Pauline Holden
38 Eastfield Road
Western Park
Leicester LE3 6FE
England

Journal of the American Musical Instrument Society
(Annual)
The American Musical Instrument Society, Inc.
c/o The Shrine to Music Museum
414 East Clark Street
Vermillion, SD 57069

Journal of the Lute Society of America, Inc. (Annual)
Beedle Hinely
Box 1328
Lexington, VA 24450

Journal of the Viola da Gamba Society of America
(Annual)
John A. Whisler, Secretary-Treasurer
1536 Third Street, Apt. 6
Charleston, IL 61920

Lute Society Journal (British) (Annual)
Diana Poulton, President
5 Wilton Square
London N1 3DL
England

The Organ Yearbook (Annual)
Frits Knuf
P.O. Box 720
4116 ZJ Buren (Gld.)
The Netherlands

APPENDIX E
Pronunciation Guides

See Chapter 4, "Languages" (p. 38), for introductory guidelines. As stated there, every language has variant dialects and spellings, which make its "correct" pronunciation difficult to determine. The following pages offer suggestions for pronunciation. These were derived by the authors from writings by scholars and experts. Readers who wish to investigate a particular language in more detail may consult the pertinent books and recordings included in the Bibliography.

Editions of texts often change an original spelling to conform to a more common spelling of the period or to the modern version of the word. Before consulting a pronunciation table, the singer must discover the nature of the spellings and diacritical marks that appear in the edition.

ENGLISH

Middle English (ca. 1100–ca. 1450) distinguishes between long and short vowels in speech. In singing, the difference is perhaps less critical; however, the short vowels sound more like modern English vowels, the long vowels less so. Most consonants have their usual modern sounds.

TABLE E-1.   Selected Phonetic Symbols

[a]	(French) salle	[λ]	(Spanish) llamar, (Italian) figlio
[ɑ]	cot	[b]	bob
[æ]	cat	[d]	dad
[aɪ]	bite	[f]	fun
[au]	house	[g]	gag
[e]	eight	[h]	he
[ɛ]	bet	[k]	kick
[ɛɪ]	say	[l]	lull
[ə]	above	[m]	mom
[i]	beet	[n]	nun
[ɪ]	bit	[ŋ]	sing
[ɪu]	feud	[ɲ]	(French) agneau
[o]	boat	[p]	pup
[ɔ]	bought	[r]	roar
[œ]	(French) jeune, (German) schön	[R]	(French) coeur
[ɔɪ]	boy	[s]	sis
[u]	boot	[t]	tot
[ʊ]	put	[v]	valve
[ʌ]	but	[w]	we
[y]	French une, German für	[x]	(German) ach
		[z]	zoos
[Y]	similar to [y]; a half-close back vowel	[ʒ]	azure
		[dʒ]	judge
[ɥi]	French nuit	[ʃ]	shy
[~]	indicates a nasal vowel	[tʃ]	church
		[θ]	thin
[j]	yes	[ð]	this

TABLE E-2.   Middle English Pronunciation

a	[ɑ] or [a]
aa	[ɑ]
ai, ay	[ɛɪ]
au, aw	[au]
e	[e] or [ɛ]; possibly [ə] in a medial or final syllable; final e is pronounced [ə] before ca. 1400, and is silent later; final e is elided, within a phrase, to the following word if it begins with h or a vowel.
ee	[e] or [ɛ]
ei, ey	[æɪ]; rarely [i] or [e]
eo	[œ]
eu, ew	[ɛu]; also [ɪu] or [ju]
i, y	[i] or [ɪ]
ie, ye	[i]; sometimes [e]
o	[o], [ɔ], or [ʊ]; occasionally [œ] or [ɔʊ]
oo	[o] or [ɔ]
oi, oy	[ɔɪ]
ou, ow	[u] or [ɔʊ]
u	[y] or [ʊ]; also [ɪu] or [ju]; occasionally [Y]
ui	[y]
ch, cch	[tʃ]
g	[g] or [dʒ], as in modern usage
gg	[g] or [dʒ]
gh	[x]
gn	[gn] at the beginning of a word; otherwise [n]
h	sometimes silent initially
kn	[kn]
ng	[ŋg]
r	possibly trilled initially
sch	[ʃ]
wr	[wr]
þ	[θ]
ƿ	[w]

Table E-2 represents the Midland dialect, that of London and of Chaucer. This table provides several phonemes for some vowels. The correct choice depends on the etymology of the word, a subject too involved to be explained here. The table lists only differences from modern standard English (American). It also reduces the more than 80 spelling symbols of Middle English to a basic list. The letters *i* and *j* were written interchangeably; likewise *u* and *v*.

Table E-3 lists pronunciations for Elizabethan English. Consonants are equivalent to modern English consonants, with few exceptions. Vowels are closer to modern English than to Middle English. The variety of possible pronunciations relates to etymological differences. Unstressed syllables may use [ə].

TABLE E-3. Elizabethan English Pronunciation

a	[ɑ], [æ], or [e]; also [ɑ] before *r*, [ɛ] before *re* or *ir*
ai, ay	[e] or [ɛ]
au	[æ] or [ɔ]
aw, sometimes al	[ɔ]
e	[i], [ɪ], or [e]; also [a] before *r*, [ɛ] before *re, ar, ir*
ee	[i]
ea	[e]; also [ɛ] or [i]
ei	[e] or [ɛ]
ey	[e], [əɪ], or [ɛ]
ew	[ju]
i, y	[ɪ], [i], or [əɪ]
ie	[i] or [əɪ]
o	[u], [o], [ɔ], or [ʌ]
oo	[ʊ], [u], or [ʌ]
oa	[o]
oe	[u] or [o]
oi, oy	[əɪ] or [ɔɪ]
ou	[o], [ɔ], [ʌ], or [əʊ]
ough	[əʊ] or [ɔ]
ow	[o] or [əʊ]
u	[ʊ], [ʌ], or [u]
ue	[ju]
g	often silent in unstressed *ing*
h	often silent initially
t	[t], occasionally [θ]

FRENCH

Table E-4 provides pronunciations for Francien or Parisian French, 1100–1600, and does not cover

Provençal, Picard, or Norman. The table lists only differences from modern educated Parisian French. The information that follows comes from *Bele buche e bele parleure*, by Jeannine Alton and Brian Jeffery, used with permission of the publisher (Tecla Editions, London).

Final consonants were generally pronounced until 1250, silent from 1250 to 1500, and sometimes pronounced in the sixteenth century. They were voiced in liaison, or at the end of a phrase or sentence; they could also be voiced for poetic rhyme.

GERMAN

Middle High German is the general form of German used from ca. 1050 to ca. 1500. Viewed more specifically, it is the language of the period ca. 1150–ca. 1350, when minnesingers were active.

Vowels carry an important distinction between long and short values, although the difference may not be apparent in singing, especially if metrical rhythm is employed. Long vowels comprise *â, ê, î, ô, û, ae, iu,* and *oe.* Diphthongs include *ei, eu, ie, öi, ou, öu, üe,* and *uo.* All other vowel sounds are short. Unstressed syllables may use [ə]. Consonants may be pronounced as Modern High German, with the basic exceptions noted in Table E-5.

ITALIAN

Pronunciation of early Italian lies beyond the scope of this book. Spellings and dialects show extreme variation.

Italian of the fourteenth and fifteenth centuries bears many resemblances to modern Italian. Variant spellings of the period apply mainly to consonants. An attempt was made in the sixteenth century to standardize spellings. Some sixteenth-century secular vocal works have texts that deliberately employ regional dialects.

TABLE E-4. French Pronunciation*

VOWELS

	a when followed by an *s* that becomes silent, as in pas, mât, âne	*ai* faire, mais, raison	*ai* in verb endings j'aimai	*au* aube, autre	*ei* mei, curteis	*eu* fleur, cheveux	*e* final or in monosyllables père, je	*eau* beau
1100		[ai]	[ai]		[ei]	[εu]	as in English *get*	[εau]
1200			[ε]	[au]	[ɔi] / [uε]			
1300	[a]	[ε]						
1400			[e]	[ao]	[wε], [ε], [wa]	[œ]	as in English *sofa*	[εao]
1500								[əo]
1600	[ɑ]			[o]			as in modern French	

VOWELS   **NASAL VOWELS**

	ie pied, fièvre	*oi* voix, joie, gloire	*ui* nuit, conduire		*a* + nasal consonant chant, âme, agneau	*ai* + nasal consonant faim, aime	*e* + nasal consonant temps, vent, femme	*ei* + nasal consonant sein, pleine
1100	[ie]	[oi]	[yi]	1100				[ei] and the consonant
1200	[je]	[uε], [wε]	[ɥi]	1200				
1300				1300	[ã] and the consonant	[ẽi] and the consonant	[ã] and the consonant	[ẽi] and the consonant
1400	as in modern French	[wε], [ε], [wa]		1400				
1500				1500	[ã], [a]	[ẽ], [ε]	[ã], [a]	[ẽ], [ε]
1600				1600				

*From Jeannine Alton and Brian Jeffery, *Bele buche e bele parleure* (London: Tecla Editions, 1976), 32–39. Reproduced with permission.

TABLE E-4 (*cont.*)

NASAL VOWELS

	i + nasal consonant *vigne, fin*	*ie* + nasal consonant *bien, viennent*	*o* + nasal consonant *ombre, donner*	*oi* + nasal consonant *loin, point*	*u* + nasal consonant *un, lune*
1100	[i] and the consonant	[ie] and the consonant	[o] and the consonant	[oi] and the consonant	[y] and the consonant
1200					
1300		[jẽ], [jã] and the consonant	[ɔ̃], [ũ], and the consonant	[uẽ] [wẽ], and the consonant	
1400	[ĩ] and the consonant				[ỹ] and the consonant
1500		[jẽ], [jã], [jɛ]	[ɔ̃], [ũ]		[ỹ], [œ̃], [y]
1600	[ĩ], [ɛ̃]				

CONSONANTS

	c + *e, i* *cité, ciel*	*ch* *chanter, cher*	*g* + *e, i* *rouge, argent*	initial *h*, in words marked * in modern dictionaries *haïr, honte*	*j* *jaloux joie*	*r* *rose, avril, finir*	*z* final *aimez*
1100	[ts]	[tʃ]	[dʒ]		[dʒ]		[ts]
1200							[s]
1300							
1400	[s]	[ʃ]	[ʒ]	[h]	[ʒ]	[r] (not [R])	silent except in liaison
1500							
1600							

al   [au] after 1150, as in *albe*
el   [eu] after 1150, as in *chevels*
il, ill   [λ], as in *travail, feuille*
l   silent when final, 1300–1500, except in liaison
r   silent when final, after ca. 1300, except in liaison or in the infinitive ending *-oir*; when pronounced, *r* receives a trill, as in modern Spanish and Italian.

rr   pronounced as a double consonant, as in *mourrai*
s   silent when final after ca. 1200, except in liaison, where it is [z]; followed by *f, l,* or *m, s* is silent after ca. 1050; followed by *t, k,* or *p, s* is silent after ca. 1150.
x   [us] when final, as in *Dex (Deus)*, in early texts, before ca. 1300

TABLE E-5.	Middle High German Pronunciation
a, â	[ɑ]
ä, ae	[ɛ]
ay	[aɪ]
e	[ɛ]
ê	[ɛ]; rarely [e]
ei	[ɛɪ]
eu	[œɪ]
i, î	[ɪ]
ie	[ɪə]; occasionally [ɪ] before r or l, or at the end of a word when followed by a stressed syllable
iu	[Y]
o	[ɔ]
ô	[ɔ]; rarely [o]
ö, oe	[œ]
oi	[œɪ]
ou	[ɔʊ]
öu	[œɪ]
u, û	[ʊ]; u often represents [v]
ü	[Y]
üe	[Yə]
uo	[ʊɔ]
b	[b]
ch	[x]
d	[d]
h	[h] beginning a syllable; [x] next to a consonant or at the end of a word
ng	[ŋg]
ph	[pf]
qu	[kw]
r	trilled [r]
sp	[sp]
st	[st]
w	[w]
ȝ	[s]

TABLE E-6.	Latin Pronunciation
a	[ɑ]
ae*	[e], [ɛ], or [ɛɪ]
e*	[e] or [ɛ]
i	[i]; [j] as a substitute for j
o	[ɔ]
oe*	[e], [ɛ], or [ɛɪ]
u*	[u]; sometimes [v]
y	[i]
c	[tʃ] before ae, e, i, oe, or y; otherwise [k]
cc	[tʃ] before e or i; otherwise [k]
ch	[k]
g	[dʒ] before ae, e, i, oe, or y; otherwise [g]
gg	[dʒ] before e or i; otherwise [g]
gn	[ɲ]
h	[k] between two i's; otherwise silent
j	[j]
r	rolled [r] initially; otherwise flipped
s*	[s]; perhaps [z] between two vowels
sc	[ʃ] before ae, e, i, or oe; otherwise [sk]
t	[ts] before ia, ie, io, or iu, unless t follows s, t, or x, or unless the word is Greek; otherwise [t]
th	[t]
x	[ks] at end of word; [gs] or [gz] before a vowel, h, or s
xc*	[ksk] before a, o, or u; otherwise [kʃ] or perhaps [kstʃ]
z	[dz]

Table E-6 lists some common modern pronunciations of modern Latin spellings. An asterisk (*) marks spellings that receive more than one interpretation today. The table lists only differences from modern standard English.

LATIN

Latin, the international European language of the Middle Ages and Renaissance, was pronounced differently in each country where it was spoken. In 1528 Erasmus advocated a standardized pronunciation to facilitate communication. The Vatican Council of 1870 made the same recommendation, because of the diversity of local pronunciations at that time.

Modern singers use several approaches to Latin: an Italianate interpretation or a "Classical" pronunciation is favored in English-speaking countries. German singers have a distinctive style of Latin diction.

SPANISH

During the Middle Ages and Renaissance the Spanish language comprised many regional dialects, some of which persist today in modern forms. Castilian is the accepted form of modern Spanish. In the thirteenth century, the dialect of Galicia and Portugal was used for writing the Cantigas de Santa Maria.

The results of scholarly investigations into early Spanish have been published primarily in Spanish; little is available in English. The Bibliography includes some histories of Spanish, dictionaries, and a work on medieval Galician. Singers may wish to consult a specialist about Spanish pronunciations.

APPENDIX F
A Checklist of Performance Considerations

1. *Classification.* Composer, style period, form, sacred or secular, vocal or instrumental or combination, relationship to other compositions.

2. *Original Manuscript or Original Print. Symbols:* staff, clefs, accidentals, mensuration signs, notes, dots, rests, ligatures, plicas, note-grouping indications. *Text:* language(s), dialect(s), form, rhyme scheme, completeness, underlay, calligraphy, orthography, abbreviations, symbolism. *Other information:* arrangement on the page, marginal comments, correspondence of musical and textual forms, characteristics of the complete manuscript or print, history of the source. *Additional sources of the same piece:* If identical, what is the significance? If different, what are the nature and significance of differences? Which source is earliest? Which is preferable? Also consider contrafacta and instrumental settings of vocal pieces. *Other documents:* theoretical treatises, descriptions of performances, iconographic evidence, institutional records.

3. *Analysis of the Composition.* Formal structure, cadences, melodic modes, rhythmic modes, isorhythm (color and talea), hemiola, mensuration, proportions; number, range, and relationship of parts; voice-crossing, imitation, canon, consonance and dissonance, borrowed material, cantus firmus, refrain, word painting, overall qualities of movement and sound.

4. *Composer's Intention.* Who performed the piece originally? An established ensemble? For what occasion? How many and what pitches of voice or instrument per part? Are variant instrumentations possible? What temperaments were used? What is the ideal solution, considering occasion of first performance?

5. *Media. Instruments:* types, names, ranges, functions, techniques; use in the Church, in secular functions; doubling voice(s), or independent of voices, or accompaniment to voice(s); improvisation; sustained tenors; use of percussion; significance in art, symbolism. *Voices:* tone, technique, chapel choirs, secular professional singers, trained nobility, octave doubling, high voice—boys, men, women?

6. *Decisions for Performance.* Rhythm, tempo, phrasing, articulation, timbre, tone, vibrato, intonation and inflection, temperament, *musica ficta* (*falsa*), transposition, doubling at pitch or octave, balance, dynamics; treatment of structural features such as hemiola, isorhythm, borrowed material, refrain, canon; changes in tempo or in other elements, contrast or homogeneity of sounds, ornamentation, improvisation, word accent, pronunciation, text underlay.

Abbreviations

The following abbreviations will be used throughout the Notes and Bibliography sections.

ACR	*American Choral Review*	JM	*Journal of Musicology*
Acta	*Acta Musicologica*	MD	*Musica Disciplina*
AM	*Annales Musicologiques*	ML	*Music and Letters*
CM	*Current Musicology*	MQ	*Musical Quarterly*
CMS	*College Music Symposium*	MT	*Musical Times*
EM	*Early Music*	NG	*The New Grove Dictionary of Music and Musicians.* Edited by Stanley Sadie. 20 vols. London: Macmillan, 1980.
GSJ	*Galpin Society Journal*		
JAMS	*Journal of the American Musicological Society*	PRMA	*Proceedings of the Royal Musical Association*
JVdGSA	*Journal of the Viola da Gamba Society of America*	RB	*Revue Belge de Musicologie*

Notes

The full citation for all sources listed in the notes can be found in the Bibliography.

Chapter 1. The Collegium Musicum.

1. See Kottick, *The Collegium: A Handbook*, the source of much information found in Chapter 1. See also Kottick, "State of Collegium"; Forney, ed., "Collegium Musicum"; and Blount, "Collegium Musicum."

Chapter 2. Resources for Performance.

1. See, for instance, Uberti, "Vocal Techniques"; von Ramm, "Style in Early Music Singing" and "Singing Early Music."

2. Regarding possible choral performance of ballate, chansons, laude, or conducti, see Brown, "Fantasia," 328–330; Hoppin, *Medieval Music*, 273, 294, 314, 343; and Reese, *Music in the Middle Ages*, 201–202, 220, 222, 237, 324.

3. For further information, see Craig Wright, "Voices and Instruments," 645–646, and "Performance Practices and Pedagogy at the Cathedral," 295–297, 308–311; Bray, "Performers' Guide"; Brown, "Choral Music in the Renaissance," 164–165; and d'Accone, "Performance of Sacred Music."

4. Craig Wright, "Voices and Instruments," 646, mentions the addition of instruments to court chapels.

5. See Brown, "Instruments and Voices," for references to women performers; also Borroff, "The Medium."

6. The authors have drawn primarily upon the following sources for the information concerning instruments that appears in this chapter and in Appendix B: Remnant, *Musical Instruments of the West*; Jeremy Montagu, *Medieval and Renaissance Musical Instruments*; Munrow, *Instruments of the Middle Ages and Renaissance*; Marcuse, *Musical Instruments* and *A Survey of Musical Instruments*; and Bachmann, *Origins of Bowing*.

7. Bachmann, *Origins of Bowing*, 78–81.

8. For specific information on maintenance, see, for instance, Karp, "Storage Climates for Musical Instruments"; Norris, "How to Get the Best"; Hanchet, "Adjustment and Control"; Willetts, "First Steps on the Shawm"; and Abbott and Segerman, "Gut Strings."

9. Comprehensive listings of recordings of early music may be found in the following discographies: Croucher, *Early Music Discography*; and Coover and Colvig, *Medieval and Renaissance Music*. See also Henry, *The Listener's Guide*.

Chapter 3. Approaches to Performing Medieval and Renaissance Music.

1. Ideas about "authentic" performance may be found in Taruskin et al., "Limits of Authenticity"; Dreyfus, "Early Music Defended"; Taruskin, "On Letting the Music Speak"; Planchart, "Performance of Early Music"; Morrow, "Musical Performance and Authenticity"; Jeremy Montagu, "'Authentic' Sound"; and Grout, "On Historical Authenticity."

Chapter 4. Primary Recommendations for Performance.

1. Hibberd, "On 'Instrumental Style.'"

2. Reese, *Music in the Renaissance*, 54, states that the melismas of Dufay's chansons appear to be instrumental. Many pictures show a trio of singer, flute or recorder, and lute or harp, as Brown states in "On the Performance," 6. Given that the harp or lute might play both the tenor and contratenor, the flute or recorder possibly performs the cantus part with the singer. Evidence for such performance on the lute in the early sixteenth century is cited by Brown, ed., *A Florentine Chansonnier*, text part, 168.

3. See Bray, "Performers' Guide," 437–439; Turner, "Scholarship and Performance," 203;

Craig Wright, "Performance Practices at the Cathedral," 308–311; and Kramme, "Notes on Renaissance Performance Practice," 10.

4. See, for example, Mendel, "Pitch in Western Music," 63–64; and Bray, "More Light on Early Tudor Pitch."

5. See Grocheo, *Concerning Music (De musica)*, 19; Weaver, "Sixteenth-Century Instrumentation"; Lampl, "*Syntagma Musicum III*," 202; and Bowles, "*Haut and Bas*."

6. Weber, "Some Researches into Pitch."

7. See Mendel, "Pitch in Western Music," 26–33.

8. See, for instance, Bowers, "Performing Pitch of English Polyphony," 27; Caldwell, "The 'Te Deum,'" 191–192; Mendel, "Pitch in Western Music," 58–63; and Cramer, "Significance of Clef Combinations."

9. See Lindley, "Temperaments," 661.

10. See Lindley, "Pythagorean Intonation" and "Evidence for Meantone Temperament."

11. Herlinger, "Marchetto's Division of the Whole Tone," 206.

12. For example, particular works by Johannes Ciconia, Guillaume Costeley, and Nicola Vicentino.

13. See Lowinsky, *Secret Chromatic Art*.

14. Gable, "Possibilities for Mean-Tone Temperament," presents information from Ganassi, Bermudo, et al.

Chapter 5. Rhythm.

1. See, for instance, Yudkin, "The Rhythm of Organum Purum"; Tischler, "A Propos Meter and Rhythm"; Roesner, "The Performance of Parisian Organum," 183–187; Treitler, "Regarding Meter and Rhythm"; Tischler, "On Transcribing the *Magnus Liber*"; Werf, *Chansons of the Troubadours and Trouvères*, Chapter 3; Maddrell, "*Mensura* and Rhythm"; and Waite, *Rhythm of Twelfth-Century Polyphony*.

2. See Michael Collins, "Performance of Sesquialtera and Hemiolia," for examples and information regarding both notations.

3. Sachs, *Rhythm and Tempo*, 217, cites Ramis de Pareia.

4. Brown, "Tactus."

5. For instance, Sachs, *Rhythm and Tempo*,

219; Reese, *Music in the Renaissance*, 179, n. 151; and Brown, "Tactus."

6. Glarean, *Dodecachordon*, pt. 2: 234.

7. Brown and McKinnon, "Performing Practice," 380.

Chapter 6. Musica Ficta.

1. Information in this chapter relies primarily on the conclusions of Margaret Bent, "Musica Ficta" and "Musica Recta and Musica Ficta."

2. Apel, *Harvard Dictionary of Music*. For more information consult Sadie, ed., *New Grove Dictionary*.

3. Margaret Bent, "Musica Recta and Musica Ficta," 83, cites Ugolino of Orvieto.

4. Margaret Bent, "Musica Recta and Musica Ficta," 97–100.

5. Margaret Bent, "Musica Ficta," 804, mentions this last possibility.

6. Margaret Bent, "Musica Recta and Musica Ficta," 87.

7. Lowinsky, "Function of Conflicting Signatures," 254–256.

8. See Harrán, "New Evidence for Musica Ficta" and "More Evidence for Cautionary Signs."

9. The Enchiriadis treatises (ca. 900) and other early writings recommend avoiding the tritone; exceptions to this practice are illustrated by Prosdocimus de Beldemandis (ca. 1410); see Margaret Bent, "Musica Ficta," 805. See also Samuel, "Modality, Tonality, and *Musica Ficta*," 15–18.

10. Treatises by Jehan de Murs (fourteenth century), Magister Lambertus (thirteenth century), and the author of the *Quatuor principalia* (fourteenth century), as cited by Margaret Bent, "Musica Ficta," 805, and "Musica Recta and Musica Ficta," 93.

11. See Haar, "False Relations and Chromaticism."

12. Regarding *musica ficta* in the medieval motet, see Anderson, ed., *Compositions of the Bamberg Manuscript*, xxxvi–xxxvii.

13. Margaret Bent, "Musica Recta and Musica Ficta," 83.

14. Ibid., 76.

15. Ibid., 84.

16. Treatises by Johannes de Garlandia (thirteenth century) and Jehan de Murs (fourteenth century), as cited by Margaret Bent, "Musica Ficta," 805.

17. Jehan de Murs (fourteenth century); see Margaret Bent, "Musica Ficta," 805.

18. Samuel, "Modality, Tonality, and *Musica Ficta*," 22–24.

19. Lowinsky, Foreword to *Musica Nova*, ix; and Samuel, "Modality, Tonality, and *Musica Ficta*," 24.

20. Samuel, "Modality, Tonality, and *Musica Ficta*," 20; and Bray, "Interpretation of Musica Ficta," 36.

21. Margaret Bent, "Musica Recta and Musica Ficta," 92.

22. Ibid., 74–75, 77.

23. See Lowinsky, *Secret Chromatic Art*. In a preliminary report on her study of the subject of diatonic ficta, Margaret Bent, "Diatonic Ficta," proposed a method of applying rules of *musica ficta* that would have far-reaching consequences for the editing and performance of vocal music from the fourteenth through sixteenth centuries. It seems likely that future publications on the subject of *musica ficta* will lead performers and editors to reinterpret the application of some rules.

Chapter 7. Text Underlay.

1. Treatises by Anonymous (ca. 1440), Gafori (1496), Lanfranco (1553), Vicentino (1555), Zarlino (1558), Stocker (ca. 1570), and Luchini (after 1588) are discussed in the following publications: Atlas, "Paolo Luchini's *Della Musica*"; Harrán, "In Pursuit of Origins," "Vicentino and His Rules," and "New Light on the Question"; Lowinsky, Introduction to *Petrucci, Canti B* and "A Treatise on Text Underlay." The absence of an article on text underlay in *NG* may reflect the difficulty of making generalized statements on this topic.

2. For example, Howard Mayer Brown has derived a useful set of guidelines for text underlay in the fifteenth-century chanson; see Brown, ed., *A Florentine Chansonnier*, text part, 176–179.

3. Lanfranco, Zarlino, and Stocker observe this convention.

4. See Craig Wright, "Voices and Instruments," 647.

5. See note 1 for Chapter 7.

Chapter 8. Improvisation and Ornamentation.

1. Selected examples of ornamented music and improvisatory styles appear in Ferand, *Improvisation*.

2. Instructions by Anonymous XIII (thirteenth or fourteenth century) and John of Affligem (twelfth century) appear, respectively, in MacClintock, ed., *Readings in the History of Music*, 7–11, and Ian D. Bent, "A Twelfth-Century Extemporizing Technique."

3. Sanders, "Discant."

4. Dalglish, "The Origin of the Hocket," 3, argues that hocket was originally a way of improvising on a chant melody; he points out that theorists—for example, Walter Odington—mention both improvised and composed hocket (Ibid., 14, note 40).

5. Kanazawa, "Musical Style," 637.

6. See Maynard, "Heir Beginnis Countering."

7. Margaret Bent, "*Resfacta* and *Cantare Super Librum*"; the author refutes earlier interpretations of Tinctoris that advocate improvisation, perhaps in simultaneous polyphonic voices.

8. See references in Project 2 at the end of this chapter.

9. See Brown, *Embellishing Sixteenth-Century Music*.

10. For example, Giovanni Maffei, as cited in Brown, *Embellishing Sixteenth-Century Music*, 54; also Ludovico Zacconi, cited in MacClintock, *Readings in the History of Music*, 70.

11. See Duckles, "Florid Embellishment."

12. Roesner, "The Performance of Parisian Organum," 177.

13. See Reese, *Music in the Renaissance*, 147.

14. Regarding trills and later graces, see Brown, *Embellishing Sixteenth-Century Music*, Chapter 1.

Part III. The Early Music Repertory.

1. Hucke, "Gradual."

2. Reese, *Music in the Middle Ages*, 179.

3. Ibid., note 48.

4. Pp. 22–47; see the citation under "Other transcriptions," preceding Example III–1.

5. Dalglish, "The Origin of the Hocket," 10.

6. Ibid., 11–12.

7. Brunner, "The Performance of Plainchant," 320–321; the article reproduces some of the manuscript evidence.

8. For further discussion of the arguments for each approach, see Brunner, "The Performance of Plainchant," 317–324; Berry, "Liturgical Chant" and "Gregorian Chant," 199–207; and Apel, *Gregorian Chant*, 126–132.

9. Reese, *Music in the Middle Ages*, 178–179, describes the three preceding forms.

10. Hoppin, *Medieval Music*, 127, describes these latter forms.

11. All biographical dates cited in Part III have been taken from *NG*.

12. For instance, Tischler, "On Transcribing the *Magnus Liber*"; and Waite, *Rhythm of Twelfth-Century Polyphony*.

13. For example, Yudkin, "The Rhythm of Organum Purum"; Levy, "A Dominican Organum Duplum," 197, 207, contrasts the freer rhythm of Leonin's time with the measured rhythm of late organum.

14. See Bowles, "Were Musical Instruments Used"; also McKinnon, "Musical Instruments," 4.

15. See McKinnon, "Polemic against Musical Instruments".

16. See McKinnon, "Musical Instruments," 12.

17. Bowles, "Organ in the Service," 20.

18. Roesner, "The Performance of Parisian Organum," 174.

19. Bowles, "Organ in the Service," 20.

20. For instance, Van Wye, "Ritual Use of the Organ," 288.

21. Peter Williams, *New History of the Organ*, 46.

22. See Roesner, "The Performance of Parisian Organum," 175.

23. For a table of consonances according to Johannes de Garlandia, see Yudkin, "The Rhythm of Organum Purum," 375. Exceptions provided by Anonymous IV to this principle are listed by Yudkin, "The Rhythm of Organum Purum," 373–374.

24. Hoppin, *Medieval Music*, 242.

25. Ibid., 245–246.

26. Ibid., 250–251.

27. Reese, *Music in the Middle Ages*, 307, appears to favor this solution.

28. Ibid., 324, mentions this possibility; see also Bowles, "Organ in the Service," 21, note 3.

29. Hoppin, *Medieval Music*, 245.

30. Ibid., 245.

31. This discussion of the liturgical context is based on information in Ibid., 94–96, and in Anderson, ed., *Latin Compositions*, pt. 1: 33.

32. Bowles, "Organ in the Service," 22, supports the concept of doubling but doubts the likelihood of purely instrumental tenors. See the discussion preceding Example III–2.

33. See Anderson, "Notation of Manuscripts," 19 et passim.

34. See Reese, *Music in the Middle Ages*, 312; and Seay, *Music in the Medieval World*, 113.

35. See Grocheo, *Concerning Music (De musica)*, 19–20.

36. Peter Jeffery, "A Four-Part *In seculum*," 17, note 30.

37. For example, Hoppin, *Medieval Music*, 349.

38. Apel, *Harvard Dictionary of Music*, 389.

39. Peter Jeffery, "A Four-Part *In seculum*," 18–19, refers to Jerome of Moravia.

40. For example, Dalglish, "The Origin of the Hocket," 4.

41. Peter Jeffery, "A Four-Part *In seculum*," 17–18.

42. See Apel, *Notation of Polyphonic Music*, 318–324.

43. For example, Grout, *A History of Western Music*, 103; see also Hoppin, *Medieval Music*, 341, regarding instrumental performance of textless tenors borrowed from trouvère chansons and dances.

44. Reese, *Music in the Middle Ages*, 322.

45. Ibid., 323–324, suggests these three options.

46. Hoppin, *Medieval Music*, 342–343, suggests these two options.

47. Ibid., 369–370, describes the MS.

48. See Fallows, *Dufay*, 118, on thirteenth-and fourteenth-century motets.

49. Christopher Page has found evidence to suggest that French vocal music ca. 1300 should be transposed down a fourth; see Holman, Report on Symposium, 8.

50. See Page, "Machaut's 'Pupil.'"

51. See, for instance, Grout, *A History of Western Music*, 124; Reese, *Music in the Middle Ages*, 353; Reaney, "Voices and Instruments," 94; Seay, *Music in the Medieval World*, 144; and Hoppin, *Medieval Music*, 432.

52. See Page, "Machaut's 'Pupil,'" 490, note 24.

53. Support comes from Reaney, "Voices and Instruments," 96–97, 103; rejection from Godwin, "'Main divers acors,'" 159.

54. Bowles, "Musical Instruments at the Medieval Banquet," 48 and 48, note 3; instrumental arrangements of works by Machaut and other fourteenth-century composers appear in Codex Faenza 117.

55. Godwin, "'Main divers acors,'" 158.

56. Hoppin, *Medieval Music*, 474–475.

57. Ibid., 476.

58. Reaney, "Philippus de Caserta," 653.

59. von Fischer, "Giovanni da Cascia," 400.

60. See Pettit, Review, 7; see also Fallows, Review.

61. See, for instance, Reese, *Music in the Middle Ages*, 367.

62. Grout, *A History of Western Music*, 133, cites this as a possibility.

63. Reese, *Music in the Middle Ages*, 384–385.

64. Marrocco, ed., *Italian Secular Music*, xvi.

65. Brown, "Fantasia."

66. White, "Performing Fourteenth-Century Music," 86.

67. See Pirrotta, ed., *Maestro Piero*, ii–iii; the attribution is on stylistic grounds.

68. von Fischer, "Caccia," 576.

69. For example, Lowinsky, "Canon Technique," 639; Hoppin, *Medieval Music*, 443; and Grout, *A History of Western Music*, 130.

70. Nádas, "Structure of MS Panciatichi 26," 394, 409, et passim.

71. von Fischer, "Ballata," 88, defines various types of ballata.

72. Ibid, 87.

73. Schrade, *Commentary to Volume IV*, 112.

74. Hoppin, *Medieval Music*, 459–461.

75. See Nádas, "Structure of MS Panciatichi 26," 422–427.

76. For instance, Hoppin, *Medieval Music*, 459–460.

77. Grout, *A History of Western Music*, 133.

78. Reese, *Music in the Middle Ages*, 386.

79. Margaret Bent, *Dunstable*, iv.

80. See Ibid., 1, 6; also Hoppin, *Medieval Music*, 522.

81. Margaret Bent, *Dunstable*, 87.

82. See Hughes, "Mensural Polyphony," 362 et passim; see also Hughes, "Non-Mensural Polyphony."

83. See Craig Wright, *Music at the Court of Burgundy*, 52, note 205.

84. See Fallows, *Dufay*, 19.

85. Reese, *Music in the Renaissance*, 764.

86. Brown, *Music in the Renaissance*, 21.

87. John Stevens, "Carol," 807. Caldwell, *Medieval Music*, 215, questions both the participation of a chorus in carols and their use in processions.

88. Bukofzer, *Studies*, 154, states this and also raises the possibility that the sign represents a chorus section omitted by the scribe.

89. See Bukofzer, Review, 63.

90. Reese, *Music in the Renaissance*, 10.

91. Fallows, *Dufay*, 255.

92. Ibid., 99.

93. See note 2, Chapter 4.

94. See Page, "Performance of Songs," 449; Fallows, *Dufay*, 4, 87, 132; and Leech-Wilkinson, Review.

95. This approach is taken by the singers reviewed in Leech-Wilkinson, Review, 559.

96. Craig Wright, "Voices and Instruments," 644, 648; also Brown, "Instruments and Voices," 93.

97. Craig Wright, "Voices and Instruments," 644, 648; and Brown, "On the Performance," 5.

98. Perkins, "Toward a Rational Approach," 104.

99. Brown, "Instruments and Voices," 104–106, and "On the Performance," 5.

100. Page, "Performance of Songs," 447, 449; and Brown, "On the Performance," 5.

101. Brown, "On the Performance," 5.

102. Brown, ed., *A Florentine Chansonnier*, text part, 168, and Ibid.

103. Brown, "On the Performance," 5.

104. Brown, "Instruments and Voices," 112.

105. Brown, ed., *A Florentine Chansonnier*, text part, 57–58.

106. Brown, *Music in the Renaissance*, 73–74, 79.

107. See McKinnon, "Representations of the Mass," 22, 48, 49, on *a cappella* singing.

108. See Grout, *A History of Western Music*, 187.

109. Litterick, "Performing Franco-Netherlandish Secular Music." See also Litterick, "On Italian Instrumental Ensemble Music"; and Edwards, "Songs without Words."

110. Brown, ed., *A Florentine Chansonnier*, text part, 168; and Litterick, "Performing Franco-Netherlandish Secular Music," 478–480.

111. Reese, *Music in the Renaissance*, 224, mentions the borrowed tune.

112. Wess, "Bossinensis."

113. Rubsamen, "From Frottola to Madrigal," 55, 57.

114. Prizer, "Performance Practices in the Frottola," 230–232.

115. Ibid., 232.

116. Advice regarding text underlay appears in Ibid., 233–234.

117. Brown, "Eustachio Romano."

118. See Bellingham, "Bicinium," 693.

119. Brown, *Music in the Renaissance*, 243–244, refers to the genre as *court songs*.

120. See the list in Russell, *Harpsichord and Clavichord*, 155–160; see also Reese, *Music in the Renaissance*, 867.

121. John Stevens, ed., *Music at the Court*, xix.

122. Edwards, "Instrumental Music," 276.

123. Bernstein, "Gervaise, Claude," 309.

124. Arbeau, *Orchesography*, 130, 224.

125. Ibid., 132–133.

126. Göllner, "Ott, Hans," 22.

127. Reese, *Music in the Renaissance*, 678–679.

128. Böker-Heil, "Tenorlied."

129. Reese, *Music in the Renaissance*, 684.

130. Brown, *Music in the Renaissance*, 274.

131. Neugent, "Gombert, Nicolas," 512.

132. Brown, *Music in the Renaissance*, 188.

133. Schmidt-Görg, ed., *Magnificat*, Foreword (unnumbered pages).

134. Apel, *Harvard Dictionary of Music*, 500.

135. Ibid., 591.

136. Ibid., 500.

137. Reese, *Music in the Renaissance*, 346.

138. Rumery, "Music at Seville," 16–17; also McKinnon, "Representations of the Mass," 50.

139. See Rumery, "Music at Seville," 11, 13.

140. Ibid., 14.

141. McKinnon, "Representations of the Mass," 51.

142. Brown, *Music in the Renaissance*, 222, and *Embellishing Sixteenth-Century Music*, 59.

143. Brown, *Embellishing Sixteenth-Century Music*, 57.

144. Ibid., 59.

145. Stevenson, "Ortiz, Diego," 875.

146. McKee, "Maschera, Florentio."

147. Bartlett and Holman, "Giovanni Gabrieli," 27; and Selfridge-Field, "Bassano and the Orchestra," 156–157.

148. Reese, *Music in the Renaissance*, 874.

149. Solutions to this problem have been proposed by Bernard Thomas, "The Renaissance Flute," 9–10; Harwood, "A Case of Double Standards?" 478; and Myers, "Instrumental Pitch in England *c*1600," 521.

150. Foster, "Ward," 210.

151. Dodd, Letter.

152. W. K. Lowther Clark, *Liturgy and Worship*, 856, states that the Penitential Psalms were recited on Ash Wednesday.

153. Regarding Tomkins's choirs, see Cavanaugh, ed., *Thomas Tomkins, Thirteen Anthems*, xiii.

154. See Mendel, "Pitch in Western Music,"

65; and Cavanaugh, ed., *Thomas Tomkins, Thirteen Anthems*, xii.

155. Denis Stevens, *Thomas Tomkins, 1572–1656*, 87.

156. Ibid.

Appendix A. Other Genres of Medieval and Renaissance Music.

1. Problems of interpreting the sources have been discussed by Parker, "Performance of Troubadour and Trouvère Songs"; Werf, *Chansons of the Troubadours and Trouvères*, and "Concerning the Measurability"; and Madrell, "*Mensura* and the Rhythm."

2. See Crane, "On Performing the '*Lo Estampies*,'" 31, regarding the logic of examining European folk music.

3. Modern scholars generally reject the notion of "Southern" style, owing to the lack of concrete evidence of Moorish influence on performance practice. Because Moorish influences on sciences, letters, and the arts (including musical instruments) profoundly affected the culture of Spain, some modern performers have extrapolated a similar influence on musical performance practice. For information on Andalusian Arabic styles of performance, see Malm, *Music Cultures*, Chapter 3; and Pacholczyk, "Secular Classical Music."

4. See Crane, "On Performing the '*Lo Estampies*,'" 31, regarding the improbability of Arabic dance style in Europe.

5. Hoppin, *Medieval Music*, 351.

6. For important studies of the basse danse, see Gombosi, "About Dance and Dance Music"; Bukofzer, *Studies*, 190–216; Ward, "The Maner of Dauncynge"; see also notes 7–12, which follow.

7. See Crane, *Materials for Study*, 33–61; and Heartz, "The Basse Dance."

8. See Apel, "A Remark about the Basse Danse"; and Heartz, "Hoftanz and Basse Dance."

9. Heartz, "Hoftanz and Basse Dance," 14, 15, 17, 26.

10. Mullally, "Polyphonic Theory of the *Basse Danse*," 246–248, and "Polyphonic Theory of the *Bassa Danza*," 9.

11. Rooley, "Dance and Dance Music," 79–80.

12. Crane, *Materials for Study*, 114–117, lists 19 artistic representations, which he identifies as *basse danses*, showing various instruments accompanying.

13. See Bowles, "*Haut and Bas*."

14. For information on the performance of liturgical drama, see Bowles, "Role of Musical Instruments"; Fletcher Collins, Jr., *Production of Medieval Church Music-Drama*; and Smoldon, *Music of Medieval Church Dramas*, 478, 490–496.

Appendix B. Principal Instruments of the Middle Ages and Renaissance.

1. The figures in Appendix B, executed by Elizabeth Blair Matisz, are drawn from a variety of sources: treatises, paintings, sculptures, photographs, and (in a few cases) modern reproductions. The figures are intended to illustrate general characteristics more than specific examples; for this reason, some illustrations are composites. See also note 6, Chapter 2.

2. Marcuse, *A Survey of Musical Instruments*, 215.

3. Jeremy Montagu, *Medieval and Renaissance Musical Instruments*, 13–14.

4. See Laurence Wright, "Medieval Gittern and Citole."

5. Ibid., 29.

6. Page, "Jerome of Moravia," 82.

7. See Woodfield, "Early History of the Viol."

8. Brown, "Notes on the Viol," examines evidence from treatises by Argicola (1528), Ganassi (1542/43), and Gerle (1546). Harwood, "A Case of Double Standards?" 470–477, suggests two sets of viol sizes, a fourth apart. Andrew Parrott argues for playing English viol music a fourth lower than notated; see Harwood, "A Case of Double Standards?" 481, note 19, and Holman, Report on Symposium, 8.

9. See Edmunds, "Venetian Viols"; Harwood, "An Introduction to Renaissance Viols"; and Harwood and Edmunds, "Reconstructing Sixteenth-Century Venetian Viols."

10. Boyden, *History of Violin Playing*, 4, 49–64.

11. See Ripin, "Towards an Identification";

Page, "The Myth of the Chekker"; Meeùs, "Keyboard Scholarship" and Page's reply.

12. Wraight, "Italian Harpsichords."

13. Bernard Thomas, "The Renaissance Flute."

14. See Marcuse, *Musical Instruments*, 438, on twelfth-century documentation; regarding the fourteenth-century specimens, see Weber, "Recorder Finds."

15. Weber, "Tournebout-Pifia-Bladderpipe (*Platerspiel*)," 68.

16. For information on this instrument, see Frances Palmer, "Musical Instruments from the *Mary Rose*"; and Myers, "The *Mary Rose* 'Shawm.'" Further information on the douçaine appears in Boydell, *Crumhorn and Other Windcap Instruments*, 404–408.

17. Regarding the conjectural nature of the cornamuse, see Macmillan, "The Mysterious Cornamuse"; Fallows, Letter; Moeck, Letter; and Boydell, Letter.

18. Downey, "Renaissance Slide Trumpet," argues that this trumpet did not slide. Figure B-43 depicts a modern reconstruction that exhibits a more flared bell than would have been likely on a period instrument.

Bibliography

Abbott, Djilda, and Ephraim Segerman. "Gut Strings." *EM* 4 (1976): 430–437.

Abrams, Meyer H., ed. *The Norton Anthology of English Literature.* 3rd ed. 2 vols. New York: Norton, 1974.

Algeo, John, and Thomas Pyles. *Problems in the Origins and Development of the English Language.* New York: Harcourt, Brace, and World, 1966.

Allaire, Gaston. "Peculiar Signatures in Fourteenth-, Fifteenth-, and Sixteenth-Century Sources." *Canadian Association of University Schools of Music Journal* 7 (1977): 52–90.

————. *The Theory of Hexachords, Solmization, and the Modal System.* Musicological Studies and Documents, vol. 24. N.p.: American Institute of Musicology, 1972.

Allen, W. Sidney. *Vox Latina: A Guide to the Pronunciation of Classical Latin.* Cambridge: Cambridge University Press, 1965.

Alton, Jeannine, and Brian Jeffery. *Bele buche e bele parleure: A Guide to the Pronunciation of Medieval and Renaissance French for Singers and Others.* London: Tecla Editions, 1976.

Anderson, Gordon A. "The Notation of the Bamberg and Las Huelgas Manuscripts." *MD* 32 (1978): 19–67.

————. "The Rhythm of the Monophonic Conductus in the Florence Manuscript As Indicated in Parallel Sources in Mensural Notation." *JAMS* 31 (1978): 480–489.

————, ed. *Compositions of the Bamberg Manuscript.* Corpus Mensurabilis Musicae, vol. 75. N.p.: American Institute of Musicology, 1977.

————, ed. *The Latin Compositions in Fascicules VII and VIII of the Notre Dame Manuscript Wolfenbüttel Helmstadt 1099 (1206).* Musicological Studies, vol. 24. Brooklyn: Institute of Mediaeval Music, n.d.

————, ed. *Motets of the Manuscript La Clayette, Paris, Bibliothèque Nationale, nouv. acq. f. fr. 13521.* Corpus Mensurabilis Musicae, vol. 68. N.p.: American Institute of Musicology, 1975.

Apel, Willi. *Gregorian Chant.* Bloomington: Indiana University Press, 1958.

————. *Harvard Dictionary of Music.* 2nd ed. Cambridge: Belknap Press of Harvard University Press, 1969.

————. *The History of Keyboard Music to 1700.* Translated and edited by Hans Tischler. Bloomington: Indiana University Press, 1972.

————. *The Notation of Polyphonic Music, 900–1600.* 5th ed., rev. Cambridge, MA: Medieval Academy of America, 1961.

————. "The Partial Signatures in the Sources up to 1450." *Acta* 10 (1938): 1–13.

————. "A Remark about the Basse Danse." *Journal of Renaissance and Baroque Music* 1 (1946/47): 139–143.

————, ed. *French Secular Music of the Late Fourteenth Century.* Cambridge, MA: Medieval Academy of America, 1950.

Aplin, John. "The Survival of Plainsong in Anglican Music: Some Early English Te-Deum Settings." *JAMS* 32 (1979): 247–275.

Arbeau, Thoinot [Jehan Tabourot]. *Orchesography.* Translated by Mary Stewart Evans and revised by Julia Sutton. 2nd ed. New York: Dover, 1967.

Arnold, Denis. "Brass Instruments in Italian Church Music of the Sixteenth and Early Seventeenth Centuries." *Brass Quarterly* 1 (1957/58): 81–92.

————. "Con ogni sorte di stromenti." *EM* 4 (1976): 167–171.

————. "The Grand Motets of Orlandus Lassus." *EM* 6 (1978): 170–181.

Atlas, Allan. "Paolo Luchini's *Della Musica:* A Little-Known Source for Text Underlay from the Late Sixteenth Century." *JM* 2 (1983): 62–80.

Avenary, Hanoch. "The Northern and Southern Idioms of Early European Music: A New Approach to an Old Problem." *Acta* 49 (1977): 27–49.

Bachmann, Werner. *The Origins of Bowing and the Development of Bowed Instruments up to the Thirteenth Century.* Translated by Norma Deane. London: Oxford University Press, 1969.

Baines, Anthony, ed. *Musical Instruments Through the Ages.* Baltimore: Penguin, 1961.

Baines, Francis. "Introducing the Hurdy-Gurdy." *EM* 3 (1975): 33–37.

Ball, Christopher. "Renaissance and Baroque Recorders: Choosing an Instrument." *EM* 3 (1975): 11–19.

Barbour, James Murray. *Tuning and Temperament: A Historical Survey.* 2nd ed. East Lansing: Michigan State College Press, 1953.

Bartlett, Clifford, and Peter Holman. "Giovanni Gabrieli: A Guide to the Performance of His Instrumental Music." *EM* 3 (1975): 25–32.

Beck, Sydney, ed. *The First Book of Consort Lessons, Collected by Thomas Morley, 1599 and 1611.* New York: C. F. Peters for the New York Public Library, 1959.

Bedbrook, G. S. "The Problem of Instrumental Combination in the Middle Ages." *RB* 25 (1971): 53–67.

Bellingham, Bruce A. "Bicinium." *NG* 2: 692–694.

Bent, Ian D. "A Twelfth-Century Extemporizing Technique." *MT* 111 (1970): 33–37.

Bent, Margaret. "Diatonic Ficta." Paper presented at the annual meeting of the American Musicological Society, Louisville, October 1983.

———. *Dunstaple.* Oxford Studies of Composers, no. 17. London: Oxford University Press, 1981.

———. "Musica Ficta, I, i–iv." NG 12: 802–806.

———. "Musica Recta and Musica Ficta." MD 26 (1972): 73–100.

———. "The Old Hall Manuscript." EM 2 (1974): 2–14.

———. "*Resfacta* and *Cantare Super Librum.*" JAMS 36 (1983): 371–391.

Bernstein, Lawrence F. "Gervaise, Claude." NG 7: 309–310.

Berry, Mary. "Gregorian Chant: The Restoration of the Chant and Seventy-five Years of Recording." EM 7 (1979): 197–217.

———. "Liturgical Chant." *Gramophone* 59, no. 703 (December 1981): 861–862.

———. "The Practice of Alternatim: Organ-Playing and Polyphony in the Fifteenth and Sixteenth Centuries with Special Reference to the Choir of Notre-Dame de Paris." *Diapason* 859 (June 1981): 5–11.

Besseler, Heinrich, and Peter Gülke. *Schriftbild der mehrstimmigen Musik.* Musikgeschichte in Bildern, vol. 3, pt. 5. Leipzig: Deutscher Verlag für Musik, 1973.

Blades, James. "Percussion Instruments of the Middle Ages and Renaissance." EM 1 (1973): 11–18.

Blades, James, and Jeremy Montagu. "Capriol's Revenge." EM 1 (1973): 84–92.

———. *Early Percussion Instruments: From the Middle Ages to the Baroque.* Early Music Series, no. 2. London: Oxford University Press, 1976.

Blezzard, Judith. "Editing Early English, Some Further Evidence." MT 119 (1978): 265–268.

Blount, Gilbert. "The Collegium Musicum: Complacency or Commitment?" CMS 15 (1975): 70–77.

Blume, Friedrich, ed. *Die Musik in Geschichte und Gegenwart.* 14 vols. and supplements. Kassel: Bärenreiter, 1949–1968; supplements, 1968-

Boase, Roger. *The Origin and Meaning of Courtly Love: A Critical Study of European Scholarship.* Manchester: Manchester University Press, 1977.

Böker-Heil, Norbert. "Tenorlied." NG 18: 691.

Bonnin, G. M. *A Phonetic System for Middle High German.* University of Queensland Papers, vol. 1, no. 3. Brisbane: University of Queensland Press, 1960.

Borroff, Edith. "The Medium." CMS 10 (1970): 112–113.

———, ed. *Notations and Editions: A Book in Honor of Louise Cuyler.* Dubuque: Wm. C. Brown, 1974.

Bouterse, Curtis. "Reconstructing the Medieval Arabic Lute: A Reconsideration of Farmer's *Structures of the Arabic and Persian Lute.*" GSJ 32 (1979): 2–9.

Bowers, Roger. "The Performing Pitch of English Fif-

teenth-Century Church Polyphony." EM 8 (1980): 21–28.

Bowles, Edmund A. "*Haut* and *Bas*: The Grouping of Musical Instruments in the Middle Ages." MD 8 (1954): 115–140.

———. "Instruments at the Court of Burgundy (1363–1467)." GSJ 6 (1953): 41–51.

———. "Musical Instruments at the Medieval Banquet." RB 12 (1958): 41–51.

———. "The Organ in the Medieval Liturgical Service." RB 16 (1962): 13–29.

———. *La pratique musicale au Moyen Age: Musical Performance in the Late Middle Ages.* N.p.: Minkoff and Lattès, 1983.

———. "The Role of Musical Instruments in Medieval Sacred Drama." MQ 45 (1959): 67–84.

———. "Were Musical Instruments Used in the Liturgical Service during the Middle Ages?" GSJ 10 (1957): 40–56.

Boydell, Barra. *The Crumhorn and Other Renaissance Windcap Instruments: A Contribution to Renaissance Organology.* Buren: Frits Knuf, 1982.

———. "The Instruments in Mielich's Miniature of the Munich *Hofkapelle* under Orlando di Lasso." *Tijdschrift van de Vereniging voor Nederlandse Muziekgeschiedenis* 28 (1978): 14–18.

———. Letter. EM 7 (1979): 431–433.

Boyden, David. *The History of Violin Playing from Its Origins to 1761 and Its Relationship to the Violin and Violin Music.* London: Oxford University Press, 1965.

Bray, Roger. "The Interpretation of Musica Ficta in English Music c.1490–c.1580." PRMA 97 (1970/71): 29–45.

———. "More Light on Early Tudor Pitch." EM 8 (1980): 35–42.

———. "Performers' Guide." EM 6 (1978): 437–441.

Brittain, Frederick. *Latin in Church: Episodes in the History of Its Pronunciation.* 2nd ed. Alcuin Club Tracts, no. 28. London: A. R. Mowbray, 1955.

Brown, Howard Mayer. "Choral Music in the Renaissance." EM 6 (1978): 164–169.

———. "Continental Sacred Music of the Sixteenth Century." EM 3 (1975): 373–377.

———. *Embellishing Sixteenth-Century Music.* Early Music Series, no. 1. London: Oxford University Press, 1976.

———. "Eustachio Romano." NG 6: 316.

———. "Fantasia on a Theme by Boccaccio." EM 5 (1977): 324–339.

———. "Guillaume Dufay and the Early Renaissance." EM 2 (1974): 218–233.

———. *Instrumental Music Printed before 1600: A Bibliography.* Cambridge, MA: Harvard University Press, 1965.

———. "Instruments and Voices in the Fifteenth-

Century Chanson." In *Current Thought in Musicology*, edited by John W. Grubbs, 89–137. Austin: University of Texas Press, 1976.

———. "Instruments of the Middle Ages and Renaissance: In Memoriam David Munrow." *EM* 4 (1976): 288–293.

———. *Music in the French Secular Theatre, 1400–1550*. Cambridge: Harvard University Press, 1963.

———. *Music in the Renaissance*. Englewood Cliffs, NJ: Prentice-Hall, 1976.

———. "Notes (and Transposing Notes) on the Viol in the Early Sixteenth Century." In *Music in Medieval and Early Modern Europe*, edited by Iain Fenlon, 61–78. Cambridge: Cambridge University Press, 1981.

———. "On the Performance of Fifteenth-Century Chansons." *EM* 1 (1973): 3–10.

———. *Sixteenth-Century Instrumentation: The Music for the Florentine Intermedii*. Musicological Studies and Documents, vol. 30. N.p.: American Institute of Musicology, 1973.

———. "Tactus." *NG* 18: 518.

———. "Training Early Musicians." *EM* 3 (1975): 218–219.

———, ed. *A Florentine Chansonnier from the Time of Lorenzo the Magnificent: Florence, Biblioteca Nazionale Centrale MS Banco Rari 229*. Monuments of Renaissance Music, vol. 7. Chicago: University of Chicago Press, 1983.

Brown, Howard Mayer, and Joan Lascelle. *Musical Iconography: A Manual for Cataloguing Musical Subjects in Western Art before 1800*. Cambridge: Harvard University Press, 1972.

Brown, Howard Mayer, and James W. McKinnon. "Performing Practice." *NG* 14: 370–393.

Brunner, Lance W. "The Performance of Plainchant: Some Preliminary Observations of the New Era." *EM* 10 (1982): 317–328.

Bukofzer, Manfred. "Changing Aspects of Medieval and Renaissance Music." *MQ* 44 (1958): 1–18.

———. Review of *Medieval Carols*, edited by John Stevens. *JAMS* 7 (1954): 63–78.

———. *Studies in Medieval and Renaissance Music*. New York: Norton, 1950.

Byler, Arthur. "The Music for Cittern and Gittern in the Mulliner Book." *JAMS* 5 (1952): 142.

Caldwell, John. *English Keyboard Music before the Nineteenth Century*. New York: Praeger, 1973.

———. *Medieval Music*. London: Hutchinson, 1978.

———. "The 'Te Deum' in Late Medieval England." *EM* 6 (1978): 188–194.

Carpenter, Hoyle. "Tempo and Tactus in the Age of Cabezon." *Anuario Musical* 21 (1966): 123–130.

Carré Alvarellos, Leandro. *El idioma gallego en la edad media: Discurso leída en el acto de su recepción el día 3 de marzo de 1945*. Vigo: Artes Gráficas Galicia, 1973.

Carvell, Bruce Ray. "A Practical Guide to Musica Ficta Based on an Analysis of Sharps Found in the Music Prints of Ottaviano Petrucci (1501–1519)." Ph.D. dissertation, Washington University in St. Louis, 1982.

Casa, Girolamo dalla. *Il vero modo di diminuir con tutte le sorti di stromenti*. Venice: Angelo Gardano, 1584. Facsimile. Bologna: Forni, 1970.

Castellani, Marcello. "A 1593 Veronese Inventory." *GSJ* 26 (1973): 15–24.

Cavanaugh, Robert W., ed. *Thomas Tomkins, Thirteen Anthems*. Recent Researches in the Music of the Renaissance, vol. 4. New Haven: A-R Editions, 1968.

Chambers, Edmund K. *The Mediaeval Stage*. 2 vols. London: Oxford University Press, 1903.

Charlton, Andrew. "Embellishment in Renaissance and Baroque Music." *Soundboard* 9, no. 4 (Winter 1982–83): 335–339; 10, no. 1 (Spring 1983): 32–35; 10, no. 2 (Summer 1983): 132–135.

Clark, John Williams. *Early English: A Study of Old and Middle English*. Rev. ed. London: Andre Deutsch, 1967.

Clark, W. K. Lowther. *Liturgy and Worship: A Companion to the Prayer Books of the Anglican Communion*. London: SPCK, 1932.

Cohen, Albert. "A Study of Notational and Performance Problems of an Early *Air de cour: Je voudrois bien, ô Cloris* (1629) by Antoine Boësset (c.1586–1643)." In *Notations and Editions*, edited by Edith Borroff, 55–68. Dubuque: Wm. C. Brown, 1974.

Collins, Fletcher, Jr. *The Production of Medieval Church Music-Drama*. Charlottesville: University Press of Virginia, 1972.

———, ed. *Medieval Church Music-Dramas: A Repertory of Complete Plays*. Charlottesville: University Press of Virginia, 1976.

Collins, Michael. "The Performance of Sesquialtera and Hemiolia in the Sixteenth Century." *JAMS* 17 (1964): 5–28.

Coover, James, and Richard Colvig. *Medieval and Renaissance Music on Long-Playing Records*. Detroit Studies in Music Bibliography, no. 6. Detroit: Information Service, 1964. *Supplement, 1962–1971*. Detroit Studies, no. 26. Detroit: Information Coordinators, 1973.

Corominas, Joan. *Breve diccionario etimológico de la lengua castellana*. 2nd ed. Madrid: Editorial Gredos, 1967.

———. *Diccionario crítico etimológico de la lengua castellana*. 4 vols. Bern: Francke, 1954.

Cramer, Eugene. "The Significance of Clef Combinations in the Music of Tomás Luis de Victoria." *ACR* 18, no. 3 (July 1976): 3–11.

Crane, Frederick. *Extant Medieval Musical Instruments: A Provisional Catalogue by Types*. Iowa City: University of Iowa Press, 1972.

———. *Materials for the Study of the Fifteenth Century Basse Danse*. Musicological Studies, vol. 16. Brooklyn: Institute of Mediaeval Music, 1968.

———. "On Performing the 'Lo Estampies.'" EM 7 (1979): 25–33.

Crawford, David. "Musica Ficta." CMS 10 (1970): 107–111.

Crocker, Richard L. *A History of Musical Style*. New York: McGraw-Hill, 1966.

Croucher, Trevor. *Early Music Discography: From Plainsong to the Sons of Bach*. 2 vols. Phoenix: Oryx Press, 1981.

Cummings, Anthony M. "Toward an Interpretation of the Sixteenth-Century Motet." JAMS 34 (1981): 43–59.

Cuyler, Louise. *The Emperor Maximilian I and Music*. London: Oxford University Press, 1973.

d'Accone, Frank. "The Performance of Sacred Music in Italy during Josquin's Time, c. 1475–1525." In *Josquin des Prez*, edited by Edward E. Lowinsky, 601–618. London: Oxford University Press, 1976.

Dalglish, William. "The Hocket in Medieval Polyphony." MQ 55 (1969): 344–363.

———. "The Origin of the Hocket." JAMS 31 (1978): 3–20.

Dart, Thurston. "The Cittern and Its English Music." GSJ 1 (1948): 46–63.

———. *The Interpretation of Music*. London: Hutchinson's University Library, 1954.

Diagram Group. *Musical Instruments of the World: An Illustrated Encyclopedia*. N.p.: Paddington Press, 1976. Reprint. New York: Bantam, 1978.

Dodd, Gordon. Letter to author (Phillips), 10 March 1979.

Doe, Paul. "Another View of Musica Ficta in Tudor Music." PRMA 98 (1971/72): 113–122.

Donington, Robert. *The Interpretation of Early Music: New Version*. New York: St. Martin's Press, 1974.

Downey, Peter. "The Renaissance Slide Trumpet: Fact or Fiction?" EM 12 (1984): 26–33.

Dreyfus, Laurence. "Early Music Defended Against Its Devotees: A Theory of Historical Performance in the Twentieth Century." MQ 69 (1983): 297–322.

Dronke, Peter. *The Medieval Lyric*. 2nd ed. Cambridge: Cambridge University Press, 1977.

Duckles, Vincent. "Florid Embellishment in English Song of the Late Sixteenth and Early Seventeenth Centuries." AM 5 (1957): 329–345.

Dunn, Charles W., and Edward T. Byrnes. *Middle English Literature*. New York: Harcourt Brace Jovanovich, 1973.

Edmunds, Martin. "Venetian Viols of the Sixteenth Century." GSJ 33 (1980): 74–91.

Edwards, Warwick. "The Instrumental Music of Henry VIII's Manuscript." *Consort* 34 (1978): 274–282.

———. "Songs without Words by Josquin and His Contemporaries." In *Music in Medieval and Early Modern Europe*, edited by Iain Fenlon, 79–92. Cambridge: Cambridge University Press, 1981.

Einstein, Alfred. *The Italian Madrigal*. Translated by Alexander H. Krappe, Roger H. Sessions, and Oliver Strunk. 3 vols. Princeton: Princeton University Press, 1949. Reprint. 1971.

Falck, Robert. *The Notre Dame Conductus: A Study of the Repertory*. Musicological Studies, vol. 33. Henryville, PA: Institute of Mediaeval Music, 1981.

Fallows, David. *Dufay*. The Master Musicians Series. London: J. M. Dent and Sons, 1982.

———. "Early English." MT 118 (1977): 949–952.

———. Letter. EM 7 (1979): 135.

———. Review of Machaut Songs [*The Mirror of Narcissus*]. Gothic Voices, directed by Christopher Page. *Gramophone* 61, no. 728 (January 1984): 898.

Farrell, Peter. "Diego Ortiz' *Tratado de glosas*." JVdGSA 4 (1967): 5–9.

Fenlon, Iain, ed. *Music in Medieval and Early Modern Europe: Patronage, Sources, and Texts*. Cambridge: Cambridge University Press, 1981.

Ferand, Ernest T. *Improvisation in Nine Centuries of Western Music*. Anthology of Music, vol. 12. Cologne: Arno Volk Verlag, 1961.

———. "Improvised Vocal Counterpoint in the Late Renaissance and Early Baroque." AM 4 (1956): 129–174.

Finscher, Ludwig. "Historical Reconstruction versus Structural Interpretation in the Performance of Josquin's Motets." In *Josquin des Prez*, edited by Edward E. Lowinsky, 627–632. London: Oxford University Press, 1976.

Fitzpatrick, Horace. "The Medieval Recorder." EM 3 (1975): 361–364.

Ford, Terence. "Index to the Facsimiles of Polyphonic Music before 1600 Published in *Die Musik in Geschichte und Gegenwart*." *Notes* 39 (1982–83): 283–315.

Forney, Kristine, ed. "The Collegium Musicum: A Survey of Thirty-two American Universities." CM 22 (1976): 24–40.

Foster, Michael W. "Ward, John." NG 20: 210–211.

Frischmann, Charles. "What is This Thing Called Organum?" *Journal of Church Music* 17, no. 3 (March 1975): 2–3.

Fuller, Sarah. "Additional Notes on the Fifteenth-Century Chansonnier Bologna Q 16." MD 23 (1969): 81–103.

Gable, Frederick K. "Possibilities for Mean-Tone Temperament Playing on Viols." JVdGSA 16 (1979): 22–39.

Gaffurius, Franchinus, *Practica Musicae*. Translated by Clement A. Miller. Musicological Studies and Documents, vol. 20. N.p.: American Institute of Musicology, 1968.

———. *Practica Musicae*. Translated and edited by Irwin

Young. Madison: University of Wisconsin Press, 1969.

Gajard, Joseph. *The Rhythm of Plainsong According to the Solesmes School.* Translated by Aldhelm Dean. Liverpool: Rushworth and Dreaper, 1943.

Gill, Donald. "The Elizabethan Lute." *GSJ* 12 (1959): 60–62.

———. "The Orpharion and Bandora." *GSJ* 13 (1960): 14–25.

———. "Vihuelas, Violas, and the Spanish Guitar." *EM* 9 (1981): 455–462.

Glarean, Heinrich. *Dodecachordon: Translation, Transcription and Commentary.* Edited by Clement A. Miller. Musicological Studies and Documents, vol. 6. N.p.: American Institute of Musicology, 1965.

Godt, Irving. "Choral Conductors Forum: The Motets in the Josquin Edition: A Contribution to Performance." *ACR* 18, no. 1 (January 1976): 17–20.

———. "A Lesson in *Musica ficta* from Guillaume Costeley and Le Roy & Ballard, 1570–1579." *Music Review* 38 (1977): 159–162.

Godwin, Joscelyn. "Instruments in Robert Fludd's *Utriusque Cosmi . . . Historia.*" *GSJ* 26 (1973): 2–14.

———. "'Main divers acors': Some Instrument Collections of the Ars Nova Period." *EM* 5 (1977): 148–159.

———. "Playing from Original Notation." *EM* 2 (1974): 15–19.

———. "The Renaissance Flute." *Consort* 28 (1972): 70–81.

Goldin, Frederick. *German and Italian Lyrics of the Middle Ages: An Anthology and a History.* Garden City, NY: Anchor, 1973.

———. *Lyrics of the Troubadours and Trouvères: An Anthology and a History.* Garden City, NY: Anchor, 1973. Reprint. Gloucester, MA: Peter Smith, 1983.

Göllner, Marie Louise. "Ott, Hans." *NG* 14: 22–23.

Gombosi, Otto. "About Dance and Dance Music in the Late Middle Ages." *MQ* 27 (1941): 289–305.

Gottfried von Strassburg. *Tristan.* Translated by A. T. Hatto. Harmondsworth: Penguin, 1960.

Graham-Jones, Ian. "Some Random Thoughts on Pitch in English Viol Consort Music in the Seventeenth Century." *Chelys* 11 (1982): 20–23.

Greenberg, Noah. "Early Music Performance Today." In *Aspects of Medieval and Renaissance Music,* edited by Jan La Rue, 314–318. 2nd ed. New York: Pendragon, 1978.

Greene, Gordon. "The Schools of Minstrelsy and the Choir-School Tradition." *Studies in Music* (University of Western Ontario) 2 (1977): 31–40.

Grijp, Louis Peter. "Fret Patterns of the Cittern." *GSJ* 34 (1981): 62–97.

Grocheo, Johannes de. *Concerning Music (De musica).* Translated by Albert Seay. Colorado College Music Press Translations, no. 1. 2nd ed. Colorado Springs: Colorado College Music Press, 1974.

Groeneveld, Dagmar. "A Bibliography of the European Harp to 1600." *CM* 16 (1973): 92–102.

Grout, Donald Jay. *A History of Western Music.* 3rd ed. New York: Norton, 1980.

———. "On Historical Authenticity in the Performance of Old Music." In *Essays on Music in Honor of Archibald T. Davison by His Associates,* 341–347. Cambridge: Harvard University, Department of Music, 1957.

Grubbs, John W. "Ornamentation and Other Performance Problems." *CMS* 10 (1970): 114–120.

Haar, James. "False Relations and Chromaticism in Sixteenth-Century Music." *JAMS* 30 (1977): 391–418.

———, ed. *Chanson and Madrigal, 1480–1530: Studies in Comparison and Contrast. A Conference at Isham Memorial Library, September 13–14, 1961.* Isham Library Papers, no. 2. Cambridge: Harvard University Press, 1964.

Hadaway, Robert. "Another Look at the Viol." *EM* 6 (1978): 530–539.

———. "The Cittern." *EM* 1 (1973): 77–81.

Hagopian, Viola L. *Italian Ars Nova Music: A Bibliographic Guide to Modern Editions and Related Literature.* 2nd ed., rev. Berkeley and Los Angeles: University of California Press, 1973.

Hanchet, John F. "Adjustment and Control of Double Reeds for Direct Blown Early Instruments." *EM* 8 (1980): 361–365.

Harden, Jean. "'Musica Ficta' in Machaut." *EM* 5 (1977): 473–477.

Harrán, Don. "In Pursuit of Origins: The Earliest Writing on Text Underlay (c. 1440)." *Acta* 50 (1978): 217–240.

———. "More Evidence for Cautionary Signs." *JAMS* 31 (1978): 490–494.

———. "New Evidence for Musica Ficta: The Cautionary Sign." *JAMS* 29 (1976): 77–98.

———. "New Light on the Question of Text Underlay Prior to Zarlino." *Acta* 45 (1973): 24–56.

———. "Vicentino and His Rules of Text Underlay." *MQ* 59 (1973): 620–632.

Harrison, Frank Ll. *Music in Medieval Britain.* 4th ed. Buren: Frits Knuf, 1980.

———. "Tradition and Innovation in Instrumental Usage, 1100–1450." In *Aspects of Medieval and Renaissance Music,* edited by Jan La Rue, 319–335. 2nd ed. New York: Pendragon, 1978.

Harrison, Frank Ll., and Eric J. Dobson. *Medieval English Lyrics.* Argo (Z)RG(5)443. 1965. Sound recording and brochure.

Harwood, Ian. "A Case of Double Standards?: Instrumental Pitch in England c1600." *EM* 9 (1981): 470–481.

———. "Instrumental Pitch in England c1600." *EM* 11 (1983): 76–77.

————. "An Introduction to Renaissance Viols." EM 2 (1974): 235–246.

Harwood, Ian, and Martin Edmunds. "Reconstructing Sixteenth-Century Venetian Viols." EM 6 (1978): 519–525.

Heartz, Daniel. "The Basse Dance: Its Evolution circa 1450 to 1550." AM 6 (1958–63): 287–340.

————. "Hoftanz and Basse Dance." JAMS 19 (1966): 13–36.

Henry, Derrick. The Listener's Guide to Medieval and Renaissance Music. New York: Facts on File, 1983.

Herlinger, Jan W. "Marchetto's Division of the Whole Tone." JAMS 34 (1981): 193–216.

Hibberd, Lloyd. "On 'Instrumental Style' in Early Melody." MQ 32 (1946): 107–130.

Hines, Robert S. Singer's Manual of Latin Diction and Phonetics. New York: Schirmer Books, 1975.

Holman, Peter. Report on Symposium on Performance Practice, Oxford, September 24–25, 1983. Early Music News 69 (November 1983): 8–9.

Holoman, D. Kern. "Staging the Play of Daniel." EM 4 (1976): 159–163.

Holst, Imogen. "A Learner's Questions [on Eastern Influences]." EM 5 (1977): 364–368.

Hoppin, Richard H. "Conflicting Signatures Reviewed." JAMS 9 (1956): 97–117.

————. Medieval Music. New York: Norton, 1978.

————. "Partial Signatures and Musica Ficta in Some Early Fifteenth-Century Sources." JAMS 6 (1953): 197–215.

Horsley, Imogene. "The Diminutions in Composition and Theory of Composition." Acta 35 (1963): 124–153.

————. "Improvisation, I, i." NG 9: 32–35.

————. "Improvised Embellishment in the Performance of Renaissance Polyphonic Music." JAMS 4 (1951): 3–19.

Hucke, Helmut, "Gradual." NG 7: 599.

Hughes, Andrew. "The Choir in Fifteenth-Century English Music: Non-Mensural Polyphony." In Essays in Musicology in Honor of Dragan Plamenac on His Seventieth Birthday, edited by Gustave Reese and Robert J. Snow, 127–145. Pittsburgh: University of Pittsburgh Press, 1969.

————. Manuscript Accidentals: Ficta in Focus, 1350–1450. Musicological Studies and Documents, vol. 27. N.p.: American Institute of Musicology, 1972.

————. Medieval Music: The Sixth Liberal Art. Toronto Medieval Bibliographies, no. 4. Rev. ed. Toronto: University of Toronto Press, 1980.

————. "Mensural Polyphony for Choir in Fifteenth-Century England." JAMS 19 (1966): 352–369.

————. "Some Notes on the Early Fifteenth-Century Contratenor." ML 50 (1969): 376–387.

Jackson, John, and Elizabeth Phillips. "Some Guidelines for Early Music Performance." Divisions 1, no. 2 (December 1978): 5–17.

Jeffery, Brian. "Instrumentation in the Music of Anthony Holborne." GSJ 19 (1966): 20–26.

Jeffery, Peter. "A Four-Part In seculum Hocket and a Mensural Sequence in an Unknown Fragment." JAMS 37 (1984): 1–48.

Jones, Charles. An Introduction to Middle English. New York: Holt, Rinehart and Winston, 1972.

Kanazawa, Masakata. "The Musical Style of Polyphonic Hymns in the Fifteenth Century." In International Musicological Society, Report of the Twelfth Congress, Berkeley, 1977, edited by Daniel Heartz and Bonnie Wade, 634–639. Kassel: Bärenreiter, 1981.

Karp, Cary. "Storage Climates for Musical Instruments." EM 10 (1982): 469–476.

Kerman, Joseph. The Elizabethan Madrigal: A Comparative Study. American Musicological Society Studies and Documents, no. 4. N.p.: AMS, 1962.

Kirby, Frank. "Hermann Finck on Methods of Performance." ML 42 (1961): 212–220.

Kirkendale, Warren. "Ciceronians versus Aristotelians on the Ricercar as Exordium, from Bembo to Bach." JAMS 32 (1979): 1–44.

Knapp, Janet. "Musical Declamation and Poetic Rhythm in an Early Layer of Notre Dame Conductus." JAMS 32 (1979): 383–407.

Kökeritz, Helge. A Guide to Chaucer's Pronunciation. New Haven: Whitlock, 1954. Reprint. Toronto: University of Toronto Press, 1978.

————. Shakespeare's Pronunciation. New Haven: Yale University Press, 1953.

————. A Thousand Years of English Pronunciation. EAV Lexington LE 7650/55. Sound recording.

Kohn, Karl. "The Renotation of Polyphonic Music." MQ 67 (1981): 29–49.

Kottick, Edward L. The Collegium: A Handbook. Stonington, CT: October House, 1977.

————. "The State of Collegium in America." CMS 16 (1976): 137–148.

Kramme, Joel. "Notes on Medieval Performance Practice." ACR 19, no. 1 (January 1977): 17–19.

————. "Notes on Renaissance Performance Practice." ACR 19, no. 3 (July 1977): 7–12.

Lampl, Hans. "A Translation of Syntagma Musicum III by Michael Praetorius." D.M.A. dissertation, University of Southern California, 1957.

Lane, George B. The Trombone in the Middle Ages and Renaissance. Bloomington: Indiana University Press, 1982.

La Rue, Jan, ed. Aspects of Medieval and Renaissance Music: A Birthday Offering to Gustave Reese. 2nd ed. New York: Pendragon, 1978.

Lasocki, David. "Professional Recorder Playing in England, 1500–1740; I: 1500–1640." EM 10 (1982): 22–29.

Leech-Wilkinson, Daniel. Review of Dufay, Complete Secular Music. Medieval Ensemble of London. EM 10 (1982): 557–559.

Le Huray, Peter. *Music and the Reformation in England, 1549–1660*. London: Oxford University Press, 1967.

Lenaerts, René Bernard. "Musical Structure and Performance Practice in Masses and Motets of Josquin and Obrecht." In *Josquin des Prez*, edited by Edward E. Lowinsky, 617–626. London: Oxford University Press, 1976.

Levy, Kenneth. "A Dominican Organum Duplum." JAMS 27 (1974): 183–211.

The Liber Usualis, with Introduction and Rubrics in English. Edited by the Benedictines of Solesmes. Tournai: Desclée, 1952 and other editions.

Lindley, Mark. "Fifteenth-Century Evidence for Meantone Temperament." PRMA 102 (1975/76): 37–51.

———. "Pythagorean Intonation and the Rise of the Triad." *Research Chronicle* 16 (1980): 4–61.

———. "Temperaments." NG 18: 660–674.

Litterick, Louise. "On Italian Instrumental Ensemble Music in the Late Fifteenth Century." In *Music in Medieval and Early Modern Europe*, edited by Iain Fenlon, 117–130. Cambridge: Cambridge University Press, 1981.

———. "Performing Franco-Netherlandish Secular Music of the Late Fifteenth Century: Texted and Untexted Parts in the Sources." EM 8 (1980): 474–485.

Lockwood, Lewis. "A Dispute on Accidentals in Sixteenth-Century Rome." *Analecta Musicologica* 2 (1965): 24–40.

———. "A Sample Problem of *Musica Ficta*: Willaert's *Pater Noster*." In *Studies in Music History: Essays for Oliver Strunk*, edited by Harold Powers, 161–182. Princeton: Princeton University Press, 1968.

Lockwood, William B. *An Informal History of the German Language, with Chapters on Dutch and Afrikaans, Frisian, and Yiddish*. New ed. London: Deutsch, 1976.

Longyear, Rey M. "Some Aspects of Sixteenth-Century Instrumental Terminology and Practice." JAMS 17 (1964): 193–198.

Lowinsky, Edward E. "Canon Technique and Simultaneous Conception: A Comparison of North and South." In International Musicological Society, *Report of the Twelfth Congress, Berkeley, 1977*, edited by Daniel Heartz and Bonnie Wade, 639–640. Kassel: Bärenreiter, 1981.

———. "Conflicting Views on Conflicting Signatures." JAMS 7 (1954): 181–204.

———. Foreword to *Musica Nova*. Edited by H. Colin Slim. Monuments of Renaissance Music, vol. 1. Chicago: University of Chicago Press, 1964.

———. "The Function of Conflicting Signatures in Early Polyphonic Music." MQ 31 (1945): 227–260.

———. Introduction to *Ottaviano Petrucci, Canti B numero cinquanta*. Edited by Helen Hewitt. Monuments of Renaissance Music, vol. 2. Chicago: University of Chicago Press, 1967.

———. *Secret Chromatic Art in the Netherlands Motet*. Translated by Carl Buchman. Columbia Studies in Musicology, no. 6. New York: Columbia University Press, 1946. Reprint. New York: Russell and Russell, 1967.

———. "A Treatise on Text Underlay by a German Disciple of Francisco de Salinas." In *Festschrift Heinrich Besseler zum sechzigsten Geburtstag*, 231–251. Leipzig: Deutscher Verlag für Musik, 1961.

———. ed. *The Medici Codex of 1518*. Monuments of Renaissance Music, vols. 3–5. Chicago: University of Chicago Press, 1968.

Lowinsky, Edward E., ed., in collaboration with Bonnie J. Blackburn. *Josquin des Prez: Proceedings of the International Josquin Festival-Conference Held at the Juilliard School at Lincoln Center in New York City, 21–25 June 1971*. London: Oxford University Press, 1976.

MacClintock, Carol, ed. *Readings in the History of Music in Performance*. Bloomington: Indiana University Press, 1979.

McGee, Timothy J. "Eastern Influences in Medieval European Dances." In *Cross-Cultural Perspectives on Music*, edited by Robert Falck and Timothy Rice, 79–100. Toronto: University of Toronto Press, 1982.

McKee, W. E. "Maschera, Florentio." NG 11: 745.

McKinnon, James W. "The Meaning of the Patristic Polemic against Musical Instruments." CM 1 (1965): 69–82.

———. "Musical Instruments in Medieval Psalm Commentaries and Psalters." JAMS 21 (1968): 3–20.

———. "Representations of the Mass in Medieval and Renaissance Art." JAMS 31 (1978): 21–52.

Macmillan, Douglas. "The Mysterious Cornamuse." EM 6 (1978): 75–77.

McPeek, Gwynn S. "Medieval Monophonic Song: *Kalenda Maia* by Raimbault de Vaqueiras (c. 1155–1205)." In *Notations and Editions*, edited by Edith Borroff, 1–7. Dubuque; Wm. C. Brown, 1974.

Maddrell, J. E. "Grocheo and *The Measurability of Medieval Music*: A Reply to Hendrik Vanderwerf." CM 11 (1971): 89–90.

———. "*Mensura* and the Rhythm of Medieval Monophonic Song." CM 10 (1970): 64–69.

Malm, William P. *Music Cultures of the Pacific, the Near East, and Asia*. 2nd ed. Englewood Cliffs, NJ: Prentice-Hall, 1977.

Maniates, Maria R. "*Maniera*: The Central Issue in Sixteenth-Century Musical Controversy." *Canadian Association of Schools of Music Journal* 7 (1977): 1–30.

Marcuse, Sibyl. *Musical Instruments: A Comprehensive Dictionary*. Corrected ed. New York: Norton, 1975.

———. *A Survey of Musical Instruments*. New York: Harper and Row, 1975.

Marrocco, W. Thomas, ed. *Italian Secular Music.* Polyphonic Music of the Fourteenth Century, vol. 11. Monaco: Editions de l'Oiseau-Lyre, 1978.

Mather, Christine K. "Maximilian I and His Instruments." *EM* 3 (1975): 42–46.

Maynard, Judson D. "Heir Beginnis Countering." *JAMS* 20 (1967): 182–196.

"The Medieval, Renaissance and Baroque Lute in Pictures." *EM* 3 (1975): 137–139.

Meer, J. H. van der. "A Contribution to the History of the Clavicytherium." *EM* 6 (1978): 247–259.

Meeùs, Nicolas. "Keyboard Scholarship." *EM* 8 (1980): 222–223. Reply by Christopher Page, 223–226.

Mendel, Arthur. "Pitch in Western Music since 1500— A Re-examination." *Acta* 50 (1978): 1–93, 328.

Menéndez Pidal, Ramon. *Orígenes del español: Estado lingüístico de la Península ibérica hasta el siglo XI.* 9th ed. Madrid: Espasa-Calpe, 1980.

Mersenne, Marin. *Harmonie universelle* (Paris, 1636). Facsimile edition by François Lesure. 3 vols. Paris: Editions du CNRS, 1963.

———. *Harmonie universelle, The Book on Instruments.* Translated by Roger E. Chapman. The Hague: Martinus Nijhoff, 1957.

Meyer, Kenton T. *The Crumhorn: Its History, Design, Repertory, and Technique.* Ann Arbor: UMI Research Press, 1983.

Migliorini, Bruno. *The Italian Language.* Edited and translated by T. Gwynfor Griffith. London: Faber and Faber, 1966.

Milner, Anthony. "Liturgy, Church Music, and Politics in the Carolingian Empire." *Studies in Music* (University of Western Ontario) 5 (1980): 23–34.

Moeck, Herman. Letter. *EM* 7 (1979): 431.

Monk, Christopher. "First Steps Towards Playing the Cornett." *EM* 3 (1975): 132–133, 244–248.

Montagu, Gwen, and Jeremy Montagu. "Beverley Minster Reconsidered." *EM* 6 (1978): 401–415.

Montagu, Jeremy. "The 'Authentic' Sound of Early Music." *EM* 3 (1975): 242–243.

———. "Choosing Brass Instruments." *EM* 4 (1976): 35–38.

———. "Early Percussion Techniques." *EM* 2 (1974): 20–24.

———. *Making Early Percussion Instruments.* Early Music Series, no. 3. London: Oxford University Press, 1976.

———. Review of *The Crumhorn and Other Renaissance Windcap Instruments,* by Barra Boydell. *EM* 11 (1983): 97–100.

———. *The World of Medieval and Renaissance Musical Instruments.* Woodstock, NY: Overlook Press, 1976.

Moonen, Toon. "The Brussels Crumhorns: Hypotheses on Their Historical Construction." *GSJ* 36 (1983): 49–70.

Morehen, John. "The English Consort and Verse Anthems." *EM* 6 (1978): 381–385.

Morrow, Michael. "Musical Performance and Authenticity." *EM* 6 (1978): 233–246.

———. "The Renaissance Harp." *EM* 7 (1979): 499–510.

———. "Sixteenth Century Ensemble Viol Music." *EM* 2 (1974): 160–163.

Mullally, Robert. "The Polyphonic Theory of the *Bassa Danza* and the *Ballo.*" *Music Review* 41 (1980): 1–10.

———. "The Polyphonic Theory of the *Basse Danse.*" *Music Review* 38 (1977): 241–248.

Munrow, David. "The Art of Courtly Love." *EM* 1 (1973): 195–199.

———. *Instruments of the Middle Ages and Renaissance.* London: Oxford University Press, 1976.

Myers, Herbert W. "Instrumental Pitch in England c1600." *EM* 10 (1982): 519–522.

———. "The *Mary Rose* 'Shawm.'" *EM* (1983): 358–360.

Mynett, Alan. "On the Reconstruction of a Medieval Tabor." *EM* 1 (1973): 223–227.

Nádas, John. "The Structure of MS Panciatichi 26 and the Transmission of Trecento Polyphony." *JAMS* 34 (1981): 393–427.

Neugent, George. "Gombert, Nicolas." *NG* 7: 512–516.

New Oxford History of Music: Vol. 2. *Early Medieval Music up to 1300.* Edited by Anselm Hughes. Rev. ed. London: Oxford University Press, 1955; Vol. 3. *Ars Nova and the Renaissance, 1300–1540.* Edited by Anselm Hughes and Gerald Abraham. London: Oxford University Press, 1960; Vol. 4. *The Age of Humanism, 1540–1630.* Edited by Gerald Abraham. London: Oxford University Press, 1968.

Newcomb, Anthony. *The Madrigal at Ferrara, 1579–1597.* 2 vols. Princeton Studies in Music, no. 7. Princeton: Princeton University Press, 1980.

Norris, John. "How to Get the Best from Direct-Blown Double Reeds." *EM* 10 (1982): 201–207.

Ortiz, Diego. *Tratado de glosas.* Edited by Max Schneider. Kassel: Bärenreiter, 1967.

Pacholczyk, Jozef M. "Secular Classical Music in the Arabic Near East." In *Musics of Many Cultures: An Introduction,* edited by Elizabeth May, 253–268. Berkeley and Los Angeles: University of California Press, 1980.

Page, Christopher. "An Aspect of Medieval Fiddle Construction." *EM* 2 (1974): 166–167.

———. "Early Fifteenth-Century Instruments in Jean de Gerson's 'Tractatus de Canticis.'" *EM* 6 (1978): 339–349.

———. "The Fifteenth-Century Lute: New and Neglected Sources." *EM* 9 (1981): 11–21.

———. "Fourteenth-Century Instruments and Tunings: A Treatise by Jean Vaillant? (Berkeley, MS 744)." *GSJ* 33 (1980): 17–35.

———. "German Musicians and Their Instruments: A

Fourteenth-Century Account by Konrad of Megen-berg." *EM* 10 (1982): 192-200.

———. "Jerome of Moravia on the Rubeba and Viella." *GSJ* 32 (1979): 77-98.

———. Letter. *EM* 8 (1980): 223-226.

———. "Machaut's 'Pupil' Deschamps on the Performance of Music: Voices or Instruments in the Fourteenth-Century Chanson?" *EM* 5 (1977): 484-491.

———. "The Medieval *Organistrum* and *Symphonia* 1: A Legacy from the East?" *GSJ* 35 (1982): 37-44.

———. "The Medieval *Organistrum* and *Symphonia* 2: Terminology." *GSJ* 36 (1983): 71-87.

———. "The Myth of the Chekker." *EM* 7 (1979): 482-489.

———. "The Performance of Songs in Late Medieval France: A New Source." *EM* 10 (1982): 441-451.

———. "The *Pes* of 'Sumer is icumen in.'" *EM* 2 (1974): 263.

———. "String-Instrument Making in Medieval England and Some Oxford Harpmakers, 1380-1466." *GSJ* 31 (1978): 44-67.

———. See also Meeùs.

Palmer, Frances. "Musical Instruments from the *Mary Rose*: A Report on Work in Progress." *EM* 11 (1983): 53-57.

Palmer, Leonard R. *The Latin Language*. London: Faber and Faber, 1954.

Palmer, Susann, with Samuel Palmer. *The Hurdy-Gurdy*. Newton Abbot, England: David and Charles, 1980.

Panum, Hortense. *The Stringed Instruments of the Middle Ages: Their Evolution and Development*. Translated and edited by Jeffrey Pulver. London: Wm. Reeves, n.d.

Parker, Ian. "The Performance of Troubadour and Trouvère Songs: Some Facts and Conjectures." *EM* 5 (1977): 184-207.

Parkinson, Andrew. "Guesswork and the Gemshorn." *EM* 9 (1981): 43-46.

Parrish, Carl. *The Notation of Medieval Music*. New York: Norton, 1957. Reprint. New York: Pendragon, 1978.

Parrott, Andrew. "Grett and Solompne Singing." *EM* 6 (1978): 182-187.

Perkins, Leeman L. "Toward a Rational Approach to Text Placement in the Secular Music of Dufay's Time." In *Papers Read at the Dufay Quincentenary Conference, Brooklyn College, December 6-7, 1974*, edited by Allan W. Atlas, 102-114. New York: Brooklyn College, 1976.

Petersen, Alice Vanette Neff. "A Guide to the Development and Direction of an Early Music Performance Program." D.A. dissertation, Ball State University, 1980.

Pettitt, Stephen. Review of a concert by Gothic Voices, directed by Christopher Page, 16 February 1984. *Early Music News* 74 (April 1984): 6-7.

Phillips, Peter. "Performance Practice in Sixteenth-Century English Choral Music." *EM* 6 (1978): 195-199.

Pinnock, Trevor. "Buying a Harpsichord." *EM* 3 (1975): 126-131, 365-367.

Pirrotta, Nino, ed. *Maestro Piero; Codex Vatican Rossi 215; Anonymous Madrigals and Cacce from Other Manuscripts*. Part 2 of *The Music of Fourteenth-Century Italy*. Corpus Mensurabilis Musicae, vol. 8. N.p.: American Institute of Musicology, 1960.

Planchart, Alejandro Enrique. "The Performance of Early Music in America." *JM* 1 (1982): 19-29.

Pope, Mildred K. *From Latin to Modern French, with Especial Consideration of Anglo-Norman: Phonology and Morphology*. 2nd, rev. ed. Manchester: Manchester University Press, 1952. Reprint. New York: Barnes and Noble, 1973.

Powell, Newman. "The Function of the Tactus in the Performance of Renaissance Music." *Musical Heritage of the Church* 6 (1963): 64-84.

Praetorius, Michael. *The Syntagma musicum of Michael Praetorius, Volume Two, De organographia: First and Second Parts*. Translated by Harold Blumenfeld. 3rd ed. New York: Da Capo, 1980.

———. See also Lampl.

Price, Glanville. *The French Language: Present and Past*. Rev. ed. London: Edward Arnold, 1975.

Prizer, William F. "Performance Practices in the Frottola." *EM* 3 (1975): 227-235.

Puglisi, Filadelfio. "The Renaissance Flutes of the Biblioteca Capitolare of Verona: The Structure of a 'Pifaro.'" *GSJ* 32 (1979): 24-37.

Pyles, Thomas. *The Origins and Development of the English Language*. 2nd ed. New York: Harcourt Brace Jovanovich, 1971.

Rahn, Jay. "Text Underlay in French Monophonic Song ca. 1500." *CM* 24 (1977): 63-79.

Rastall, Richard. "Music for a Royal Entry, 1474." *MT* 118 (1977): 463-466.

Reaney, Gilbert. "Accidentals in Early Fifteenth Century Music." In *Renaissance-Muziek, 1400-1600: Donum natalicum René Bernard Lenaerts*, edited by Jozef Robijns, 223-231. Musicologica Lovaniensia, vol. 1. Leuven: Catholic University, 1969.

———. "The Performance of Medieval Music." In *Aspects of Medieval and Renaissance Music*, edited by Jan La Rue, 704-722, 2nd ed. New York: Pendragon, 1978.

———. "Philippus de Caserta." *NG* 14: 653-654.

———. "Text Underlay in Early Fifteenth-Century Musical Manuscripts." In *Essays in Musicology in Honor of Dragan Plamenac on His Seventieth Birthday*, edited by Gustave Reese and Robert J. Snow, 245-251. Pittsburgh: University of Pittsburgh Press, 1969.

———. "Voices and Instruments in the Music of Guillaume de Machaut." *RB* 10 (1956): 3-17, 93-104.

Reese, Gustave. *Fourscore Classics of Music Literature*.

New York: Liberal Arts Press, 1957. Reprint. New York: Da Capo, 1970.

———. *Music in the Middle Ages, with an Introduction on the Music of Ancient Times.* New York: Norton, 1940.

———. *Music in the Renaissance.* Rev. ed. New York: Norton, 1959.

Remnant, Mary. "The Diversity of Medieval Fiddles." *EM* 3 (1975): 47–49.

———. *Musical Instruments of the West.* New York: St. Martin's Press, 1978.

———. "Rebec, Fiddle and Crowd in England." *PRMA* 95 (1968/69): 15–27.

———. "Rebec, Fiddle and Crowd in England: Some Further Observations." *PRMA* 96 (1969/70): 149–150.

———. "The Use of Frets on Rebecs and Mediaeval Fiddles." *GSJ* 21 (1968): 146–151.

Ribera y Tarragó, Julian, ed. *La música de las cantigas.* Volume 3 of *Cantigas de Santa María.* Madrid: Tipografía de la Revista de Archivos, 1922.

Ripin, Edwin M. "Towards an Identification of the Chekker." *GSJ* 28 (1975): 11–25.

Robertson, Daniel. "Anyone for the Galliard?" *EM* 2 (1974): 83–84.

Roche, Jerome, and Elizabeth Roche. *A Dictionary of Early Music: From the Troubadours to Monteverdi.* New York: Oxford University Press, 1981.

Roesner, Edward H. "The Performance of Parisian Organum." *EM* 7 (1979): 174–189.

Rooley, Anthony. "Dance and Dance Music of the Sixteenth Century." *EM* 2 (1974): 78–83.

Rowen, Ruth Halle. *Music Through Sources and Documents.* 2nd ed. Englewood Cliffs, NJ: Prentice-Hall, 1979.

Rubsamen, Walter H. "From Frottola to Madrigal: The Changing Pattern of Secular Italian Vocal Music." In *Chanson and Madrigal, 1480–1530,* edited by James Haar, 51–72. Cambridge, MA: Harvard University Press, 1964.

Rumery, Leonard R. "Music at Seville under a Renaissance Master." *ACR* 23, no. 2 (April 1981): 11–17.

Russell, Raymond. *The Harpsichord and Clavichord: An Introductory Study.* Revised by Howard Schott. 2nd ed. New York: Norton, 1973.

Sachs, Curt. *The History of Musical Instruments.* New York: Norton, 1940.

———. *Rhythm and Tempo: A Study in Music History.* New York: Norton, 1953.

Sadie, Stanley, ed. *The New Grove Dictionary of Music and Musicians.* 20 vols. London: Macmillan, 1980.

Sage, Jack. Review of *A Short History of Spanish Music,* by Ann Livermore. *EM* 2 (1974): 185–187.

Samuel, Rhian. "Modality, Tonality, and *Musica Ficta* in the Sixteenth-Century Chanson." Ph.D. dissertation, Washington University in St. Louis, 1978.

Sanders, Ernest H. "Cantilena and Discant in Fourteenth-Century England." *MD* 19 (1965): 7–52.

———. "Consonance and Rhythm in the Organum of the Twelfth and Thirteenth Centuries." *JAMS* 33 (1980): 264–286.

———. "Discant, II. English Discant." *NG* 5: 492–495.

———. "The Medieval Hocket in Practice and Theory." *MQ* 60 (1974): 246–256.

Schmidt-Görg, Joseph, ed. *Magnificat,* by Nicolai Gombert. Part 4 of *Opera Omnia.* Corpus Mensurabilis Musicae, vol. 6. N.p.: American Institute of Musicology, 1957.

Scholl, Evelyn H. "New Light on Seventeenth Century Pronunciation from the English School of Lutenist Song Writers." *Publications of the Modern Language Association* 59 (1944): 398–445.

Schrade, Leo. *Commentary to Volume IV, The Works of Francesco Landini.* Polyphonic Music of the Fourteenth Century, vol. 4, commentary volume. Monaco: Editions de l'Oiseau-Lyre, 1958.

Seay, Albert. *Music in the Medieval World.* 2nd ed. Englewood Cliffs, NJ: Prentice-Hall, 1975.

Selfridge-Field, Eleanor. "Bassano and the Orchestra of St Mark's." *EM* 4 (1976): 152–158.

Senn, Alfred, *An Introduction to Middle High German: A Reader and Grammar.* New York: Norton, 1937.

Shiloah, Amnon. "The Arabic Concept of Mode." *JAMS* 34 (1981): 19–42.

Smoldon, William L. *The Music of the Medieval Church Dramas.* Edited by Cynthia Bourgeault. London: Oxford University Press, 1980.

Spaulding, Robert K. *How Spanish Grew.* Berkeley and Los Angeles: University of California Press, 1943.

Spencer, Robert. "Chitarrone, Theorbo and Archlute." *EM* 4 (1976): 407–423.

Stevens, Denis. "Ceremonial Music in Medieval Venice." *MT* 119 (1978): 321–327.

———. "Some Observations on Performance Practice." *CM* 14 (1972): 159–163.

———. *Thomas Tomkins, 1572–1656.* London: Macmillan, 1957. Reprint. New York: Dover, 1967.

Stevens, John. "Carol, 1, 2." *NG* 3: 802–811.

———. *Music and Poetry in the Early Tudor Court.* Rev. ed. Cambridge: Cambridge University Press, 1979.

———, ed. *Medieval Carols.* Musica Britannica, vol. 4. 2nd ed. London: Stainer and Bell, 1970.

———, ed. *Music at the Court of Henry VIII.* Musica Britannica, vol. 18. 2nd ed. London: Stainer and Bell, 1969.

Stevenson, Robert M. "Ortiz, Diego." *NG* 13: 875–876.

———. *Spanish Cathedral Music in the Golden Age.* Berkeley and Los Angeles: University of California Press, 1961. Reprint. Westport, CT: Greenwood, 1976.

———. *Spanish Music in the Age of Columbus.* The Hague: Martinus Nijhoff, 1960. Reprint. Westport, CT: Hyperion, 1979.

Strecker, Karl. *Introduction to Medieval Latin*. Translated by Robert B. Palmer. 4th ed. Dublin: Weidmann, 1967.

Strunk, Oliver. *Source Readings in Music History: From Classical Antiquity through the Romantic Era*. New York: Norton, 1950. Reprint in 5 vols. New York: Norton, 1965.

Taruskin, Richard. "On Letting the Music Speak for Itself: Some Reflections on Musicology and Performance." *JM* 1 (1982): 338–349.

Taruskin, Richard, Daniel Leech-Wilkinson, Nicholas Temperley, and Robert Winter. "The Limits of Authenticity: A Discussion." *EM* 12 (1984): 3–25.

Thomas, Bernard. "An Introduction to the Crumhorn Repertoire." *EM* 1 (1973): 142–146.

———. "Playing the Crumhorn: First Steps." *EM* 2 (1974): 151–156.

———. "The Renaissance Flute." *EM* 3 (1975): 2–10.

———. "Renaissance Music in Modern Notation." *EM* 5 (1977): 4–11.

Thomas, W. R., and J. J. K. Rhodes. "Schlick, Praetorius and the History of Organ-Pitch." *Organ Yearbook* 2 (1971): 58–76.

Tiella, Marco. "The Violeta of S. Caterina de' Vigri." *GSJ* 28 (1975): 60–70.

Tinctoris, Johannes. *The Art of Counterpoint (Liber de arte contrapuncti)*. Translated and edited by Albert Seay. Musicological Studies and Documents, vol. 5. N.p.: American Institute of Musicology, 1961.

Tischler, Hans. "A Propos Meter and Rhythm in the Ars Antiqua." *Journal of Music Theory* 26 (1982): 313–329.

———. "How Were Notre Dame Clausulae Performed?" *ML* 50 (1969): 273–277.

———. "Musica Ficta in the Parisian Organa." *Journal of Music Theory* 17 (1973): 311–319.

———. "Musica Ficta in the Thirteenth Century." *ML* 54 (1973): 38–56.

———. "On Transcribing the *Magnus Liber*." *RB* 32–33 (1978–79): 9–22.

———. "Rhythm, Meter, and Melodic Organization in Medieval Songs." *RB* 28–30 (1974–76): 5–23.

Treitler, Leo. "Regarding 'A Propos Meter and Rhythm in the Ars Antiqua.'" *Journal of Music Theory* 27 (1983): 215–222.

———. "Regarding Meter and Rhythm in the Ars Antiqua." *MQ* 65 (1979): 524–558.

Turner, Bruno. "Scholarship and Performance." Interview by Peter Phillips. *EM* 6 (1978): 199–203.

Tyler, James. "A Checklist for the Cittern." *EM* 2 (1974): 25–29.

———. *The Early Guitar: A History and Handbook*. Early Music Series, no. 4. London: Oxford University Press, 1980.

———. "The Renaissance Guitar, 1500–1650." *EM* 3 (1975): 341–347.

Uberti, Mauro. "Vocal Techniques in Italy in the Second Half of the Sixteenth Century." Translated by Mark Lindley. *EM* 9 (1981): 486–495.

Ulrich, Homer, and Pisk, Paul A. *A History of Music and Musical Style*. New York: Harcourt, Brace, and World, 1963.

Ultan, Lloyd. *Music Theory: Problems and Practices in the Middle Ages and Renaissance*. Minneapolis: University of Minnesota Press, 1977.

van der Meer. See Meer.

van der Werf. See Werf.

Van Wye, Benjamin. "Ritual Use of the Organ in France." *JAMS* 33 (1980): 287–325.

Vinquist, Mary, and Neal Zaslaw, eds. *Performance Practice: A Bibliography*. New York: Norton, 1971. Supplements issued in CM 12 (1971): 129–149; CM 15 (1973): 126–136.

Virdung, Sebastian. *Musica getutscht* (Basel, 1511). Facsimile edition by Klaus Niemöller. Documenta Musicologica, ser. 1, vol. 31. Kassel: Bärenreiter, 1970.

von Fischer, Kurt, "Ballata." NG 2: 87–88.

———. "Caccia." NG 3: 574–576.

———. "Giovanni da Cascia." NG 7: 400–401.

von Ramm, Andrea. "Singing Early Music." *EM* 4 (1976): 12–15.

———. "Style in Early Music Singing." *EM* 8 (1980): 17–20.

Waite, William G. *The Rhythm Of Twelfth-Century Polyphony, Its Theory and Practice*. Yale Studies in the History of Music, no. 2. New Haven: Yale University Press, 1954.

Walls, Peter. "Common Sixteenth-Century Dance Forms: Some Further Notes." *EM* 2 (1974): 164–165.

Ward, John M. "The Maner of Dauncynge." *EM* 4 (1976): 127–142.

Weaver, Robert L. "Sixteenth-Century Instrumentation." *MQ* 47 (1961): 363–378.

Weber, Rainer. "Recorder Finds from the Middle Ages, and Results of Their Reconstruction." *GSJ* 29 (1976): 35–41.

———. "Some Researches into Pitch in the Sixteenth Century with Particular Reference to the Instruments in the Accademia Filarmonica of Verona." *GSJ* 28 (1975): 7–10.

———. "Tournebout-Pifia-Bladderpipe (*Platerspiel*)." *GSJ* 30 (1977): 64–69.

Weigand, George. *Lute Improvisation*. London: Shattinger, 1977.

Weisman, Maish. "The Paris Vihuela Reconstructed." *GSJ* 35 (1982): 68–77.

Weiss, Piero, and Richard Taruskin. *Music in the Western World: A History in Documents*. New York: Schirmer Books, 1984.

Wells, Marcus. "The Crumhorn: Historical Sources." *EM* 1 (1973): 139–141.

Werf, Hendrik van der. *The Chansons of the Troubadours and Trouvères: A Study of the Melodies and Their Relation to the Poems.* Utrecht: A. Oosthoek, 1972.

————. "Concerning the Measurability of Medieval Music." CM 10 (1970): 69–73.

Wess, Joan. "Bossinensis, Franciscus." NG 2: 80.

White, John Reeves. "Lyonel Power's *Sanctus* (ca. 1410)." In *Notations and Editions,* edited by Edith Borroff, 17–32. Dubuque: Wm. C. Brown, 1974.

————. "Performing Fourteenth-Century Music." CMS 9 (1969): 85–90.

Wilkins, Nigel. "Music in the Fourteenth Century 'Miracles de Nostre Dame.'" MD 28 (1974): 39–75.

Wilkinson, L. P. *Golden Latin Artistry.* Cambridge: Cambridge University Press, 1970.

Willetts, Carl. "First Steps on the Shawm." EM 5 (1977): 342–351.

Williams, Peter. *A New History of the Organ: From the Greeks to the Present Day.* Bloomington: Indiana University Press, 1980.

Williams, Sarah J. "Vocal Scoring in the Chansons of Machaut." JAMS 21 (1968): 251–257.

Wiltshire, Jacqueline. "Medieval Fiddles at Hardham." GSJ 34 (1981): 142–146.

Winternitz, Emanuel. *Musical Instruments and Their Symbolism in Western Art.* 2nd ed. New Haven: Yale University Press, 1979.

————. "Secular Musical Practice in Sacred Art." EM 3 (1975): 221–226.

Wolf, Johannes. "Die Tänze des Mittelalters." *Archiv für Musikwissenschaft* 1 (1918–19). Reprint. Hildesheim: Georg Olms, 1964. 10–64.

Woodfield, Ian. "The Early History of the Viol." PRMA 103 (1976/77): 141–157.

————. "Posture in Viol Playing." EM 6 (1978): 36–40.

————. "Viol Playing Techniques in the Mid-Sixteenth Century: A Survey of Ganassi's Fingering Instructions." EM 6 (1978): 544–549.

Wraight, Denzil. "Italian Harpsichords." EM 12 (1984): 151.

Wright, Craig. "Dufay at Cambrai: Discoveries and Revisions." JAMS 28 (1975): 175–229.

————. *Music at the Court of Burgundy, 1364–1419: A Documentary History.* Musicological Studies, vol. 28. Henryville, PA: Institute of Mediaeval Music, 1979.

————. "Performance Practices and Pedagogy at the Cathedral of Cambrai, 1475–1550." Paper presented at the annual meeting of the American Musicological Society, Washington, D.C., November 1976.

————. "Performance Practices at the Cathedral of Cambrai." MQ 64 (1978): 295–328.

————. "Voices and Instruments in the Art Music of Northern France during the Fifteenth Century: A Conspectus." In International Musicological Society, *Report of the Twelfth Congress, Berkeley, 1977,* edited by Daniel Heartz and Bonnie Wade, 643–649. Kassel: Bärenreiter, 1981.

Wright, Laurence. "The Medieval Gittern and Citole: A Case of Mistaken Identity." GSJ 30 (1977): 8–42.

————. "Sculptures of Medieval Fiddles at Gargilesse." GSJ 32 (1979): 66–76.

Yeston, Maury Alan. *The Stratification of Musical Rhythm.* New Haven: Yale University Press, 1976.

Young, Karl. *The Drama of the Medieval Church.* 2 vols. Oxford: Clarendon Press, 1933.

Yudkin, Jeremy. "The Rhythm of Organum Purum." JM 2 (1983): 355–376.

Zadro, Michael. "Guide to the Restoration of Woodwind Instruments." EM 2 (1974): 169–173.

————. "Woods Used for Woodwind Instruments since the Sixteenth Century." EM 3 (1975): 134–136, 249–251.